Go West, Mr. President

Go West, Mr. President

Theodore Roosevelt's Great Loop Tour of 1903

Michael F. Blake

TWODOT®

Helena, Montana
Guilford, Connecticut

To Kim,
my daughter, my friend,
and to
Abigail Cannon,
the best granddaughter a guy could have

A · TWODOT® · BOOK

An imprint and registered trademark of The Rowman & Littlefield Publishing Group, Inc.
4501 Forbes Blvd., Ste. 200
Lanham, MD 20706
www.rowman.com

Distributed by NATIONAL BOOK NETWORK

British Library Cataloguing in Publication Information available

Library of Congress Cataloging-in-Publication Data

Names: Blake, Michael F. (Michael Francis), 1957- author.
Title: Go West, Mr. President : Theodore Roosevelt's Great Loop Tour of 1903 / Michael F. Blake.
Other titles: Theodore Roosevelt's Great Loop Tour of 1903
Description: Helena, Montana : TwoDot, [2020] | Includes bibliographical references and index.
Identifiers: LCCN 2020001761 (print) | LCCN 2020001762 (ebook) | ISBN 9781493048465
  (hardcover) | ISBN 9781493048472 (e-book)
Subjects: LCSH: Roosevelt, Theodore, 1858-1919—Travel—West (U.S.) | Presidents—Travel—
  West (U.S.)--History--20th century. | West (U.S.)—Description and travel.
Classification: LCC E757 .B6483 2020 (print) | LCC E757 (ebook) | DDC
  917.804/0904—dc23
LC record available at https://lccn.loc.gov/2020001761
LC ebook record available at https://lccn.loc.gov/2020001762

♾™ The paper used in this publication meets the minimum requirements of American National Standard for Information Sciences—Permanence of Paper for Printed Library Materials, ANSI/NISO Z39.48-1992.

Contents

Author's Note

Newspapers covered every aspect of Theodore Roosevelt's presidency from his filing of the Sherman Antitrust lawsuit against the Northern Securities Company, to his Mississippi bear hunt, to his last day in office. Theodore made, in newspaper parlance, good copy.

I have relied on the numerous 1903 newspapers that covered all or part of Theodore's Great Loop Tour, from the big city presses like the *New York Times* and the Washington, DC, *Evening Star*, to small-town papers. Local papers provided more personal insights into his visit as compared to the larger papers or press syndicates like the Associated Press. After all, how many small towns can boast that they've had a visit from the president of the United States?

One aspect of these newspaper articles that I found particularly fascinating was the way the reporters crafted their stories. Their words flowed with a style that brought to mind the characters in the play and movie versions of *The Front Page*. One particular story was about a man who attempted to assassinate Theodore. The reporter noted that the police arrested him and "sweated him." No writer today could equal such expository description.

The reader may find some of the comments quoted from the newspapers of the time to be particularly insensitive by today's standards, but these comments were wholly acceptable in 1903. As a historian, I have chosen not to edit them. Whether we like it or not, they are part of history.

Preface

Bully!

According to *Webster's Unabridged Dictionary*, the definition of this word means "fine; excellent; very good"; a more informal definition is "well done."[1]

No other single word has been so readily identified with a U.S. president than "bully" with Theodore Roosevelt. The word fit perfectly the man and his life. He used it to describe anything that pleased or entertained him. The American public took to using the word to express their delight; even newspapers occasionally used the word in reference to anything relating to Theodore.[2]

By the end of 1901, a scant three months after Theodore assumed office as the youngest president of the United States at age forty-two, the American public—not to mention Washington, DC—came to realize that the new man in the White House was not a typical commander in chief. Theodore Roosevelt quickly stepped into this leadership role with a gusto never before experienced. It was said that when Theodore entered a room, it was like a cyclone blowing in. His magnetic personality overshadowed anyone else in the room. His full mustache sat above a broad grin that bared his even, white teeth, and his blue eyes sparkled behind his glasses. Even those who disagreed with his policies could not help but admire the man; many grudgingly admitted to liking him.

One group that loved Theodore was newspaper correspondents. Although they may have disagreed with his administration on various things, they "love[d] him for the copy he has made!"[3] Theodore learned early in his public service career that making friends with newspaper reporters was not only smart but necessary. During the Spanish-American War, reporters gave him and his Rough Riders more coverage than the army during the fighting in Cuba. The press turned Theodore into a national hero and helped pave his way to the White House. Once inside the Executive Mansion—it was Theodore who renamed it the White House—he continued to cultivate relationships with the press but was not afraid to take them to task if he felt they were wrong. Political cartoonists loved him, as well, since Theodore provided them a never-ending wealth of material.

———

In 1903, Theodore planned a tour of the midwestern and western states, which he was careful to avoid calling a campaign tour, even though he intended to seek reelection the following year. Theodore was adamant that his speeches be devoid of any partisan rhetoric nor would he meet solely with Republican officeholders in the various cities and towns. He happily shook hands with Democratic mayors or senators, just as he would Republicans. Theodore's speeches, which he wrote himself, covered subjects of good citizenship, a square deal for every man, a strong navy, and the positive aspects of the irrigation bill he had recently signed into law. Then there were his speeches relating to conservation of the land, forests, rivers, and wildlife. Nowhere did these subjects become more important to him than when he visited Yellowstone, the Grand Canyon, and Yosemite. Still three years away from enacting the law that would anoint him the "conservationist president," Theodore already was making his mark by preserving the country's resources.

The trip was dubbed the Great Loop Tour because of its route, coming out of Minnesota and Wisconsin, through the Midwest to the Southwest, up along the Pacific Coast, and across the northern states of Montana, Idaho, and Wyoming, before sweeping back across Iowa and Illinois, and returning to Washington, DC. Theodore was gone for two months, visiting twenty-one states and two territories and giving 265 speeches. As word of this planned excursion was announced, every city and hamlet along the way (and some out of the way) clamored for a presidential visit. It fell to William Loeb, Theodore's secretary, to choose when and where the president would visit. (Some states, like Texas, were not included in this trip, and the residents made their feelings known.) Each city or town chosen for a visit was free to plan a program during the time that was allotted for Theodore's stopover. Some cities tried to monopolize his time down to the last second, compelling him to announce that all visits and speeches were to be concluded by ten o'clock in the evening.

Theodore relished the opportunity to visit with the people. It was not uncommon for him to say he had to retire to his train car while continuing to talk with the people. Those moments were not forced; they were completely honest and real. He genuinely liked speaking to the people, especially those in the western states, as he easily related to them. In doing so, he showed the people that, unlike previous occupants of the White House, he was not unreachable or indifferent. Theodore spoke a common language with the ranchers, farmers, and cowboys. The fact that he had owned his own cattle ranch and understood the hardships faced by stockmen and farmers gave him the ability to speak plainly with them. None of them had to explain the problems of overgrazing or the need for irrigation to help crops thrive.

During a stop in Kalispell, Montana, a man told Theodore that he reminded him of a fellow he knew in a timber camp who liked good whiskey or rotgut. The man told Theodore that a lot of them knew the difference between good whiskey and bad whiskey, and there was no man who wouldn't take the right kind of whiskey if he could get it. "Mr. Roosevelt, you are the best sort of whiskey we have had for a good many years," he stated.[4]

His charismatic personality and heartfelt words invited all the people to join him in pursuing their own dreams, as well as Theodore's dreams for the country. Hardships would happen, he warned, but together they would face them as the country's predecessors had done and, in the end, emerge victorious. No person, no matter his race, creed, or social standing, Theodore noted, was entitled to anything but a "square deal." It was up to the individual to succeed. Yet, if a person tripped, Theodore said, it was up to all of us to help our fellow countryman get up. After that, a person's success or failure was up to him. "No one who heard the President will wonder why the word strenuous is associated with his name," commented the *Salt Lake Tribune* during his visit. "His words are fraught with conviction and his opinions are delivered with over-powering earnestness. He wins others to his views because he so thoroughly believes in himself."[5]

The Great Loop Tour allowed the people to meet the hero of San Juan Hill, who was now their president. In some cases, a visit by Theodore was just a brief stop at a train depot while his train took on water. It allowed citizens to see, hear, and—if they were lucky—shake the hand of the president of the United States. Even if his train was passing through a station without stopping, he ordered the engineer to slow down as he stood on the back of the car's platform to wave to the crowd, which likely had been standing there for hours just to get a brief glimpse of their leader. In other towns and cities, people came from several miles by horse, wagon, or a special train to see and hear him. The *Caldwell Tribune* observed that Theodore's visit "brought the government nearer to the people and the people nearer to the government."[6]

The words Theodore spoke came from his personal beliefs and his faith in the people, in fair play, and in what was best for America. His speeches are just as important and relevant today as they were more than a hundred years ago.

It would be one "bully" of a tour—not just for Theodore, but for the country and its people.

A Presidential Tour Unlike Any Other

I wanted them to understand that if they so desire, they shall have all the fight they wish.

TODAY, A PRESIDENTIAL APPEARANCE IN ANY TOWN OR CITY DRAWS supporters as well as critics. Everything a president does or says is closely monitored by a ubiquitous media (television, radio, newspapers, and the internet). With smartphones, average citizens can turn themselves into would-be journalists by capturing an image or pronouncement (positive or negative) by a president, circulating it worldwide within minutes and making or breaking a political career.

Prior to 1866, a president leaving the nation's capital for any extended length of time was simply not contemplated. (President Lincoln's historic trip to Gettysburg lasted only twenty-four hours.) For President Andrew Johnson (1865–1869), it might have been better if he had never left Washington, DC. His 1866 tour, dubbed the "swing around the circle," was designed to increase support for his Reconstruction policies in the South. It was nothing short of a disaster.[1]

Johnson was not at his finest when speaking spontaneously, and his aides heartily urged him to use prepared speeches. At first, his speeches were positively received, but all that changed in Cleveland, Ohio, when someone in the crowd taunted Johnson, shouting that former Confederate president Jefferson Davis should be hung. Johnson took the bait, replying that zealous abolitionists Thaddeus Stevens and Wendell Phillips should be hung instead. After that, his appearances were overshadowed by hecklers.

I

Given the calamity of this tour, Ulysses S. Grant (1869–1877) never made a trip while in office. However, Rutherford B. Hayes (1877–1881) took an expansive trip in 1880, hoping it would help heal the scars caused by the Civil War. Lasting seventy-one days, Hayes traveled by train, stagecoach, and steamship, visiting twelve states.[2] Since the Secret Service had yet to be assigned to protect the president, the duty fell to the U.S. Army, under the supervision of General William T. Sherman, who not only arranged the trip, but was at the president's elbow the entire time.[3] Protecting the president was not an easy task, but the greater disquietude came when the presidential party switched to stagecoaches in Yerka, California, to travel to Oregon. Sherman, concerned that a bandit might attempt to rob the stagecoaches, chose to discourage this by personally riding shotgun on the coach carrying President Hayes.[4]

Grover Cleveland (1885–1889; 1893–1897) launched a twenty-two-day tour in the fall of 1887 covering five thousand miles.[5] Although his trip was deemed a success, Cleveland lost his reelection bid two years later to Benjamin Harrison. (In 1893, Cleveland ran once again and won, making him the only American president to serve two nonconsecutive terms.) Benjamin Harrison (1889–1893) exceeded the tour of President Hayes by covering more than nine thousand miles in 1891.[6] Eight weeks after being sworn in for his second term, William McKinley (1897–1901) and his wife, Ida, planned an extensive seven-week trip across the country in late April 1901. They traveled down the Atlantic coast, through the South and Southwest, then up the Pacific Coast and across the northern part of the country, culminating with a stop in Buffalo, New York.[7] By the time the tour had reached Los Angeles, one of Ida McKinley's thumbs had become infected from a small cut. A few days later she began running a fever, but once in San Francisco, the crisis seemed to have passed. President McKinley, on the advice of Dr. Marion Rixley, decided to return to Washington and forego the remainder of the planned tour. Ironically, McKinley was scheduled to finish his tour at the opening of the Pan-American Exposition in Buffalo, New York. Instead, he rescheduled his appearance for early September, when he was assassinated.

Theodore traveled light when it came to his train. Whereas most presidential trains pulled at least eight cars, Theodore's had only six: two for baggage and four sleeper cars.[8] (The baggage cars carried both winter and spring clothing for the party.) All the cars were electrically lit and equipped with all the conveniences a traveler would need. The president's car, called *Elysian* (traditionally the last car of the train), was "the handsomest ever placed on the tracks by the Pullman Company." His car was fitted with an observation parlor, three staterooms, a dining room, kitchen, and servants' quarters. The kitchen was supervised by "the best chef in the employ of the [Pullman] company."[9]

The next car, *Texas*, was a compartment sleeper, and *Senegal* was a Pullman section sleeper "of the handsome type." *Gilsey*, a dining car, was next, followed by *Atlantic*, a buffet car, and the two baggage cars behind the engine. Pullman conductor William H. Johnson was in charge of the entire train, and a short, balding, gray-mustached waiter by the name of Spencer Murray attended to Theodore's needs. Murray was known to have "attended Chief Executives upon their journeys for half a score of years."[10] Forty books were purchased for Theodore and placed in his private quarters. An avid reader since childhood, Theodore was known to consume two books a week, reading even while sitting in a carriage. The books for this trip ranged from S. S. Pratt's *The Work of Wall Street* to Eleanor Gates's *Biography of a Prairie Girl* to his friend Richard Harding Davis's *Captain Macklin*.[11]

As the plans for his wide-ranging trip took shape, Theodore was adamant that his speeches and appearances should not be partisan in any manner. He insisted to reporters that this would not be a campaign trip. Although he had yet to publicly state that he would seek another term, it was all but a foregone conclusion that Theodore would run again. However, others were determined to make Theodore Roosevelt a one-term president.

Ever since his administration filed its antitrust lawsuit against the Northern Securities Company,[12] the Wall Street money men and business friendly Republicans were not pleased with Theodore's leadership. As the lawsuit slowly made its way through the halls of justice, Wall Street investors began to form a plan to defeat Roosevelt. "There is an ugly feeling among some of the big Wall Street men against me," Theodore wrote to his friend Seth Bullock. "Whether they will dare to come out openly I do not know. They are at present, using their organ, the *Sun*, as the chief means of attacking me."[13] Some investors favored a Democratic president "of approved conservatism" such as Grover Cleveland. Other Wall Streeters voiced concerns that should a Democratic candidate win the White House, it would lead to an increase of Democrats in the house and state legislatures. As the *Evening Star* noted, "The big industrial corporations are not ready to risk even half a democratic administration soon again."[14]

It wasn't just Wall Street that soured on Theodore. Many in the South had high hopes of his leadership when he assumed the presidency, but those hopes quickly evaporated. Tennessee's former secretary of state, William S. Morgan, pulled no punches in his assessment:

> I believe the Republicans of the South are for Senator Hanna in preference to President Roosevelt. The latter has been somewhat of a disappointment to Southern people ... because of his courage and integrity, they expected he would prove an ideal head of the Nation. But his pushing forward of the colored people has cost him many friends.[15]

In late April, the attack against Theodore went public with a biting editorial in the *Sun*. The newspaper assailed Theodore in "the most approved style of caustic invective," stating that the president was twisting every effort to secure a nomination. The editorial further stated that the president's attacks on wealth "exceeded the wildest threats of Bryanism and populism," going on to compare Theodore with Emperor William of Germany and Napoleon. The editorial ended with the observation that "while Napoleon had mowed down the mob in front of the Tuileries, Napoleon had not invited the mob to the Tuileries."[16]

Opinions regarding the editorial were split within the Republican Party. Those who supported Theodore were angry, while the other side held the opinion that he had it coming to him. (Issues of the newspaper were sold out in Washington by noon.) Speculation swirled that Wall Street and other business factions would support a Democratic candidate for president, but that was purely a tactic to scare the president into changing course. If anything, it only solidified Theodore's decision that he was correct. Opponents painted Theodore as emotional and quick to take action, whereas others suggested he was also receptive to suggestions despite these attributes. Both observations of the man were correct—to a point. Although he would listen to advice—and at times alter his decisions based on such consultation—in the end, the final decision was always based on what he felt was the right thing to do.

The *Evening Star* commented that as long as the Wall Street interests "fight Roosevelt out in the open," the president would "come out ahead." However, as the newspaper stated, Wall Street had no intention of fighting Theodore out in the open.

> The real opposition that will show results, it is said, is being developed in secret plans that will look to an absolute control over the next republican nominating convention.
>
> This, it is stated, is to be done very largely by the instrumentality of the railroads of the entire country. Everywhere railroad influence is regarded as extremely strong. The roads have their friends in every community. These are men of influence in both political parties, but especially potent in republican counsels in Pennsylvania, New York and other states in which the control of delegates to the republican convention will be of the greatest importance.
>
> Those who are relying on this plan for a control of the delegates look forward to much less interest on the part of the public in the work of nominating conventions than is shown in elections. Whatever may be the influence of Roosevelt in a general way in communities all over the country, it is not expected that this popularity will count for much in a practical way against the systematic work to be carried on by shrewd politicians, who, with maps in hand, will indicate a plan of campaign to be carried on in every county, backed by all the money that may be needed to bring success.[17]

In a letter to his close friend, Senator Henry Cabot Lodge, Theodore made it plain that he was ready for a fight. Referring to a speech he would make in Butte, Montana, he was ready for "having a knock-down and drag-out fight with [Senator Mark] Hanna and the whole Wall Street crowd, and I wanted them to understand that if they so desire, they shall have all the fighting they wish."[18]

Wall Street warmed up to the idea of Senator Mark Hanna as the Republican nominee. Hanna, who was a close ally to President McKinley, was against Theodore as the vice presidential candidate in 1900 from the beginning. When Theodore assumed office after McKinley's assassination, Hanna was heard to exclaim, "Now we've got that damned cowboy in office!" Despite the attention heaped on him, Hanna was coy about a run for the presidency. In reality, he had zero interest in running for or becoming president, preferring his Senate position. Yet he did nothing to stop the hints and rumors that he would run against Theodore for the Republican nomination. (J. P. Morgan offered to fund Hanna's run for office.) Ohio Senator Joseph B. Foraker, attending the state's annual Republican convention, unleashed a surprising resolution: convention members would endorse Theodore for president a year early. It was a squeeze play by Foraker, in the most underhanded way, to wrest from Hanna his dominance of the state's party. Hanna was forced to make a choice: go along with Foraker's move and confirm he was not running or oppose the resolution, indicating his desire for the nomination. If he chose the latter, it would create animosity with Theodore.

Hanna telegraphed Theodore that he would "oppose such a resolution." He went on to assure him that when Theodore was made aware of all the facts in the matter, he would "approve my course." Theodore spent twenty-four hours contemplating a reply. Deciding "that the time had come to stop shilly-shallying," he telegraphed Hanna that he had not asked "any man for his support," nor did he have anything to do with Foraker's actions. Since the issue was raised, "those who favor my administration and my nomination will favor endorsing both and those who do not will oppose." Realizing he was painted into a corner, Hanna replied "in view of the sentiment expressed" he would not oppose Foraker's resolution.[19]

Though many still held out hope Hanna would accept the nomination, it was all for naught. The Ohio senator, whose health was failing, died on February 15, 1904.

John Burroughs, the eminent American naturalist and writer, became friends with Theodore after sharing a lunch at the Fellowcraft Club in New York City in March 1889. Theodore told the naturalist that he gave copies of the latter's book *Wake-Robin* as gifts to underprivileged boys in New York City, with the suggestion to read it attentively, as it was "all that was good and important in life."[20]

Burroughs, who described Theodore as "a man of such abounding energy and ceaseless activity that he sets everything into motion around him," found a fellow naturalist who shared his passion for the outdoors. In early 1903, Burroughs wrote an article, "Real and Sham Natural History," for the *Atlantic Monthly* in which he attacked popular nature writers of the day for their outlandish representations regarding wildlife. It caused controversy, with some finding fault with the famed naturalist's comments. "I was delighted with your *Atlantic* article. I have long wished that something of the kind should be written," Theodore noted in his letter to Burroughs. Theodore extended an invitation for Burroughs to accompany him to Yellowstone.

> If the Senate will permit, and unless it proves impossible to dodge the infernal yellow papers [*newspapers*], I would like to visit the Yellowstone Park for a fortnight this spring. I want to see the elk, deer, sheep and antelope there, for the Superintendent of the Park, Major Pitcher, tells me they are just as tame as domestic animals. I wonder whether you could not come along? I would see that you endured neither fatigue nor hardship.[21]

At first, the sixty-five-year-old Burroughs had doubts about footslogging with Theodore in Yellowstone. Admitting he was a "non-strenuous person," wholly unlike Theodore, who lived the "strenuous life" he preached, Burroughs worried about walking in deep snow with snowshoes ("I never had the things on in my life") or whether the "infernal fires" beneath the park would melt the snow and the group would be "tearing along on horseback at a wolf-hunt pace." Ultimately, Burroughs realized that traveling with Theodore would be an adventure. "I knew nothing about big game," he wrote, "but I knew there was no man in the country with whom I should so like to see it as Roosevelt."[22]

Theodore was delighted to learn that Burroughs accepted his offer.

I am overjoyed that you can go. When I get to Yosemite, I shall spend four days with John Muir. Much though I shall enjoy that, I shall enjoy far more spending the two weeks in Yellowstone with you. . . . Bring pretty warm clothing, but that is all. Everything else will be provided in the Park. Of course, I should be delighted to have you go on the train with me from Washington, but I think it would be less tiresome for you if you joined me in Fargo. Come without fail; & let me know where you will join my special train—here or Fargo.[23]

On March 14, 1903, Theodore signed an executive order that, along with other actions during his presidency, earned him the title of "the conservationist president." Pelican Island, located on the east coast of Florida, was a haven for pelicans and white egrets, as well as other birds and wildlife. Fashion dictates for women's hats in the early 1900s demanded they be adorned with feathers, and poachers slaughtered egrets by the thousands. Members of the American Ornithologists Union (AOU) attempted to purchase the island from the U.S. government in an effort to save the birds but were met with stony silence. When he learned of the birds' fate, Theodore asked if there was any law preventing him from making Pelican Island a federal bird sanctuary. Informed that the island was federal property and that there were no laws to prevent his action, Theodore slammed his hand on his desk. "I so declare it!" he said. It marked the first time in the country's history that the U.S. government had set aside land as a federal bird reserve. Pelican Island was the first of fifty-one federal bird sanctuaries that Theodore would enact into law as president.

John Burroughs noted in his diary: "His sense of right and duty was as inflexible as adamant. Politicians found him a hard customer."[24]

Around three o'clock on the morning of April 1, Theodore rang his call bell in his bedroom at the White House. The attendant rushed up to his room, expecting the worst.

Theodore inquired if the man could call one of the telegraph offices to find out who won the fight in San Francisco. When he was informed that Young Corbett had knocked out Terry McGovern in the eleventh round, Theodore was disappointed, as he believed McGovern would win.

Thanking the man, he rolled over and went back to sleep. In five hours, he would begin his Great Loop Tour.

The Journey Begins:
Pennsylvania to Minnesota

Speak softly and carry a big stick.

THE STEAM ENGINE HUFFED AND HISSED AS IT SAT ON THE TRACKS AT the Baltimore and Potomac Station waiting for its special passenger.[1] The Pullman cars gleamed in the morning sun, as newspaper reporters and other well-wishers waited on the platform.

Striding down the platform at his usual nimble pace, Theodore arrived wearing a cutaway coat, dark-striped pants, and his familiar black slouch hat. His eyes caught the "wistful looks in the eyes" of three schoolgirls, and he stopped to talk and shake hands with them before moving to the assembled group of people.

Among the crowd was the German minister Baron Speck van Sternberg, the only member of the diplomatic corps to see Theodore off. Asking the baron if he would be in Washington in June when he returned, the German minister replied that he would. Theodore told him they would have "some more bully rides together." The baron regretfully informed Theodore that his riding horses were in India and would not arrive until June. Theodore insisted he take his horse for several rides while he was gone, to which the reedy German diplomat asked if he would be too light for Theodore's horse. This comment provided Theodore with a hearty laugh before giving orders that the baron have complete access to his horse during his absence.[2]

None of his immediate family was there to see him off, with the exception of his older sister, Anna ("Bamie"). Edith and the children had taken the presidential yacht, *Mayflower*, for a trip down the Atlantic coast to Port Royal, North Carolina. William Loeb, Theodore's assistant secretary, sent Edith a note assuring her that he would see that her husband was returned "safe and sound."[3]

Although Theodore was adamant that this trip was not a political campaign tour, the *Evening Star* commented the trip would "take another pull on the girth of his popularity and cinch it up a hole higher."[4]

The Pennsylvania House and Senate passed a motion to suspend work in order to visit Theodore at the Harrisburg train station. Although his train stopped for only five minutes to take on water, state Senator Benjamin Focht greeted Theodore and the large crowd, stating he wished the president could have been welcomed at the capitol, but at least they were within sight of Zion Lutheran Church, where President William Henry Harrison had been nominated in 1839. Briefly addressing the crowd, Theodore turned to a Civil War veteran in the crowd, proudly wearing his Grand Army of the Republic pin on his coat's lapel. Pointing to the veteran, he said,

> And you, my comrade with the little bronze button on your coat, who fought in the great war! When you thought of the man at your shoulder you did not consider whether he was a lawyer, a doctor, a bricklayer, or a millionaire. Your thought for the man next to you was only as to whether he would "stay put." This principle is vital in war and no less so in peace. Every man must pull his own weight and do his best to help his brother.[5]

When his speech was finished, the crowd surged forward to shake his hand. As the train began to slowly pull out, Theodore leaned over the rail and shook the hand of the Civil War veteran.

"First Day of Tour Finds Him Enjoying Himself in a Characteristic Way," noted the subheading of a *Chicago Tribune* article. For most of the day after leaving Harrisburg, Theodore spent his time reading one of his forty books. As the train pulled into Altoona, Pennsylvania, he stepped out on the rear platform to wave at the gathering crowd before walking down the left side of the train, followed by Secret Service agents who kept the crowd back. While greeting the train crew, he watched as a second engine was coupled to pull the cars over the Allegheny Mountains. Special Engineer Robert McLaren invited Theodore to step up into the train cab, where he sat in the fireman's seat (located on the left side).[6] As the train pulled out, people cheered, while Theodore wore one of the widest grins possible. Along the way, he viewed the famous Horseshoe Curve in Blair County from his cab seat.[7] Reporters noted that the train traversed a tunnel that was seven-eighths of a mile long, and despite the windows and doors "quite a quantity of smoke" found its way into the cab. When the train reached Gallitzin, the crest of the Allegheny Mountains, the front engine was detached, leaving the engine that Theodore was occupying to make the rest of the run to Seward. At that brief stop, Theodore climbed down from the cab, heartily shaking hands with the engineer and fireman. Although he was "rather dusty and grimy" from his experience, Theodore was nothing but "enthusiastic" over it.

Theodore's plans to make his tour nonpartisan were almost derailed by Republican Party members in Chicago. The city's "party machine" believed Theodore's appearance would be an ideal way to help their mayoral candidate, Graeme Stuart, in the upcoming municipal elections, five days after his visit. (Stuart lost to Carter Harrison Jr. despite Theodore's vain hopes of seeing the incumbent defeated.) It was their proposal to have only Republican Party members greet Theodore at the train station and attend the banquet in his honor. Senator Albert Hopkins, who spoke with the president prior to his Chicago visit, conveniently failed to inform him that only party members would be present at the train station and the banquet. Hopkins wired the Chicago Republican Party that everything had been "fixed." However, two reliable Washington-based newspaper reporters tipped Theodore off about the party's Chicago plans. Livid at being used when he had expressly stated that the tour was to be completely nonpartisan, he dashed off telegrams to the city's Republican Party stating that if Mayor Carter Harrison Jr. and other Democrat-elected leaders were not included, he would simply scratch Chicago entirely from his trip. He also demanded that the city's leading Democratic officials be placed on committees and "assigned conspicuous places on the program." Republican Party members, however reluctant, had no choice but to accede to Theodore's demands. "Not only would the original reception plan have shown bad taste, but it would have harmed Graeme Stuart and harmed the president," noted *the Minneapolis Journal.*[8]

Because Theodore's train arrived in Chicago thirty minutes ahead of schedule, it was forced to wait in the stockyard area until the suburban trains had cleared from the station. Sitting down to breakfast in his car, Theodore chuckled, "You can't come here without the Chicago people impressing upon you that they have the stock yards."[9] As his train moved into Union Station, numerous railway men ran alongside hoping for a glimpse of the president. Someone in the train notified Theodore, who quickly looked out the window and doffed his hat to the men, who "set up a cheer."

Greeted at the station platform by Mayor Harrison and a mixed delegation of Democrats and Republicans, Theodore was off on a nonstop tour of the Windy City. Noting the many families present to greet him, Theodore stated, "they are right in quantity and quality. I wish to state in all seriousness that a deficiency in either cannot be atoned for by an excellence in the other respect."

With the greetings out of the way, Theodore's train took him seventeen miles to Evanston, where he spoke to students at Northwestern University. (The university had given him a doctor of laws degree in 1893.) Greeted by a military band, a twenty-one-gun salute, and rousing cheers from the students, Theodore settled into his speech.

The President *[of Northwestern University]* has said that still, after two thousand years, it is a subject of discussion as to exactly how much a college education does for a man or woman. It seems to me that the explanation why that still is a question is, after all, simple. If either the boy or the girl, the man or the woman, has not got the right stuff in him or her, you cannot bring it out.

But if you have got the right stuff in you, why, then, surely it is the veriest truism to say that the better your training the better will be the kind of work that you can do. This, above all, to the young men going out, each to do a man's work in the world—and if he has not that purpose he is of no use whatsoever in our American life; we have no room for the idler here; we have no room for the man who merely wishes to lead a pleasant life; if that is all he desires he can never count in American work; if the man has not got in him the desire to count, the desire to do good work in whichever line he adopts, then scant is our use for him.

But if he has got it in him, then all that I ask him to remember is this—all that I ask each one of you here to remember is this: that if you go from this university—from any university—feeling merely that your course here has given you special privileges; if you feel that it has put you in a class apart, you will fail in life. If you feel, on the other hand, that the very fact of your having had special advantages imposes upon you special responsibilities, makes it especially incumbent upon you to show that you can do your duty with peculiar excellence; if you approach life in that spirit the university training will have done much for you. . . . Now, it is a great thing to have a safe and a strong and a vigorous body. It is a better thing to have a sage, a strong and a vigorous mind. But best of all is to have that which is partly made up of both, and partly made up of something higher and better—character.[10]

Returning to Chicago, he attended a luncheon before traveling to the University of Chicago, where he was to be given an LLD (doctor of laws) degree. Along the route, there was an accident that no doubt jolted the memory of many, including the president, bringing the recent tragedy in Massachusetts to mind.[11] A trooper from the First Illinois Cavalry was thrown from his horse as the party passed the Chicago Board of Trade building. His horse fell against the lead horses of Theodore's carriage, causing them to rear up and jerk the carriage to a halt. Managing to hold onto his horse's reins, the trooper quickly remounted. As the carriage continued to the university, it was stopped by three white-haired women who stood in the middle of the street. The trio of elderly ladies had been holding a meeting at the Second Presbyterian Church when they realized the president would soon be passing by. One of the ladies grabbed all the flowers in the room, making a huge bouquet of white lilies and carnations, as they walked out to the street. The trio walked up to Theodore's carriage and presented him their gift. They spoke to him for a few minutes before they returned to "clothing the heathen."

After receiving his degree, Theodore laid the cornerstone for the new law school building. He reminded those assembled that one needed to be "harmless as a dove, wise as a serpent," and have morality "that does and fears, morality that can suffer, and morality that can achieve results." If one had that, Theodore stated, coupled with the energy and power to accomplish things, he would "be of real value" to the community. The need for genius or brilliancy, he added, was not as important as "homely, commonplace, elemental virtues." Citing why the United States won the Revolutionary War in 1776 and the Union in "the great trial from 1861 to 1865," was due to the average citizen who "had in him the stuff out of which good citizenship has been made from time immemorial, because he had in him courage, honesty, common sense."

As the group returned to downtown Chicago, Theodore, in typical fashion, decided to walk to the Auditorium Annex Hotel. State's Attorney Charles Deneen elected to walk with the president, learning a lesson about the infamous "Roosevelt stride." The president's stride, according to the *Chicago Tribune*, led off with Deneen making "a brave show" of keeping up. As Theodore's nonstop gait continued, the reporter commented that his chin was up, "eyes gleaming and teeth showing in a succession of smiles" as he raised his hat to those who cheered him. By now, the majority of his party had dropped back and his Secret Service agents were doing their best "to keep up" without showing any effort, while Deneen "was losing ground." The newspaper noted that Theodore's stride was not only long but "rapid." Deneen was, as the paper mentioned, "in at the finish, but that is about all that can be said." Theodore, turning to Deneen, complimented the lake air, adding that he would like to take a five-mile walk in the evening. "Mr. Deneen made no audible reply," the reporter stated.[12]

The Monroe Doctrine, issued on December 2, 1823, by President James Monroe, became an integral part of foreign policy for the United States. The doctrine stated no European country could assert control of any independent nation within North or South America. To do otherwise would be looked upon by the United States as an act of hostility. The doctrine also declared that the United States would not interfere with any European nation that already had established colonies in either America, nor would it impede any domestic concerns of a European nation.[13] Over the decades, this declaration has been invoked by several U.S. presidents including Theodore, Ulysses S. Grant, John F. Kennedy, and Ronald Reagan.[14] Although most European nations had ignored the doctrine because the United States lacked a credible navy at the time, it went on to become a powerful tool in foreign policy.

Originally, Theodore's speech in Chicago was going to focus on the trusts, but city Republicans convinced him to change the subject in order to avoid any misinterpretation or misunderstanding among Democratic city leaders. (Mayor Harrison opposed Theodore's antitrust lawsuit against the Northwestern Securities Company.) Theodore noted in a letter to John Hay, his secretary of state, that his speech was "calculated to avoid jarring even the sensitive nerves of Carter Harrison, who as Mayor had to greet me, and who was just in the final days of a contest for re-election."[15] Agreeing with their suggestion, he went on to speak about the Monroe Doctrine, which he planned to address in Milwaukee. The hall in the Auditorium Annex Hotel room was filled to its capacity of five thousand people.

> I wish to speak to you not merely about the Monroe Doctrine, but about our entire position in the Western Hemisphere, a position so peculiar and predominant that out of it has grown the acceptance of the Monroe Doctrine as a cardinal feature of our foreign policy.... The Monroe Doctrine is not international law, and though I think one day it may become such, this is not necessary as long as it remains a cardinal feature of our foreign policy and as long as we possess both the will and the strength to make it effective.... I believe in the Monroe Doctrine with

all my heart and soul. . . . I would infinitely prefer to see us abandon it than to see us put it forward and bluster about it, and yet fail to build up the efficient fighting strength which, in the last resort, can alone make it respected by any strong foreign power whose interest it may ever happen to be to violate it. Boasting and blustering are as objectionable among nations as among individuals, and the public men of a great nation owe it to their sense of national self-respect to speak courteously of foreign powers, just as a brave and self-respecting man treats all around him courteously. But though to boast is bad, and causelessly to insult another, worse yet, worse than all is it to be guilty of boasting, even without insult, and when called to the proof to be unable to make such boasting good.

There is a homely old adage which runs: "Speak softly and carry a big stick; you will go far." If the American Nation will speak softly, and yet build and keep at a pitch of the highest training, a thoroughly efficient navy, the Monroe Doctrine will go far.[16]

After completing his speech, Theodore retired to his suite in the hotel for a late evening meal and then took a carriage to his train, which left Chicago after midnight.

—◆—

Undoubtedly, the most famous aphorism spoken by Theodore is "speak softly and carry a big stick." However, the speech in Chicago was not the first time he expressed this sentiment. The first known documentation is found in a letter dated January 26, 1900, to New York Assemblyman Henry L. Sprague when Theodore was governor.

I have always been fond of the West African proverb: "Speak softly and carry a big stick; you will go far." If I had not carried the big stick the organization would not have gotten behind me, and if I had yelled and blustered as Parkhurst and the similar dishonest lunatics desired, I would not have had ten votes.[17]

Theodore's first use of this adage in a public speech was at the Minnesota State Fair when he was vice president.[18]

A good many of you are probably acquainted with the old proverb, "Speak softly and carry a big stick—you will go far." If a man continually blusters, if he lacks civility, a big stick will not save him from trouble, and neither will speaking softly avail, if back of that softness there does not lie strength, power. In private life there are few beings more obnoxious than the man who is always loudly boasting, and if the boaster is not prepared to back up his words, his position becomes absolutely contemptible. So it is with the nation. It is both foolish and undignified to indulge in undue self-glorification, and above all, in loose-tongued denunciation of other peoples. . . . I hope that we shall always strive to speak courteously and respectfully of that foreign power. Let us make it evident that we intend to do justice. Then let us make it equally evident that we will not tolerate injustice being done to us in return. Let us further make it evident that we use no words which we are not prepared to back up with deeds, and that while our speech is always moderate, we are ready and willing to make it good.[19]

As for Theodore stating it was a West African proverb, historians question his veracity. If, in 1900, it was an old African proverb, there would be some evidence of previous citation, yet nothing has been found, nor is there any evidence that the quote was ever used in West Africa prior to Theodore's time. Some believe that Theodore invented the quote, adding the West African proverb as a way to give it greater distinction.

No matter where the dictum originated, it is synonymous with Theodore, even referring to his administration's foreign policy as the "Big Stick Policy." Today, the U.S. Navy aircraft carrier *Theodore Roosevelt* is nicknamed "The Big Stick."

Theodore's train arrived in Madison, Wisconsin, at four in the morning. There were no crowds or speeches made as the president and his traveling party slept. At nine o'clock in the morning, Theodore was greeted by Governor Robert LaFollette, Mayor John Groves, and numerous members of the state legislature assembled for the traditional welcome and photo opportunities. The party then was escorted by military guard to the front of the state capitol, where Theodore addressed two houses in a joint session as well as seven hundred invited guests.

> Our universities, our colleges and academies fill a double purpose throughout the country. In the first place there is a percentage of the members who are to be trained in pure scholarship, sometimes scholarship of a sort that has direct reference to certain pursuits in afterlife of immediate practical value; sometimes scholarship to be followed for the sake of the scholarship. . . . I want to see the student of the American university turned out, having deeply implanted in him the purpose to strive to do new work of value in the field of scholarship, not merely to go over those portions of the field that have been harrowed by ten thousand harrows before him, but to strike out and do original work of value. . . . It is a first class thing for a young fellow of twenty to be a crack halfback, but if at forty all you can say of him is that once he was a good halfback, then I am sorry for him. . . . I want to see the young men of America, whether in or out of the universities, fine of body; I want still more to see them fine of mind; but most of all we must hope that they develop well that which counts for more than body, for more than mind—character.[20]

Finishing his speech, Theodore stepped outside the capitol where he addressed the assembled crowd out in front. He told them that the country was passing through "a period of great material prosperity" and there would be occasional ups and downs, but in the long run "the tide will go on if we but prove true to ourselves" and the beliefs of "our forefathers." Theodore stated that the American people must fuse the spirit of individualism and cooperation. "Each man must work for himself. If he cannot support himself he will be but a drag on mankind, but each man must work for the common good," he added. "There is not a man here who does not at times need to have a helping hand extended to him, and shame on his brother who will not extend that helping hand."[21]

Stores around the state capitol were closed to allow employees an opportunity to see and hear the president, while newsboys worked the crowd, hawking their two-cent papers at an inflated price of five cents.

Prior to Theodore's arrival, merchants in Madison experienced an upsurge in purchases of silk top hats. Calls were made to Chicago for the desired headgear, causing some to arrive with the early morning train. Nonetheless, many dignitaries were forced to go hatless. One member of the committee halted the procession when his top hat was blown off his head in front of the city's opera house. A woman, attempting to catch the wayward hat, "fell headlong" to the ground before the top hat was recovered. Even Theodore had to contend with the blustery weather when his carriage turned onto Wilson Street; the wind kicked up and "the president barely retained his hat."[22]

The reporter covering Theodore's visit to Madison for the city's *Wisconsin State Journal* commented that the president looked like "a gentleman prize fighter" (a term that would have delighted Theodore) and noted that his speeches were "much alike" as they dealt with "decency [a favorite word], with common sense, and useful, plain strong living." Had these words been uttered by an average citizen, they "would sound commonplace," yet when spoken by Theodore they carried "immense weight, as his words are backed by character."[23]

John Burroughs described Theodore to the local newspaper reporter as a man "full of vivacity and full of action." He showed the reporter Theodore's room on the train and the leather chair where he read during the trip. The room, the reporter commented, was "arranged so comfortably" that no one could resist the temptation to "sit in a cozy corner." Several newspapers, along with copies of *The Two Van Revels, Stories of the West,* and Owen Wister's *The Virginian* (which was dedicated to Theodore) were carefully arranged next to his reading chair.[24]

Finishing his speech in front of the capitol, Theodore returned to his train, which departed at eleven o'clock. Arriving in Lake Mills, his train managed to avoid a near calamity. A crowd had gathered on the train platform to see Theodore. When the train stopped, the crowd surged to the train's rear platform, but something on the tracks (it was reported as "a jam") caused the train to back up. Train yard workers yelled at the crowd to get back, and the crowd quickly splintered, with no one seriously hurt. Theodore's train stayed in the station for only three minutes to take on water, and he stepped out on the rear platform to express his regrets that his stop was so short.[25] After another brief stop for water at Jefferson Junction, Theodore told a group of two hundred people that, having lived in the West, he was "glad to get back into a country where he could see a few overcoats."

The train moved on to Waukesha, where a platform had been set up at the west end of the train depot. Introduced by the city's mayor, George Harding, Theodore went on to speak about diplomacy and U.S. foreign policy in dealing with the world's current problems.

> I believe that we are now, at the outset of the twentieth century, face to face with great world problems; that we cannot help playing the part of a great world power; that all we can decide is whether we will play it well or ill, . . . Strength should go hand in hand with courtesy, with scrupulous regard in word and deed, not only for the rights, but for the feelings of other nations. I want to see a man able to hold his own. I have no respect for the man who will put up with injustice. . . . I have a hearty contempt for the man who is always walking about wanting to pick a quarrel, and above all, wanting to say something unpleasant about someone else. He is not an agreeable character anywhere; and the fact that he talks loud does not necessarily mean that he fights hard either. Sometimes you will see a man who will talk loud and fight hard; but he does not fight hard because he talks loud, but in spite of it. I want the same thing to be true of us as a nation. I am always sorry whenever I see any reflection that seems to come from America upon any friendly nation. To write or say anything unkind, unjust, or inconsiderate about any foreign nation does not do us any good, and does not help us toward holding our own if ever the need should arise to hold our own. . . . I do not believe the United States should ever suffer a wrong. I should be the first to ask that we resent a wrong from the strong, just as I should be the first to insist that we do not wrong the weak. As a nation, if we are to be true to our past, we must steadfastly keep these two positions to submit to no injury by the strong and to inflict no

injury on the weak. . . . But remember that a loose tongue is just as unfortunate an accompaniment for a nation as for an individual. The man who talks ill of his neighbors, the man who invites trouble for himself and them is a nuisance. The stronger, the more self-confident the nation is, the more carefully it should guard its speech as well as its action, and should make it a point, in the interest of its own self-respect, to see that it does not say what it cannot make good, that it avoids giving needless offence, that it shows genuinely and sincerely its desire for friendship with the rest of mankind, but that it keeps itself in shape to make its weight felt should the need arise. . . . Let us not boast, not insult anyone, but make up our minds coolly what is necessary to say, say it, and then stand to it, whatever the consequences may be.[26]

John Burroughs noted that the usual agenda when the president arrived in a city was to be greeted by the reception committee, which generally met Theodore in his private car before stepping out onto the train platform to greet the assembled crowd. A carriage ride through the city would take him to either a hall or open-air platform to give one or two speeches. If the city was large enough, he would attend an evening banquet and give a speech before retiring to his train, which then would make its way to the next stop. Theodore generally made eight to ten speeches in a twenty-four-hour period. The length of the speeches could be as short as five minutes (when his train stopped to take on water at a station) or more than an hour at a banquet.

"Wherever I stopped at a small city or county town I was greeted by the usual shy, self-conscious, awkward body of local committeemen, and spoke to the usual audience of thoroughly good American citizens—a term I can use in a private letter to you without being thought demagogic!" he wrote to John Hay.[27]

The schedule in Milwaukee was similar, but this visit required Theodore to give five speeches in nine hours. His train arrived at two in the afternoon, and once introductions and greetings were made, Theodore took a carriage ride to the veterans home, where he spoke to two thousand Civil War veterans. He pointed out that the man who wanted to perform "some heroic act" was not the type of man needed in the military. Instead, the man that "stood firm and ready" was the most desired. Noting that the man who waited until he had an opportunity to "do something heroic" would "never do anything," but the man who was consistent and faithful in all of his duties as a soldier would also make a good citizen. Very few of them, he went on, ever concerned themselves about the profession of the man next to them, nor questioned how they worshiped their Creator. "All you cared for was "did he stand pat?" If he had the heart in him to do his duty in camp, if you could count on his standing with you, you were for him," Theodore stated. He strongly believed it should be the same in civilian life; rich or poor, raised here or across an ocean, worshipping the way a man chooses was of no concern. What was important was that if a man has "the right kind of living in him, then accept him for his worth as a man. Gauge his worth as you did the worth of your comrades," he concluded.[28]

Another carriage ride brought him to Exposition Park where he spoke to a large crowd. Again, his words focused on treating everyone fairly and good citizenship. "Woe will surely await this people if we ever permit ourselves to draw lines of distinction as between class and class, or creed and creed, or along any other line save that which divides good citizenship from bad citizenship," he offered. If a man, he continued, is "fearless and honorable, upright in his dealings" not only with his fellows, but also his family, neighbors, and the state, that is all "we have the right to ask about him." If a man does this, he is entitled to "our regard, and to our esteem." However, Theodore added that if a man does not conduct himself in such a manner, he has "forfeited all rights to the respect of a decent man." Theodore stressed that the important qualities for good citizenship were honesty and decency, courage and strength, and the saving grace of common sense. If one lacked these attributes and was "a natural born fool," he simply said, "May the Lord be with you."[29]

Theodore attended a luncheon with the Deutscher Club and then dashed off to the Milwaukee Press Club, where it bestowed upon him an honorary membership. Returning to his room at the Plankton House, he changed clothes for the merchant and manufacturer banquet at the Plankton Hotel, where he gave a speech on the trust issue.

I think I speak for the great majority of the American people when I say that we are not in the least against wealth as such, whether individual or corporate; that we merely desire to see any abuse of corporate or combined wealth corrected and remedied; that we do not desire the abolition or destruction of big corporations but, on the contrary, recognize them as being in many cases efficient economic instruments, the results of an inevitable process of economic evolution, and only desire to see them regulated and controlled so far as may be necessary to subserve the public good. . . . There is no proper place in our society either for the rich man who uses power conferred by his riches to enable him to oppose and wrong his neighbors, or yet for the demagogic agitator, who instead of attacking, abuses as all abuses should be attacked wherever found, attacks men of wealth, as such, whether they be good or bad, attacks corporations whether they do well or ill, and seeks, in a spirit of ignorant rancor, to overthrow the very foundations upon which rest our national wellbeing.

In consequence of the extraordinary industrial changes of the last half century, and notably of the last two or three decades, changes due mainly to the rapidity and complexity of our industrial growth, we are confronted with problems which in their present shape were unknown to our forefathers. Our great prosperity, with its accompanying concentration of population and wealth, its extreme specialization of faculties, and its development of giant industrial leaders has brought much good and some evil, and it is as foolish to ignore the good as willfully to blind ourselves to the evil. The evil has been partly the inevitable accompaniment of the social changes, and where this is the case it can be cured neither by law nor by the administration of the law, the only remedy lying in the slow change of character and of economic environment. But for a portion of the evil, at least, we think that remedies can be found. We know well the danger of false remedies, and we are against all violent, radical, and unwise change. But we believe that by proceeding slowly, yet resolutely, with good sense and moderation, and also with a firm determination not to be swerved from our course either by foolish clamor or by any base or sinister influence, we can accomplish much for the betterment of conditions. . . . Many of the alleged remedies advocated are of the unpleasantly drastic type which seek to destroy the disease by killing the patient. Others are so obviously futile that it is somewhat difficult to treat them seriously or as being advanced in good faith. High among the latter I place the effort to reach the trust question by means of the tariff. You can, of course, put an end to the prosperity of the trusts by putting an end to the prosperity of the Nation; but the price for such action seems high. The alternative is to do exactly what has been done during the life of the Congress which has just closed, that is, to endeavor, not to destroy corporations, but to regulate them with a view of doing away with whatever is of evil in them and of making them subserve the public use. The law is not to be administered in the interest of the poor man as such, nor yet in the interest of the rich man as such, but in the interest of the law-abiding man, rich or poor. We are no more against organizations of capital than against organizations of labor. We welcome both, demanding only that each shall do right and shall remember its duty to the Republic. Such a course we consider not merely a benefit to the poor man, but a benefit to the rich man. We do no man an injustice when we require him to obey the law.[30]

John Burroughs, who attended his speech, noted that a "dense cloud of tobacco smoke" filled the hall and it was "enough to choke any speaker, but it did not seem to choke the President."[31] By the time he finished his speech, it was past midnight. Theodore and his group made a quick exit for his train, which left nearly a half-hour late. After his long days in Chicago and Milwaukee, Theodore let it be known that he would no longer endure late nights, and his speeches would start no later than eight-thirty in the evening in order to return to his train by eleven o'clock.[32]

One incident in Milwaukee touched Theodore deeply. Mayor David Rose, a Democrat, left the bedside of his dying son in Tucson (in what was then Arizona Territory) to greet Theodore at the train station and then promptly returned to his son's bedside.[33]

Arriving the following morning in La Crosse, Wisconsin, Theodore once again was part of a carriage ride through the city, while thousands of people cheered him on. (It was estimated that the crowd numbered ten thousand.) Stopping in Market Square, Senator Joseph Quarles, during his introduction of Theodore, noted that they were not there "as politicians" but as "Americans who are proud of the achievements of a great republic," and the president "represents the highest type of free government and the loftiest ideals of free men." Quarles noted that the president could ride a horse, but the only problem was that no one else could keep up with him. "He was trained on the hurricane deck of an American broncho," the senator stated. The comment delighted Theodore to no end.[34] As he began his speech, Theodore assured the people of Wisconsin that although they would never have the chance to see his riding abilities for themselves, he preferred the people take the word of Senator Quarles instead.

Many in the crowd were Civil War veterans; Theodore, a veteran of another war, stated what mattered most was if the man had the right spirit to fight. Calling the veterans his comrades, he noted that the Spanish-American War was different than the Civil War because those involved "suffered from a complaint that you did not suffer from at all, there was not enough war to go 'round. You didn't have any such difficulty."

> You not only taught us the lessons of war, but you taught us the lessons of peace. . . . In ordinary life we are so apt to be divided by artificial distances. Our lives are so hemmed around that we often do not have the chance to test a man on his worth as a man. You, who fought in the Great War, had to judge your comrades by the stuff there was in them. . . . You knew what it was to toil, footsore and weary, under the blazing heat of the southern sun; you knew what it was to lie in the trenches in the frozen mud of winter; you faced death by bullets, death on the fever cot of the hospital; you saw the brightest and the bravest around you shed their blood like water for the sake of an ideal; you did all that, and you knew that was the test you applied to the men around you. Little you cared whether they came from one state or another. Little you cared what their creed was; little you cared whether their ancestors had come to this country two centuries and a half

ago, or whether they themselves had been born on the other side, but came over here and proved as you did, by their valor, their loyalty to their adopted flag. You cared for none of these things, they were not the essentials; what you cared for was whether the man had the right fiber in him. You wanted to know that when the order was given to move he would move in the right direction; that was what you were concerned with then.

It is just the same in citizenship now; what we need as never before in this country, if we are to make, as we assuredly shall and will make, our scheme of government a success, what we need to keep ever before us is the fact that any distinction is artificial which divides one man from his fellow. It is just as wicked, no matter from which standpoint the line of division is drawn, whether it is from a standpoint of those who look down with arrogance upon the less well off, or from the standpoint of those who regard with mean envy and rancor and hate others who are better off. . . . We have a right to demand that each man shall do his duty by his neighbor and his state; beyond that it is not our affair. Let him manage his own private business as he wishes, so long as he infringes no right of anyone else. Let him lead his private life as he desires; it is not our concern, provided only that he is a square and decent man, who wrongs no one and does his duty in peace and war, and that is the common-sense spirit of Americanism.[35]

Theodore noted that when he was ranching in Dakota Territory, he employed a cowboy who found a cow and a growing calf. He began to make a fire and was going to put Theodore's ranch brand on the calf. Theodore objected to the action and fired the cowboy on the spot. He told the man that if he would steal *for* him, he would certainly steal *from* him. "If a man will do something crooked and asks you to back him on the ground that it will turn out to your advantage, he will do something crooked to your harm if the chance comes," Theodore stated.[36]

Leaving La Crosse, his train made brief stops in Lake City and Winona, where he urged parents to teach their children "to do and not to dodge" and in doing so "learn true manhood and womanhood."

More than one hundred thousand people were estimated to be in St. Paul, Minnesota, when Theodore's train arrived in the afternoon to the sound of a twenty-one-gun cannonade.[37] As he stepped from the train, the vast crowd broke into a deafening cheer. Theodore acknowledged the greeting by lifting his hat and bowing several times, "accompanied by that famous smile which has proved such a boon to the cartoonists."

As his carriage made its way down streets that were brightly decorated with red, white, and blue bunting and flags, the crowd watched as Theodore rode by and then raced to another spot to watch him again. A reporter noted that Theodore's ever-present smile was at its "broadest whenever his eyes beheld the babies—and there were lots of them out there to greet their staunch defender and champion."[38] The day before Theodore's arrival, an ad in the *Saint Paul Globe* urged everyone to fly their flags for the president's visit, noting every home should be "decorated in the manner befitting the President of the United States. DECORATE YOUR HOUSE!"

Many people in the crowds had the latest Kodak camera with them in hopes of snapping a picture of their president. It was reported that more than five hundred cameras were sold by various stores in St. Paul prior to the presidential stopover. One store sold two hundred cameras before restricting sales in order to avoid exhausting their supply. Newspapers dubbed citizens with cameras as "Kodak fiends." One of these "fiends" was at the corner of Fifth and Market Streets when he rushed Theodore's carriage in hopes of obtaining a rare picture. He was within a few feet and prepared to "sight his machine" at the president when a Secret Service agent stepped in front of him. The newspaper noted that the agent "quickly interposed his broad form and a spoiled plate resulted."[39]

At one point, John Burroughs was the center of attention during the procession. A group of girls from Monroe School waited for the carriage carrying Burroughs with a banner and a garland of wild flowers. Spotting Burroughs, the girls marched from the sidewalk and presented their bouquet to him. The naturalist later admitted that he didn't know who blushed more—himself or the group of girls. He noted that Theodore said he was "delighted to see you honored that way."[40]

Speaking to the Minnesota legislature, Theodore compared parenting children to a nation's role in the world theater.

So often throughout our social structure from the wealthiest down to the poorest, you see the queer fatuity of the man or the woman which makes them save their children from temporary discomfort, temporary unpleasantness, at the cost of future destruction; you see a great many men, and I am sorry to say a great many women, who say, "I have had to work hard; my boy or my girl shall not do anything." I have seen it in every rank. I have heard the millionaire say, "I have had to work all my life to make money, let my boy spend it."

It would be better for the boy never to have been born than to be brought up on that principle. On the other hand, I have seen the overworked drudge, the laborer's wife, who said, "Well, I have had to work my heart out all my days; my daughters shall be ladies"; and her conception of her daughters being ladies was to have them sit around useless and incompetent, unable to do anything, brought up to be discontented cumberers of the earth's surface. . . . Fundamentally, virtues and faults are just the same in the millionaire and the day laborer. The man or the woman who seeks to bring up his or her children with the idea that their happiness is secured by teaching them to avoid difficulties is doing them a cruel wrong. To bring up the boy and girl so sheltered that they cannot stand any rough knocks, that they shrink from toil, that when they meet an obstacle, they feel they ought to go around or back instead of going on over it—the man or the woman who does that is wronging the children to a degree that no other human being can wrong them. If you are worth your salt and want your children to be worth their salt, teach them that the life that is not a life of work and effort is worthless, a curse to the man or woman leading it, a curse to those around him or her.

Teach the boys that if they are ever to count in the world they will count not by flinching from difficulties, but by warring with and overcoming them. What utter scorn one feels for those who seek only the life of ease. . . . What a wretched life is the life of the man passed in endeavoring to shirk his share of the burden laid upon him in this world! And it makes no difference whether that man is a man of inherited wealth or one who has to earn his bread by the sweat of his brow; it is equally ignoble in either case. What is true of the individual is true of the nation. The man who counts is not the man who dodges work, but he who goes out into life rejoicing as a strong man to run a race, girding himself for the effort, bound to win and wrest triumph from difficulty and disaster. . . . No nation which has bound itself only to do easy things ever yet amounted to anything, ever yet came to anything throughout the ages. . . . We face great problems within and great problems without. We cannot if we would refuse to face those problems. All we can decide is whether we will do them well or ill; for the refusal to face them would itself mean that we were doing them ill. We are in the arena into which great nations must come. We must play our part. It rests with us to decide that we shall not play it ignobly; that we shall not flinch from the great problems that there are to do, but that we shall take our place in the forefront of the great nations and face each problem of the day with confident and resolute hope.[41]

One interesting aspect of Theodore's visit to St. Paul was the lack of crime. The *Saint Paul Globe* noted that with more than one hundred thousand people in the city to see the president, there was not one case of a pickpocket at work. Police Chief O'Connor noted that the lack of pickpockets plying their trade was due to the exhaustive detective staff that worked the crowd looking for trouble. Nor were any homes "entered by burglars," no patrol wagons summoned, and not even a drunk was arrested.[42]

Theodore and his party left St. Paul by electric trolley for the fourteen-mile ride to Minneapolis, where he took an hour's rest at the Nicollett Hotel before attending a dinner downstairs. Afterward he gave a speech at the University of Minnesota's armory. The crowd outside the hotel was disappointed that they could not see him, so at the suggestion of Minnesota governor Samuel Van Sant, Theodore gave an impromptu speech on the second floor, telling the crowd they were the state that "stands for the true Western spirit of development and devotion to country." A man from the crowd yelled, "Teddy's all right!" which spurred the crowd to repeat the statement, despite Theodore's disdain of being called "Teddy." "And I know that you are all right!" he yelled back to the crowd.[43]

Theodore made a brief stop at the university chapel where he told students that he believed in a sound and vigorous body, as well as a vigorous mind and character. "Keep the sense of proportion. Play hard; it will do you good in your work. But work hard and remember that this is the main thing," he told them. In his closing remarks, he recalled the motto of an old football player: "Don't flinch, don't foul, and hit the line hard."[44]

More than four thousand people waited for Theodore to give his speech at the university's armory. Walking into the auditorium at ten o'clock, Theodore spoke about the tariff law and its importance to all Americans—businessmen, workers, and farmers alike. "We must as a people approach a matter of such prime economic importance as the tariff from the standpoint of our business needs," he stated.

> We cannot afford to become fossilized or fail to recognize the fact that as the needs of the country change, it may be necessary to meet these new needs by changing certain features of our tariff laws. Still less can we afford to fail to recognize the further fact that these changes must not be made until the need for them outweighs the disadvantages which may result; and when it becomes necessary to make them, they should be made with full recognition of the need for stability in our economic system and of keeping unchanged the principle of that system which has now become a settled policy in our national life. We have prospered marvelously at home. As a nation we stand in the very forefront in the giant international industrial competition of the day. We cannot afford by any freak or folly to forfeit the position to which we have thus triumphantly attained.[45]

Once his speech was concluded, Theodore returned to his train at 11:00 p.m., and it left within minutes.

Theodore was now heading to an area with which he was well acquainted—North and South Dakota.

Old Stomping Grounds:
North and South Dakota

You can lift up a man if he stumbles; if he lies down you cannot carry him.

"HE GAVE HIMSELF VERY FREELY AND HEARTILY TO THE PEOPLE WHER-ever he went. He could easily match their Western cordiality and good-fellowship. Wherever his train stopped, crowds soon gathered, or had already gathered, to welcome him. His advent made a holiday in each town he visited," commented John Burroughs about Theodore's tour.[1]

Burroughs was not exaggerating about Theodore's ability to connect with the average American. He spoke with an honesty that the citizens understood and gravitated toward. There was no pretense when he met people. He was genuinely interested in them and their lives. Some critics were quick to dismiss his outgoing personality as just playing the political game. Naturally, he knew how to connect with a crowd and how to quickly size up people, as that was an integral part of being a politician; however, Theodore probably knew and understood—better than most politicians—the average American. He spent years among the hearty souls of the West, learning that one's word was one's bond and that self-reliance was as important a character trait as the fair treatment of others.

His speeches reflected that belief. He encouraged people to be fair, honest, and do what was right. Despite his healthy ego, he despised men who bragged and boasted. He was one of the few men who could walk with kings yet had a natural, common touch. He was often more comfortable sharing a meal with a bunch of cowboys.

As his tour entered the Dakotas, he no doubt felt a greater sense of comfort and contentment. He was now among the people with whom he shared a strong connection. They understood each other, and words were not always needed to express themselves. Farmers and cattlemen were workers of the soil, toiling from before sunup to well after sundown. It was demanding, hard work that pulled muscles, tanned one's skin, and produced hard-won calluses on hands. Theodore had shared that life with them. It was a bond that he never forgot.

He commented to John Hay that his audiences, as he traveled farther west, consisted partly of townspeople, though the majority were "rough-coated, hard-headed, gaunt, sinewy farmers and hired hands" who had traveled with their families from ten to thirty miles in any direction.

> For all the superficial differences between us, down at bottom these men are, I think, a good deal alike, or at least have the same ideals, and I am always sure of reaching them in speeches which many of my Harvard friends would think not only homely, but commonplace.[2]

His train arrived in Sioux Falls, South Dakota, at 8:30 on Sunday morning, April 5. Theodore had asked his planners to schedule his Sundays in smaller cities or towns so he could observe the Sabbath without making his presence a spectacle for the gaze of the multitude.[3] Aside from the usual greetings of politicians and welcoming committees, Theodore was most happy to see one person at the train station, Seth Bullock.

Bullock was a true westerner. Born in Canada in 1847, his family moved to Michigan during his childhood. He ran away from home when he was sixteen and lived with his sister, who was married to an army officer in Montana. Seth quickly found work as an auctioneer in Helena and then became interested in public service. He was elected to the Montana territorial legislature for three years and also served with the volunteer fire department before he found his true calling as a lawman. Elected sheriff of Lewis and Clark County in 1873, Bullock served his three-year term with efficiency. When his term expired in 1876, he and Sol Star decided to try their luck in the new mining town of Deadwood. Instead of digging for gold, Bullock and Star opened a hardware store before Bullock pinned on a badge as the town's marshal. His quiet assurance in enforcing the laws earned him the reputation of one not to be crossed.

Bullock and Theodore met in 1892 when Theodore was a civil service commissioner. He and two other men were riding horses from Medora when they met Bullock along the Belle Fourche River. Bullock later admitted they looked like "tin-horn gamblers." Theodore introduced himself, and when Bullock heard he was a civil service commissioner, he reportedly replied, "Well anything civil goes with me." From that point on, the two men became fast and close friends. When Theodore organized his famous Rough Rider unit, Bullock was given the rank of captain for his group, which, unfortunately for him, sat out the war in Georgia. He was appointed, at the urging of Vice President Roosevelt, to serve as the first forest supervisor of the Black Hills Forest Reserve (later named the Black Hills National Forest). In 1905, Theodore appointed him a U.S. marshal for South Dakota for the next nine years. When tiring of meeting European royalty, Theodore invited Seth and his wife to visit with him in England. The two men shared many stories and laughs, something Theodore missed.

Bullock along with Joe and Sylvane Ferris, Bill Merrifield, Bill Sewall, and Wilmot Dow were the men with whom Theodore formed a close and lasting bond.[4] Although Sewall and Dow hailed from the woods of Maine, they had the same qualities of those born and raised in the West. Theodore trusted and relied on them. They all shared rough-and-tumble times together in the western lands, a bond that is not easy to explain. When one meets another who "chewed the same dirt," an inexplicable bond forms, much like that of two war veterans meeting for the first time after a conflict. On this trip, Bullock would accompany Theodore throughout the western states, as he did during his 1900 tour as the vice presidential candidate.

Like other towns the president visited, Sioux Falls was decorated with colorful bunting and flags. Merchants had been urged to turn on their lights to illuminate the city streets for the president in the evening. The idea caught on with other businesses and even many residences illuminated their windows in honor of their special guest.

Before leaving the train platform, Theodore made it a point to thank the militia who provided an escort to the Cataract Hotel. At the train station, the crowd was told that since it was a Sunday, the president requested they refrain from any open demonstration of greetings other than clapping. The crowd happily complied. After arriving at the hotel, Theodore remained in his room reading until it was time for him to attend church services. Riding in an open carriage to the German Congregational Church, the weather was "cold and dreary, with a raw west wind." Despite the harsh weather, citizens lined the streets to wave at the president as he made his way to church.

The church services, presided over by Reverend John Single, were entirely in German, which did not bother Theodore in the least, as he was fluent in the language. "I was able to follow without effort his admirable sermon," he stated.[5] The church, he observed, was filled with "very humble folk," the women sitting on one side of the aisle while the men occupied the other. He even suggested the first hymn for the service, "Eine Feste Burg ist Unser Got" (Our Lord Is a Stronghold). After the closing of the service, Theodore walked up to shake hands with the ministers and to express his appreciation. Leaving the church, he raised his hat to the children of the Sunday School who gathered outside to greet him.[6]

After a meal at the hotel, Theodore and Seth Bullock resorted to a bit of strategy to exit the hotel without being followed by the crowd. Word was passed around that the president would be coming out the doors of the hotel on Ninth Street. As the crowd moved to that area, Theodore, now wearing his black slouch hat and riding clothes, and Seth sprinted out another door and into a carriage that had just pulled up. The two men beat a hasty exit before anyone could recognize them. They joined Dr. Marion Rixley, Theodore's physician, and O. H. Pender for a two-hour ride before returning to town, where Theodore and Seth led the horses at a "rapid pace" up the street to the Cataract Hotel's main entrance. They were able to dismount before any of the crowd recognized them. Theodore later stated that the ride was "one of the most pleasant and refreshing gallops" he had experienced in several days, adding that it reminded him of his days in North Dakota.[7] Theodore attended an evening church service at the Livingston Memorial Reform Church, and when the service was finished, the congregation remained seated until Theodore and his party left. The dual church services were not planned but merely a mix-up by the reception committee. However, Theodore later said he enjoyed both services "contrary to my expectations."

The only "unpleasant incident" in the town happened when Theodore was leaving the German Congregational Church. A man who claimed to be George F. Earl was arrested in the act of pickpocketing a man's wallet in the crowd. Witnesses told the police they observed Earl passing the man's wallet to a confederate who escaped into the crowd.[8]

On Monday morning, Theodore took a carriage to a school auditorium where he spoke to four thousand children. "I believe in work and play. I would be sorry not to see you enjoy yourselves but do not let play interfere with work," he told them. "Do things quickly and cheerfully. Boys, remember that the manlier you wish to be, the nicer you can afford to be at home. I would be ashamed of a boy who was a bully to the weak. When you play, be fair but play hard, and then work hard at your studies. ... Work with your whole heart in all things."[9] Returning to the center of town, his speech to the crowd concerned "the wage worker" and "the tiller of the soil." He noted that there were "many, many lesser problems" made up entirely of the huge and complex problems of "our modern industrial life." Theodore stated that each of the problems was connected to the others. Regarding the problems people faced in this new century, Theodore noted that the important problems were connected to "the farmers, the stock growers, soil tillers, the community at large, and those affecting the relations between employer and employed."

> In a country like ours it is fundamentally true that the well-being of the tiller of the soil and the wage-worker is the well-being of the State. If they are well off, then we need concern ourselves but little as to how other classes stand, for they will inevitably be well off too, and, on the other hand, there can be no real general prosperity unless based on the foundation of the prosperity of the wage-worker and the tiller of the soil. But the needs of these two classes are often not the same. The tiller of the soil has been of all our citizens the one on the whole the least affected in his ways

of life and methods of industry by the giant industrial changes of the last half century. . . .

The farmer himself still retains, because of his surroundings and the nature of his work, to a pre-eminent degree the qualities which we like to think of as distinctly American in considering our early history. The man who tills his own farm, whether on the prairie or in the woodland, the man who grows what we eat and the raw material which is worked up into what we wear, still exists more nearly under the conditions which obtained when the "embattled farmers" of '76 made this country a nation than is true of any others of our people.

But the wage-workers in our cities, like the capitalists in our cities, face totally changed conditions. The development of machinery and the extraordinary change in business conditions have rendered the employment of capital and of persons in large aggregations not merely profitable but often necessary for success, and have specialized the labor of the wage-worker at the same time that they have brought great aggregations of wage-workers together. . . .

Of course, fundamentally each man will yet find that the chief factor in determining his success or failure in life is the sum of his own individual qualities. He cannot afford to lose his individual initiative, his individual will and power; but he can best use that power if for certain objects he unites with his fellows. Much can be done by organization, combination, union among the wage-workers; finally, something can be done by the direct action of the State. It is not possible empirically to declare when the interference of the State should be deemed legitimate and when illegitimate. The line of demarcation between unhealthy over-interference and unhealthy lack of regulation is not always well defined, and shifts with the change in our industrial needs. Most certainly we should never invoke the interference of the State or Nation unless it is absolutely necessary; but it is equally true that when confident of its necessity we should not on academic grounds refuse it. Wise factory laws, laws to forbid the employment of child labor and to safeguard the employees against the effects of culpable negligence by the employer, are necessary, not merely in the interest of the wage-worker, but in the interest of the honest and humane employer, who should not be penalized for his honesty and humanity by being exposed to unchecked competition with an unscrupulous rival. It is far more difficult to deal with the greed that works through cunning than with the greed that works through violence. But the effort to deal with it must be steadily made.[10]

Arriving in Yankton later that morning, his visit was brief. Speaking from the back of the train car, Theodore told the residents about the need for laws. "You need wise laws. See that you get them," he advised. "You need wise and firm administration of laws; see that you have it. But do not make the mistake of shirking fundamental responsibility. As individuals, be strong and fearless. Fundamentally you must have the right stuff in you to get it out of you."[11]

From there it was whistle-stop after whistle-stop across the eastern part of South Dakota. Most of these speeches lasted from five to fifteen minutes. Theodore generally gave similar speeches to the crowds that greeted him, reminding them of his connection to the West and that good citizenship was one of the foremost attributes needed for all Americans. In Mitchell, he spent a half hour in the town, being driven by carriage to a platform on Third and Walnut Streets, where he informed the assembled crowd that the prosperity the state enjoyed had several causes that dictate its success or failure, including nature which "has to favor us" while "man can only do a certain amount to avert calamity." Noting that legislation "can do something," it is ultimately up to the "quality of the individual man." Theodore observed that no law will make a "timid, weak, and foolish man" ever match the work of a strong-hearted man. "Nothing can take the place of the individual's own place," he stated.

> Everyone at times needs help. Each of us should be only too glad to extend a helping hand in such a case; but in the long run the only help that really counts is the helping of a man to help himself. You can lift up a man if he stumbles; if he lies down you

cannot carry him. If you try to, it will not help him and it will not help you. So, fundamentally, it must rest upon yourself to win success. As I said, law can do something, wise legislation, wise administration of government can do something.

If you have bad laws, badly administered, they will spoil any prosperity. It is easy enough to get a bad law that will stop the whole business, but to get a good law is not so easy. It is easy to sit outside and say how the man inside should run the machine, but it is not so easy to go inside and run the machine yourself. . . . Ultimately our success as a nation must depend on the high average of citizenship of the individual.[12].

An afternoon snowstorm greeted Theodore in Aberdeen early in the evening, mixed with "a strong northwest wind." The welcoming committee quickly changed plans from an open-air speech to one at the local opera house. Once again, Theodore reminded the audience that one should seek the same qualities in a public servant as they would in a neighbor, a friend, or in their very home. "For one thing, you want any man with whom you have dealings to keep his word," he noted. "If he will always tell the truth, you can pardon some other shortcomings, because you know where you are. It is just as unpardonable to promise anything on the stump and not keep the promise, as to promise it off the stump and not keep it. And the man should be held to the same rugged accountability for doing it. Now there is another side to that. You must not ask him to promise what, if he is a sensible man, he knows cannot be done."[13]

Theodore's train crossed into North Dakota later in the evening, where he gave his twelfth and last speech of the day. Before his train arrived in Edgeley, Theodore had retired to his room. As the train pulled into Edgeley's station, the city's band began to play and bonfires illuminated the faces of hundreds of people waiting to greet the president. Informed of the waiting crowd, Theodore quickly dressed, throwing an overcoat across his shoulders. Stepping out onto the rear platform, he made a few brief comments, and when he finished, the crowd sang "America." Richard Sykes, who was in the crowd, stated that Theodore requested the band play "Hot Time in the Old Town Tonight," the unofficial song of his Rough Rider unit. Sykes stated that the president joined in "with great animation," before returning to his room.[14]

Newspapers reported that the snow in Yellowstone might be too heavy, preventing Theodore and John Burroughs from traveling around the park. (Many members of Theodore's party bought high, artic shoes from local Fargo merchants, anticipating heavy snows in the national park.) It was stated that the president would leave the national park a day early if the snows were too heavy, and he "made a conditional promise" to Seth Bullock to visit Deadwood. Bullock, a reporter quipped, guaranteed Theodore he would have a "regular cowboy jollification."[15]

His train eased into Fargo at 4:30 in the morning, where snow had blanketed the city the previous day. As the sun rose, it assured residents that the day would be bright but brisk for the president's visit. City and state officials arrived at the station at 8:30, where they were invited into the president's train for a few moments. Observing from his train window that the ground was covered in snow, Theodore donned a heavy coat; however, once he stood on the rear platform, the temperature proved not to be as cold as expected. Returning to his car's compartment, he wore a coat more suited to the temperature. "I thought I had reached the banana belt this morning, but I find I am mistaken," he told the welcoming committee.[16]

The obligatory carriage ride went through muddy streets with snow piled on the sidewalks. Despite this hardship, the crowd enthusiastically greeted their president. It was noted that Theodore had eschewed his silk top hat for a soft, black, wide-brimmed hat worn in the "conventional western shape with the top crushed in from front to back." When he lifted it to acknowledge the crowd, a reporter observed he grabbed it "by the middle of the top in true western fashion."[17]

A stand was erected in front of the Waldorf Hotel, where he spoke to the crowd about the Philippine Islands and the U.S. Army. The islands, which were dominated by the Spanish at the time of the Spanish-American War (1898), were now, with the assistance of the United States, working their way toward independence. Theodore stressed that the people of the Philippine Islands would "not be governed as vassals, serfs or slaves." Instead they would be given a government of "liberty, regulated by law, honestly administered," which would avoid oppression or tyranny in granting them their independence. To achieve that, Theodore noted, it necessitated the U.S. Army routing out the Spanish dominance with military intervention, as in Cuba. "To put down the insurrection and restore peace to the islands," he stated, "was a duty not only to ourselves but to the islanders also." Abandoning the Philippines would have inflicted the "most cruel wrong," dooming the people to a "bloody jumble of anarchy and tyranny."[18]

Returning to his train, he briefly shook hands with some of the crowd as his train left for Jamestown. Passing the small hamlet of Casselton, there was no plan to make a stop. Theodore noticed a large crowd at the station, including several hundred schoolchildren holding small flags. He ordered the train to back up to the station, where he spoke to the people for several minutes. John Burroughs recalled a small brown schoolhouse that stood near the tracks of the approaching train as it traveled along the Dakota prairies. Close to the tracks the teacher had assembled "her flock" in a line waiting for the train to pass. He and Theodore were having lunch when the president spotted the schoolhouse and its crowd. He quickly jumped up from the table and rushed to the rear platform. Standing outside, he waved to the teacher and her students as the train passed by. Returning to his chair, he told Burroughs, "Those children wanted to see the President of the United States, and I could not disappoint them. They may never have another chance. What a deep impression such things make when we are young!"[19]

Another band and cheering crowds greeted his arrival in Jamestown. He recalled to the welcoming committee how years earlier he had traveled these same railroad tracks through "Jimtown" (the nickname old-timers had for the city) with his cattle. A reporter noted that Theodore said he saw "as much of the city at night as by day."[20] Before leaving his train, Theodore wanted to thank George Kingsley, the train engineer, for his careful run from Edgeley during the night. The engineer's skill allowed Theodore to sleep fitfully without being jarred awake. When Kingsley could not be found, the president wrote him a brief letter expressing his gratitude.[21]

Grand Army of the Republic veterans marched alongside his carriage as it made its way through the city. In almost every city he was greeted by members of the Grand Army of the Republic or members of his Rough Riders unit. Theodore always made a point in his speeches to thank them for their service. In a letter to John Hay, Theodore noted that the Civil War veterans "claimed a certain right of comradeship with me that really touched me deeply."

> To them I could invariably appeal with the certainty of meeting an instant response. Whatever their faults and shortcomings, and however much in practice they had failed to come up to their ideal, yet they had this ideal, and they had fought for it in their youth of long ago, in the times when they knew "how good was life the mere living," and yet when they were willing lightly to hazard the loss of life itself of being true to the purposes, half hidden often from themselves, which spurred them onward to victory . . . after all it is because of what they did that I am President at all, or that we have a country at all.[22]

Inside Jamestown's opera house, Theodore spoke to a packed house, with others outside straining to hear him. Citing the recent success in Congress with passing legislation that equally benefitted workers and businessmen, Theodore stated that any legislation must offer "square and equal justice" to every man, whether rich or poor.

> No legislation can make some men prosperous; no legislation can give wisdom to the foolish, courage to the timid, strength to the shiftless. All that legislation can do, and all that honest and fearless administration of the laws can do is to give each man as good a chance as possible to develop the qualities he has in him, and to protect him so far as is humanly possible against wrong of any kind at the hands of his fellows. That is what legislation can do, and that I think I may say we have successfully tried to do both by legislation and by the administration of the law.[23]

A twenty-one-gun salute from the cannons of Fort Abraham Lincoln signaled the arrival of Theodore's train in the state capital of Bismarck.

Three large portraits of Theodore were displayed along his carriage route past the Hotel Northwest. One was of him on his horse, Manitou, entitled "At the Ranch." The other two depicted him at San Juan Hill and a copy of the recent painting by John Singer Sargent. The *Evening Star* noted that Sargent's portrait, which was displayed at the V. G. Fischer Gallery before being placed in the White House, had captured the president's "energy, his alertness, his aggressiveness and unyielding disposition." The newspaper noted that the only thing the artist left out was Theodore's "kindness and geniality, which have won for Mr. Roosevelt the regard of his subordinates and the affection of his friends."[24]

His carriage stopped at the state capitol, where he "sprang up the stairs with the energy and muscular enthusiasm that characterizes all his actions." (It was noted that his escort had to keep moving to keep up with him.) Ushered into the governor's office, he met several friends from his days as a cattle rancher in nearby Medora. After greeting the assembled politicians, he was introduced to a delegation of chiefs from the Sioux, Mandan, Arikara, and Gros Ventre Tribes. Many were dressed in their finest buckskins and headdresses. Theodore first met Water Chief of the Mandan Tribe. "Tell him I am glad to see him," he told his interpreter. "Mandans have always done well." A reporter noted that the wrinkled chief showed "as near an approach to a smile as an Indian is capable of" and solemnly grunted. Theodore asked where Sitting Owl and Two Shields were, whom he knew well from many years ago. His interpreter informed him that Sitting Owl could not make the trip and that Two Shields had passed on.[25]

John Grass, the orator and chief justice of the Sioux Nation, gave the president a handsomely carved peace pipe made of pipestone, along with a tobacco pouch. Theodore was then introduced to Red Fish, Red Toma-hawk (who reportedly killed Sitting Bull), Black Bull, Standing Soldier, Wakutamant, High Bear, Charger, George Siaka, Middle, Cross Bear, Two Bears, Little Bull, Crow Ghost, Medicine Word, Red Earth Nation, and Bear's Ghost. John Grass then spoke to the "great father."

We have never seen the Great Father. We are glad he has come here. We want to see him and shake him by the hand. We would like him to have a nice journey and hope he will reach safe home.

We would like permission to request that the Great Father see a delegation of Sioux chiefs at Washington. We have many important matters to say to him. We are thankful for our new agent, Major Carignan. He has been with us for many years. He is a good Christian man. We hope in future we will get along and progress with our new agent.

We have had missionaries and teachers among us for many years who have taught our children in their splendid schools, and now we see the benefit in good education for our children. We also appreciate all their doings in our nation. We hear our Great Father will build a large school here, near home. We have thought when our children went far away east to school, it was not as good for them as near home. They have come back sick from changing country. We desire to offer our thanks for building a large school here. We have been treated well by the Great Father and we hope he will be again Great Father when his time is over and for our new agent, Major Carignan we hope the same. To show our good feeling in Great Father we present this pipe of peace and this tobacco pouch. We hope the Great Father may have good health and love of his people.[26]

The April 9 *Evening Star* ran an editorial cartoon of Theodore in his traditional western clothes, smiling and shaking hands with an Indian chief as four other chiefs watch and smile. Four of the five chiefs depicted have names on the blankets that cover their shoulders (Cross Bear, Standing Bear, John Bear, and Little Bear) with the caption, "The President Encounters a Few Bears."

Theodore then walked out to the balcony of the capitol to speak to the large crowd. Commenting that as his train brought him closer to his "home country," he recalled that during his first trip there, North Dakota was just a territory. "I can claim to be a pretty old settler myself," he joked, recalling that he often traveled to Bismarck on a cattle or freight train. "It just does me good to get back here and I can't say how glad I am," he stated. Many in the audience were old neighbors he worked with on the range. Theodore said there were two ways to become acquainted with a man out there: working with him or fighting with him. "There are a few men from the ranges with whom I had both experiences," he noted. Explaining that laws could either help or hurt people, the most important thing, he observed, was citizens and elected officials having "the stuff in them" to do what was right.

> What you want to know of any man in public life is what you want to know of him in private life: how does he treat his wife; how does he fulfill the promises he made on the stump as well as those made in private life; does he deal squarely with his neighbors; does he try to administer or make laws that will neither injure the rich man as such, nor the poor man as such, but will protect every honest man, be he rich or poor? That is what we want to know. That is what we have a right to know. That is what we have a right to ask. If he has these qualities we are for him; and if he has not we are against him, because he has no proper place in the American body politic.[27]

Returning to the train station, the president's carriage passed a barbecue where he made a quick stop to eat a roast beef sandwich with a glass of cider. "This is like old times," he said between bites. Before he boarded his train, Theodore told E. H. Walker, the local committeeman, "I want to say to you, and through you to the people of Bismarck, that they have put one of the cap sheaves of enjoyment to my trip." After he entered his train car, the crowd's cheers brought him back onto the rear platform. Displaying a "cordial smile on his face," he waved a good-bye "as far as the train could be seen, while the echo of cheering was in his ears until the train passed from sight."[28]

———

"As soon as I got west of the Missouri [River] I came into my own former stomping ground," Theodore later recalled to Secretary of State John Hay.

> At every station there was somebody who remembered my riding in there when the Little Missouri roundup went down to the Indian reservation and then worked north across Cannon Ball *[Creek]* and up Knife and Green Rivers; or who had been an interested and possibly malevolent spectator when I had ridden east

with other representatives of cow men to hold a solemn council with the leading grangers on the vexed subject of mavericks; or who had been hired as a train hand when I had been taking a load of cattle to Chicago, and who remembered well how he and I at the stoppages had run frantically down the line of cars and with our poles jabbed the unfortunate cattle who had laid down until they again stood up and thereby gave themselves a chance for their lives; and who remembered how when the train started we had to clamber hurriedly aboard and make our way back to the caboose along the tops of the cattle cars.[29]

Although his remembrance of prodding cattle and running atop moving cattle cars sounds adventurous, questions arise regarding its veracity. Although it's entirely possible that his recollection is true, there is no record of him (written or spoken) previously mentioning it, especially in any of his published books or magazine articles. For example, in *Ranch Life and the Hunting Trail* (1888), Theodore details his encounters with a drunken cowboy in Mingusville, two stampedes, roundups, and the arrest of three boat thieves. Had such a situation taken place during his time in the Dakota Territory, it is certain he would have written about it, taking a delight in recalling the event to readers. This is not to say it did not happen, but additional documentation to support this claim is lacking at the moment.

In Mandan, Theodore met up with his old friends Joe and Sylvane Ferris. Joe had been the less-than-willing guide for Theodore's first buffalo hunt in 1883. From that point on, the two men became close friends, remaining so until Theodore's death. Sylvane, Joe's brother, and Bill Merrifield were also close friends and managers of Theodore's Maltese Cross Ranch. As president, he reappointed Joe to the post of postmaster for the area, a position he held until 1908. In 1897, Sylvane bought Theodore's remaining cattle stock after the disastrous 1886–1887 winter, then later became the auditor for Billings County in North Dakota.[30]

John Burroughs was a witness to their reunion.

He was as happy with them as a schoolboy ever was in meeting old chums. He beamed with delight all over. The life which those men represented, and of which he had himself once formed a part meant so much to him; it had entered into the very marrow of his being, and I could see the joy of it all shining in his face as he sat and lived parts of it over again with those men that day. He bubbled with laughter continually.

The men, I thought, seemed a little embarrassed by his open-handed cordiality and good-fellowship. He himself evidently wanted to forget the present, and to live only in the memory of those wonderful ranch days—that free, hardy, adventurous life upon the plains. It all came back to him with a rush when he found himself alone with these heroes of the rope and stirrup. How much more keen his appreciation was, and how much quicker his memory, than theirs! He was constantly recalling to their minds incidents which they had forgotten, and the names of horses and dogs which had escaped them. His subsequent life, instead of making dim the memory of his ranch days, seemed to have made it more vivid by contrast.[31]

Later on, Burroughs told Theodore that his affection for his old friends was "very beautiful." Theodore said he couldn't help it. Burroughs noted that few men "in your station would bother to go back and renew such friendships."

"Then I pity them," Theodore replied.

In Dickinson, he was again greeted by many people ("with wild and not entirely sober enthusiasm") who remembered him from twenty years earlier. On July 4, 1886, he made one of his first important public speeches that truly launched him into the political arena. Theodore found it difficult to make much of a speech "as there were dozens of men each earnestly desirous of recalling to my mind some special incident."

One of the men who hailed him was Eldridge "Jerry" Paddock, who had "shot and killed an equally objectionable individual" years ago. Though the two men recalled Paddock loaning him the hammer from his Sharps rifle to replace the broken hammer on Theodore's gun, there was no mention of another less-than-friendly exchange they had years before. While Theodore was away on a hunting trip, Paddock had boasted that Theodore's Elkhorn Ranch belonged to him and that if "four eyes" wanted it so badly, he could pay for it—even in blood. Arriving back at his ranch, Bill Sewall informed Theodore of Paddock's threats. Without taking a moment, Theodore rode directly to Paddock's cabin, banging on the front door. When Paddock stepped out, Theodore wasted no time. "I understand you have threatened to kill me on sight. I have come over to see when you want to begin the killing, and to let you know that, if you have anything to say against me, now is the time for you to say it," he announced. Paddock could only sputter that he had been misquoted. The matter ended there, and neither man ever spoke of the incident again.[32]

Medora. Built in 1883, it was part of the ambitious dreams of a French aristocrat known as the Marquis de Morés. Hoping to earn wealth in the growing western cattle industry, he, along with his father-in-law, invested close to a million dollars building a slaughterhouse, as well as ice-packed rail cars to ship the dressed beef to various eastern markets. His dreams proved to be greater than their execution, and three years later he closed the slaughterhouse and returned to France. His large home, known as the chateau, was situated on a bluff overlooking the town that was named after his wife. The home was kept in order awaiting his return, which never happened.[33]

Most of the inhabitants of Medora left after the blizzards of 1886 and 1887, which killed most of the cattle herds. Businesses closed, moving to Dickinson or other locations. Only a small handful remained, including Joe Ferris's general store, which serviced the needs of the ranchers who managed to survive.

In 1900, as the vice presidential candidate, Theodore undertook a whirlwind whistle-stop tour to meet as many voters as possible. He was greeted in Medora by many who welcomed their old neighbor, and Theodore even managed to step into the saddle for a ride up to the bluffs.

Once again, the hero had returned home. This time, he was the leader of the nation.

"I know all this country like a book," he told John Burroughs as they looked out the train windows. "I have ridden over it, and hunted over it, and tramped over it, in all seasons and weather, and it looks like home to me."

It was his home. The land welcomed him twenty years earlier, offering him an opportunity to heal from a broken heart and to grow as a person. Many historians state that the seeds of his belief in conservation began here in Medora. Living in this region he came to realize that all resources—animals, trees, and water—were not inexhaustible. Without careful monitoring of these precious assets, the country would have nothing. It is ironic that Theodore's passion for conservation began because he wanted to hunt buffalo.[34]

Theodore quickly learned that no one conquers the land or nature. To believe otherwise is foolhardy. He learned, as did others before him, that the best any man can do is to exist and live with what the land and nature delivers. No mortal can control a summer heat wave, a winter blizzard, or a raging rainstorm. The only thing one can do is to survive. Theodore learned to exist in the wilds of the Dakota Territory, happily meeting the challenges of nature. The tougher they were, the better he liked it. He needed this challenge to test his spirit. Losing his mother and his wife within hours of each other and only a day after she gave birth to their only child left him a broken man. Family members feared he would go mad over his grief. He needed to rebuild himself, to become whole again. Theodore often said he would never have been president if it were not for his time in the West. The West and the western people transformed him. Even though he was born in New York City, he was and always would remain a westerner at heart.

"At Medora, which we reached after dark, the entire population of the Bad Lands down to the smallest baby had gathered to meet me," Theodore reminisced. "The older men and women I knew well; the younger ones had been wild towheaded children when I lived and worked along the Little Missouri [River]."[35]

Every cowboy from 150 miles had ridden to Medora to greet him. The buildings were lined with bunting and several bonfires burned in the streets. Many old neighbors pressed to shake his hand, and Theodore had to decline an offer to mount a horse and go for another ride. The party made its way to what was known as the town's meeting hall, where Theodore gave a brief speech to his old friends.

I am very glad to see you all. I made up my mind that come what would I would stop at Medora. I first came to Medora twenty years ago, so I am a middling old settler. I meet boys, great big strapping men, and mothers of families who were children about three feet high when I knew them here. It is a very pleasant thing for me to see you. I shall not try to make you more than a very short talk, because I want to have the chance to shake hands with you. Most all of you are old friends. I have stopped at your houses and shared your hospitality. With some of the men I have ridden guard around the cattle at night, worked with them in the roundup, and hunted with them, so that I know them pretty well. It is the greatest possible pleasure to me to come back and see how you are getting along, to see the progress made by the State, to see the progress made up at this end in the place that I know so well, and it does me good to come here and see you. There is not a human being who is more proud of what you have done, and more pleased with your welfare and progress, than I am.[36]

"They all felt I was their man, their old friend," Theodore recalled. "And even if they had been hostile to me in the old days when we were divided by the sinister bickering and jealousies and hatreds of all frontier communities, they now finally believed they had always been my staunch friends and admirers. They had all gathered in the town hall, which was draped for a dance—young children, babies, everybody being present. I shook hands with them all and almost each one had some memory of special association with me which he or she wished to discuss. I only regretted I could not spend three hours with them."[37]

Interlude with Nature: Yellowstone

Yellowstone Park is something absolutely unique in the world.

PRIVATELY THEODORE HAD BEEN THINKING ABOUT HUNTING MOUNTAIN lions in Yellowstone before he ever left Washington. However, the chagrin he felt over his inferior black bear hunt in Mississippi was enough to give pause about hunting in Yellowstone. Even though the Mississippi trip did have a silver lining for him in the form of the creation of the teddy bear, he was still somewhat sensitive about having another failed hunting trip detailed in the press.[1] Theodore equally was aware that the public sentiment regarding hunting was changing. Long accepted as a ritual of manhood, wherein fathers took their sons on their first deer or elk hunt, many Americans, especially in larger cities, began to view hunting as a brutal pastime. He also had to evaluate the potential public backlash from hunting in America's first national park. The Boone and Crockett Club, which he founded in 1887, had pushed Congress into passing the Yellowstone Game Preservation Act in 1894. The law gave the U.S. Army the ability to arrest and prosecute poachers, as well as to safeguard the park from timber harvesting and mining. If he chose to hunt in Yellowstone, many would view him as a hypocrite. All of this weighed on his mind as his trip there approached.

On February 14, 1903, Theodore sent a letter to Secretary of the Interior Ethan Hitchcock asking for approval of the application by the park's superintendent, Major John Pitcher, for "hounds to kill mountain lions." "I would like to know at once," he wrote, "because I would like to get the hounds up there in all probability by the last week in March. If possible, although it is not very probable, [Secretary of War Elihu] Root and I will try to be present at some of the hunting of the varmints—in which case you can guarantee that we will obey to the letter of the regulations of the Park and that not a shot shall be fired excepting in the presence of one of the proper government officials."[2]

Theodore held the belief that killing mountain lions in Yellowstone was beneficial to protecting the elk herds. However, if one eliminated a predator's place in nature, in this case the mountain lion, the elk herd would increase to the point of endangering the rest of the park's ecosystem. Nature, however harsh or brutal it may seem, has its own set of checks and balances.

Several weeks later, Theodore wrote to Pitcher, informing him that he had asked the secretary of the interior to send three hunting dogs from Texas to the park, adding that without a good pack of dogs to hunt, it would be "a waste of time to go after mountain lions." One of the most telling sentences in this letter is the following: "There must be no slip-up if I go hunting at all, and we must be dead sure we get our mountain lion."[3] It illustrates Theodore's concern that the hunt could repeat the blunders of Mississippi. If he did go hunting in Yellowstone and came back empty-handed, no bear, alive or stuffed, could enhance his image this time.

"If I do not go hunting I shall try to get out to the Park anyway just to spend a fortnight in the open—seeing the game and going about on horseback, or if I get into trim, perhaps on snowshoes. But I of course would greatly like a week or ten days during which we could hunt mountain lions," he conceded.[4]

Ultimately, despite his personal desire, hunting mountain lions would not happen. Theodore came to realize that mountain lions serve a purpose in the park, and he wanted to avoid any public criticism. In this case, discretion was the better part of valor.

Some people believed Theodore's decision not to hunt in Yellowstone was influenced by John Burroughs. That was far from the truth. Burroughs stated he was never disturbed by Theodore's hunting trips. "It is to such men as he that the big game legitimately belongs—men who regard it from the point of view of the naturalist as well as from that of the sportsman—men who are interested in preservation, and who share with the world the delight they experience in the chase," he wrote.[5]

Burroughs admitted that he was "cherishing the secret hope" that he would have an opportunity to shoot a cougar or a bobcat. He noted that Theodore stated if he did not fire a weapon in Yellowstone, he would not have to offer any explanation. Although, Burroughs wrote, the president did confess one day in the park that he felt he "ought to keep the camp in meat" as he always had done.[6]

The "Roosevelt Special," as his train was now known, arrived at nine in the morning at Livingston, Montana. It was stated that five thousand people from various outlying areas had traveled to Livingston's depot to greet Theodore.

As his train came to a stop at the depot, several people noticed that a tramp had climbed down from the top of one of the passenger cars. Attempting to blend in with the crowd, Secret Service men, undoubtedly abashed about letting the man ride on top of the train without their knowledge, grabbed the man. Claiming he meant no harm, the man stated he only "wanted to swipe a ride." The Secret Service men quickly realized the tramp was not a threat to the president and "complimented him on his nerve." The man replied that he enjoyed a great trip and went on his way. Two reporters followed him in hopes of getting his story, but he refused to say anything except that he had boarded the train during the night in Miles City. Theodore, when informed about the man, was not concerned. "If I had seen him," he stated, "I would have been tempted to help him a trifle."[7]

Walking past the crowd to deliver his speech, he noticed a young boy, Egbert Scram, smiling broadly at him. Striding over, Theodore picked up the child in his arms. "I have a whole raft of them at home just like you," he said to the little boy, before kissing his cheek. Speaking to the crowd, he stated he was not coming to Montana as a stranger. "I feel as though I was coming home. Yesterday and today and this morning I have been travelling through the ground that I know so well; and Montana has done very much for me, in fact helped to train me."[8]

Theodore went on to express his regret that his train could not pass through Miles City in daylight, as he had been to the town many times attending meetings of the Montana Stockgrowers Association when he lived in the Dakota Territory. He added that his knowledge of irrigation came from those he worked with in Medora and in Montana. Theodore was a big proponent of the national government encouraging an irrigation program for the arid and semiarid regions of the country. The recent Newlands Reclamation Act of 1902 gave him "greater satisfaction." Theodore understood that if the waters in Western rivers were not being used to help people, such as farmers, the water was simply being wasted.[9]

Noting that for the past eighteen months he had "taken everything as it came," from the coal strike to his trolley car accident, he now felt he was "entitled to a fortnight to myself." Bidding the crowd farewell, he spotted Ed Becker in the group. "Hi there, Ed! Don't you imagine for a moment that I don't know you," Theodore smiled, shaking his old friend's hand. Becker, who was now the editor of the *Billings Gazette*, had held the same position for the newspaper in Miles City in 1885.[10]

On the train to Gardiner, a conversation between Theodore and Montana congressman Joseph Dixon turned to a young girl who threw a handful of red, white, and blue paper flowers into his carriage in Bismarck. When Theodore asked how many children Dixon had, the congressman replied three. Theodore took a White House notecard and addressed it "to Margaret, Florence and Dorothy, with the best wishes of Theodore Roosevelt." He handed the card and a red, white, and blue flower to Dixon to give to his children.[11]

Theodore's train arrived in Gardiner, the closest stop to Yellowstone Park, at 12:30. Twenty-five mounted members of U.S. Cavalry Troop C under the command of Captain F. O. Johnson were lined up to greet the president.

Bounding off the steps, Theodore warmly greeted Major Pitcher. "My dear Major, I am back in my own country again," he stated. After greeting other dignitaries, the group had lunch inside Theodore's train. After lunch, a dapple-gray horse, Napoleon, who belonged to one of the privates in Troop C, was brought over for the president. Quickly mounting the steed and checking his stirrups, he grinned and said they were just perfect. As he was about to speak to the crowd, a cowboy sitting on his horse yelled, "Three cheers for Teddy Roosevelt!" Grinning at the cowboy, Theodore acknowledged that he was happy to greet everyone and felt that "this is my own country." Remembering he had worked with men of the West and pointing to the cowboy, he said he was proud of the Montana people and wished them "the best of luck and unbounded prosperity." With that, Theodore wheeled his horse around and left at a gallop with Major Pitcher and the cavalry detachment following.[12] One reporter commented that as Theodore galloped off, he "was a boy again."

One group was forbidden to follow Theodore into the park—the newspapermen. This edict had been announced before the trip began, and all members of the press who accompanied the presidential tour had agreed. However, as the days wore on, the ink slingers were hungry for a story and idleness drove most of them to frustration.

John Burroughs, who was sixty-six when he made this trip, rode in a military ambulance (a wagon with benches on either side in the back). Observing that Theodore and his group were "off at a lively pace," his ambulance followed along at the same clip, forcing Burroughs to grip his bench with both hands. "Well," he said to himself, "they are giving me a regular Western send-off." Burroughs would have been happy if his driver did not attempt to keep up with Theodore; however, he was unaware that the wagon's two-horse team had been "excited beyond control by the presidential cavalcade" and did not come to a halt for nearly two miles. (Burroughs's view of the driver and horses was blocked by a curtain.) At one point the wagon bounced over some logs, sending Burroughs flying off his seat and hitting the canvas roof of the ambulance before coming back down to his bench. After that jolt, the naturalist commented to himself, "This is a lively send-off!"[13]

Arriving ahead of Theodore's group at Fort Yellowstone, Burroughs had his first view of Mammoth Hot Springs. Founded under the Department of the Interior in 1872, Yellowstone became the nation's first national park; however, the department could not manage and protect the park effectively. It was inferred the department was complicit with certain special interest groups that sought special privileges within the park. Poachers, timber harvesters, and mining interests ravaged resources in its early years, while railroad interests drooled over the prospects of running a rail line through the park. In 1886, the War Department took over the park's administration, and General Philip Sheridan ordered facilities built to house a U.S. Army cavalry unit that would patrol and protect Yellowstone. Originally named after General Sheridan, it was renamed Fort Yellowstone in 1891, when permanent structures were built.[14]

John Burroughs had never seen anything like Mammoth Hot Springs, noting that the springs built enormous mounds that were terraced, scalloped, and fluted, suggesting "some vitreous formation, or rare carving of enormous, many-colored precious stones." Commenting that it was "quite unearthly," he climbed to the top where he thought the "water seemed as unearthly in its beauty and purity as the gigantic sculpturing that it held." He observed many a bird had hopped into the little pockets of rocks, called Stygian caves, in the quest for food or shelter, only to never come back out. Although the water even today is clear and ranges from sky blue to darker blue, its boiling temperature is dangerous to animals and humans. Burroughs observed two mallards swimming in an acre-size lakelet. The birds, he discovered, were in the cooler waters of the pond, but if they had approached him, "we could have had boiled mallard for dinner."[15]

Meanwhile, Theodore and his group encountered a small herd of elk. Turning in his saddle, he yelled at the troopers following him, "After them, boys!" Nudging Napoleon with his heels, Theodore was off at a gallop, chasing the herd. The herd finally slowed and turned to look at Theodore. Thrilled with following the elk at a run, he sat in his saddle and studied the herd for nearly a half hour. Theodore's group finally arrived at Fort Yellowstone three hours later.[16]

Charles Jones was a legend by the time of Theodore's arrival in 1903. A year earlier, the president had appointed him Yellowstone's first game warden. His knowledge of buffalo (second only to William Hornaday and Theodore) earned him the nickname "Buffalo Jones." He was born in 1847 in McLean County, Illinois. The family farm did not suit him, and he enrolled at Wesleyan University, but he left school after a bout of malaria. Arriving in Troy, Kansas, in 1865 with a new wife and a bag full of Osage orange seeds, he began building a nursery. Despite his success, farming was not in his blood. The lure of hunting buffalo on the plains beckoned him. After a few years, Jones had enough of slaughtering the shaggy beasts. Purchasing 160 acres in Kansas, he established the town of Garden City and persuaded the Atchison, Topeka, and Santa Fe Railroad to build a depot in the town. Once this was secured, Kansas state officials named Garden City as the county seat, and Jones became Garden City's first mayor. But all of this was not enough for him.

Realizing that he had a hand in the near extinction of buffalo, he reversed course and worked to save them. Jones bought herds wherever they could be found, including some from Texas rancher Charlie Goodnight, and by 1888, he had amassed nearly 150 buffalo. Concerned about the dwindling size of the buffalo herd in Yellowstone, Jones petitioned Congress in 1900 to relocate his buffalo herd to Yellowstone. His petition was met with indifference until Theodore became president.[17] At Fort Yellowstone, Jones showed Theodore the buffalo corrals that had been built, which held fifteen cows and one bull. Another corral was built near Pelican Creek housing another bull in hopes of attracting the buffalo cows in the area.[18] The rebirth of Yellowstone's buffalo herd had begun.

Newspapers reported that Theodore was having the time of his life in Yellowstone. However, it was another story for the reporters. Excluded from any contact with the president's party, they were left with little to do. One reporter noted that Cinnabar, three and a half miles north of Gardiner (where Theodore's train was located), was not a very attractive place. "It has no public parks, no theatres, no extensive society, no charming homes, and no palatial hotel," the disgruntled reporter flatly stated. "In fact, there isn't much at Cinnabar except a depot, a few houses, a store, a livery stable, two saloons, and, at present, a bunch of exceedingly bored gentlemen from Washington." The reporters were left to sit around and grouse about the lack of anything to do. They attempted to obtain some horses so they might enjoy a ride in the country, but the livery had nothing for them. Then the reporters decided to try their hand at fishing, but the fish refused to bite. It was hinted that one possible reason the fish refused to take their bait was because of "the loud golf stockings and quaint attire of the fishermen" that scared them off. With no luck at the river, the malcontent group returned to the depot and "stared at the rails."[19]

Desperate for anything to write about as the days dragged on, reporters turned their attention to Theodore's secretary, William Loeb. "While he [Theodore] is absent from his train, Secretary Loeb is virtually head of the United States government," wrote a reporter for *the Butte Inter-Mountain*. In an attempt at humor, the reporter noted that Loeb was not a great fisherman. He said that Loeb "fished industriously every day since they moved to this lonesome piece of track" but had yet to catch anything. Changing location one day to farther down the river, several members of the party "whipped the stream to good effect, but Acting President Loeb did not get a nibble."

Although other reporters grumbled about having no story, *the Butte Inter-Mountain* boasted in its April 10 issue that it had obtained the only photographs of Theodore's departure into Yellowstone. A pilot train had left Livingston fifteen minutes before Theodore's train departed. Realizing that covering Gardiner would be an important story, local reporters (not traveling with Theodore) tried in vain to get on the pilot train. Railroad officials refused. The correspondent for the *Butte Inter-Mountain* sought the help of A. M. Alderson, editor of the *Livingston Post*. Alderson agreed to help, taking the camera from the correspondent. As the pilot train left Livingston, Alderson managed to get on the engine. Along the way, people mistook Alderson, described as "thickset, wears glasses and, save for the mustache, at a distance looks a trifle like the president." Realizing that they thought he was Theodore, Alderson would take off his hat and bow as people cheered.[20] When Theodore and his train arrived in Gardiner, Alderson snapped many shots. He was the only local reporter to get pictures of the president's arrival and cover the story for both the *Butte Inter-Mountain* and the *Livingston Post*.

One aggressive reporter, who was identified as Bradley for the *New York World*, ignored the warnings that newspaper reporters were strictly forbidden to follow the president into the park. Attempting to ride to Fort Yellowstone the day after Theodore's arrival, he was arrested and his dog was shot by soldiers before he reached the post. The reporter was locked up in the guardhouse for a while before being released. He then attempted to get information from the manager of the Western Union office with little success. Stating that he had a letter of introduction from Iowa governor Albert Cummings, Bradley believed that if he was able to show the president the letter, he would be allowed to remain in his party. Though Bradley declared he would get into the park to talk to Theodore (he didn't), other reporters derided his bluster. They knew that the only way for anyone to reach Fort Yellowstone was over a road that was patrolled night and day by the cavalry.[21]

With nothing but time on their hands, the newspaper reporters organized a baseball team to play against members of the train crew. One day, the game was called on account of rain in the second inning, with the train crew leading fifteen to ten. Once the weather cleared, train crew members wanted to resume the game, but various ballplayers "were too lame" to resume play. It was called a draw by the newspaper reporters, while the train crew claimed a victory. As days went on, the reporters, dubbed "the president's nine," were defeated in every game.[22]

Traveling eight miles in a buggy whose driver managed to maintain control of the horses, John Burroughs, suffering from a head cold, proceeded to Theodore's camp on the third day. For the final few miles, the naturalist mounted a horse. Having done very little horseback riding in his life, Burroughs stated that having a spirited and powerful animal under you was "a little disturbing." The camp, located in an uninhabited valley east of Mammoth Hot Springs, was dotted with pine trees and close to the Yellowstone River, where trout were abundant. Reaching the campsite, he noticed that Theodore was not there. Major Pitcher informed him that the president wanted to go alone into the wilderness for the day. (His Secret Service detail was back in Cinnabar.) Theodore had refused Pitcher's offer to have an orderly accompany him, requesting that a lunch be packed for him. As he left the camp, Theodore assured Pitcher he would come back.[23]

At five o'clock in the evening he did just that, walking briskly down the path after an eighteen-mile hike. Theodore informed Burroughs the previous day that he had gotten within fifty yards to observe the elk herd for well over an hour. During his stay in Yellowstone, Theodore took a careful head count of elk, which he later reported to his friend and head of the ornithology section of the Department of Agriculture, Clinton Merriman. Merriman, like Theodore, became fascinated with wildlife at an early age, and at age sixteen, he was appointed a naturalist for the 1872 Hayden Geological Survey, which explored much of the Yellowstone area. After graduating college, Merriman, one of the original founders of the National Geographic Society, was not only a respected naturalist, but also extremely knowledgeable about many western Indian tribes. Knowing Merriman's expertise relating to Indians, Theodore requested the naturalist supply him with "reliable information" relating to the "present conditions, necessities and treatment by the Government" of various tribes prior to his departure from Washington.

Theodore related that during his hike he had seen and heard a bird that was new to him. From the description, Burroughs believed it was a Townsend's solitaire. Having never seen one himself, he was eager to look for it. The following morning, as the camp moved to another location, Theodore and Burroughs went on a hunt to find this bird. They found the Townsend's solitaire sitting atop a cedar tree singing. Riding on, the two men stopped at the bottom of a steep hill where they heard "plaintive, musical, bird-like chirps" from the grass around them. Believing it was a bird, they gently kicked about the tufts of grass, hoping to flush it out. It turned out both men were wrong. The noise did not come from a bird but a gopher. Although he didn't know its specific name, Burroughs suggested it be called the singing gopher.[24]

After arriving at their second campsite, Theodore and Burroughs heard "a strange note, or call, in the spruce woods." Neither man recognized the sound, which sounded like that which a boy would make by blowing into the neck of an empty bottle. Their guide, Billy Hoffer, stated it was an owl, but Burroughs quickly dismissed that idea, as "the sun was shining brightly."[25] With the sound once again repeating itself, Theodore told Burroughs they should "run that bird down," and the two men were off on another adventure. Scanning the treetops, they found their quarry sitting on a tall spruce tree. Looking through their binoculars, they discovered it was indeed an owl—a pigmy owl, which is no larger than a bluebird.[26] "I was rather ashamed to find how much better his eyes were than mine in seeing the birds and grasping their difference," Theodore later wrote.[27]

Making an eastern swing through the northern portion of the park, the group would head south to Tower Falls the next morning. Theodore motioned for Burroughs to follow him on his horse. Like anyone else who attempted to walk or ride with Theodore, Burroughs had trouble keeping up with his friend. He finally caught up to Theodore, who had managed to corral a herd of elk on a hillside. Theodore, Burroughs noted, laughed like a boy, sensing the spectacle "meant much more to him than it did me." Gazing at the herd "to our heart's content," the two men rode off to a spot where they dismounted. The naturalist watched Theodore do something he rarely did—loafing for nearly an hour stretched out on a flat rock.[28]

Tower Falls, situated among a forest of spruce, drops 132 feet into the Tower River, which merges into the Yellowstone River. Where the falls drop, several volcanic spires stand like towers, hence the name. (Others have described them as resembling alligator's teeth.) "Nature shows you what an enormous furrow her plough can open through the strata when moving horizontally, at the same time that she shows you what delicate and graceful columns her slower and gentler aerial forces can carve out of the piled strata," Burroughs wrote of the area.[29]

While Burroughs and others fished the next day, Theodore put a lunch in his pocket and went off on a hike to see if he could find the big-horn sheep they spotted the previous day. (Theodore was not enchanted with fly fishing, finding it much too sedate for his liking. Those few occasions he did fish were only for food while camping.) After one of his solo hikes, Theodore sent word back to Cinnabar that he wanted Loeb to send him his books on botany, as he had come across some ferns and shrubs he had never seen before.[30]

Much of Theodore's time was spent studying the various animals in the park and taking careful notes, which he detailed in letters to Clinton

Merriman. His keen eye and attention to detail regarding the elk he studied was what would be expected from an experienced naturalist. At Harvard he wanted to major in natural science but found the courses anchored in a laboratory, studying specimens only under a microscope. Theodore could not stand such study, honestly believing the only way to truly understand nature was to be out in the field. In his April 16 letter, Theodore informs Merriman that the game in the park was "certainly more plentiful" than during his last visit twelve years ago. He praised Buffalo Jones as a great hunter and frontiersman, noting his "admirable work with his buffalo" but felt he was "not always an accurate observer" when it came to his report on elk herds in Yellowstone.

> The elk in the southern half of the Park winter outside of it to the south, chiefly in Jackson's Hole, and of them I know little; but those in the northern half of the Park winter within its borders and I have spent the last eight days among them. From very careful estimates, based for instance on counting the individuals in several different bands, I am convinced that there are at least fifteen thousand of these elk which stay permanently within the Park. . . . There are rather too many for the winter feed, and so it is evident, from the carcasses I have seen, that a somewhat larger portion than is normal dies, especially among the yearlings.
>
> The cougars are their only enemies, and in many places these big cats, which are quite numerous, are at this season living purely on the elk, killing yearlings and an occasional cow; this does no damage; but around the [Mammoth] hot springs the cougars are killing deer, antelope and sheep, and in this neighborhood they should certainly be exterminated. . . . Evidently the elk had spent the winter in the bottoms of the valleys, in great bands, browsing on the quaking asp, the willows, and the lower limbs of the conifers. They rarely drank, eating snow instead. Where there was open water, however—as by beaver dams—they drank regularly. Sometimes they would leave the valleys and feed on the side hills nearby during the daytime. . . . The bands evidently wander very little at this season, staying, as I myself saw, for days, and doubtless for weeks, within a radius of two or three miles. They

sometimes sleep in the ravines; but some of them pass their entire time on the bare places. Others live chiefly in the snow, feeding on the patches of old grass, seeming not to feel the cold at all.[31]

Theodore also informed Merriman that the deer were "common and tame," adding that the blacktail deer was "tamer than the whitetail." He also noted that the bighorn sheep were the tamest of all the creatures he encountered. He seated himself within fifteen yards of seven of them and "they hardly paid any heed to me." He found their mountaineering feats to be "marvelous."

The camp consisted of two Sibley tents and one wall tent, all without wood floors. A picket line for the horses and pack mules stood nearby.[32]After the evening meal, everyone sat on logs or camp chairs around a big campfire near their tents and listened to Theodore talk. "What a stream of it he poured forth! And what a varied and picturesque stream!" Burroughs recounted. The subject matter could range from history to his days in the Dakotas to his presidency. Burroughs was always surprised by Theodore's candor, astonished by his memory and his humor. One evening, he talked about a letter he received from a former Rough Rider who was in jail accused of horse theft. Theodore loaned the man two hundred dollars to hire an attorney and did not expect to be repaid. However, the man did indeed pay his colonel back, adding that he never went to trial because "We elected our district attorney." Theodore's laughter "rang out over the tree-tops" at the story. Another night he was discussing paleontology, giving "the outlines of the science, and the main facts" as if he had just read them.[33]

William Loeb notified the newspaper reporters on April 17 that Theodore and his party had returned to Fort Yellowstone, where they stayed overnight. "The party is in excellent health and not an accident of any kind occurred," Loeb stated. "They start today for the interior of the park to visit the geysers, and perhaps the falls of Yellowstone. They will go in sleighs, on horseback or on skis, according to the condition of the snow." Loeb also stated that Theodore "would not under any circumstances fire a shot at anything in the park," adding the president did not bring his rifle or shotgun on the trip.[34] Numerous newspapers from the *New York Times* to the *Butte Inter-Mountain* had been running stories ever since Theodore entered Yellowstone that he would hunt mountain lions. When he learned of these comments, he was livid with the papers and instructed Loeb to issue the statement that he would not be hunting any animals within the park. It seems one of the sources for the story was Buffalo Jones, who told reporters he had offered to "round up a lion or two for the president to shoot at."[35] It is certain that Theodore had a quiet discussion with Jones on the subject of his comments.

—— ——

"The novelty of the geyser region soon wears off," Burroughs later wrote. "Steam and hot water are steam and hot water the world over, and the exhibition of them did not differ, except in volume, from what one sees by his own fireside." He commented that the Growler was a "boiling tea-kettle" on a larger scale and that Old Faithful reminded him as if the lid were to fly off and "the whole contents of the kettle should be thrown high into the air." He disliked seeing so much steam and hot water go to waste, wondering how many towns could be warmed by such things. He noted that a large area of ground around these formations was bare but for a solitary buttercup only an inch in height in full bloom. As far as Burroughs could tell, it was the earliest wildflower to bloom in the Rockies.[36]

There is no evidence that Theodore shared his friend's opinion. Instead, he seemed to be in awe of the park's magnificent beauty, the vast numbers of wildlife, and the true wonders it revealed. His private hikes into various regions gave him a chance to view nature alone, much like he did in his Dakota days. As Burroughs noted, Theodore longed "to be alone with nature." For Theodore, a trip into the wilds was his way of taking a break from the demands of being president, allowing the naturalist in him to freely explore and discover things that had excited him as a boy.

As they made their way to the Upper Geyser region, they dismounted from their horses because the snow became too deep. From there on they would travel by sleigh, drawn by four horses, on a path that had been shoveled clear by soldiers. Theodore, Burroughs observed, always rode on the seat with the driver, the seat he had always preferred as a child. It allowed him a clear view of the land before him, much like when he rode his horse Manitou in the Dakotas. When the snow abated and the sleigh came to bare ground, Theodore was the first to jump down and walk, with Burroughs and the others following his example. "Walking at that altitude is no fun, especially if you try to keep pace with such a walker as the President," Burroughs commented.

The party spent the night at the Norris Hotel, with Theodore and Burroughs sharing a room that was heated by a huge box stove. Both men found the room too hot, so Theodore opened a window and the two men slept soundly. Burroughs recalled that the caretaker of the hotel commented that the president of the United States slept in a room with the window open without a soldier outside to guard him.[37]

As they made their way along in the sleigh, Theodore suddenly leaped from his seat on the sleigh and, using his slouch hat, scooped up a ground mouse. Believing it might be a new species (it wasn't), Theodore skinned the animal (the *only* animal he killed in the park) and sent it to Merriman for examination. His careful measurements reveal the naturalist in his element.

> I send you a small tribute in the shape of a skin, with the attached skull, of a microtus—a male, taken out of the lower geyser basin, National Park, Wyoming, April 18, 1903. Its length, head and body, was 4.5 inches; tail to tip, 1.3 inches, of which .2 were the final hairs. The hind foot was .7 of an inch long. I had nothing to put on the skin but salt. I believe it of no value to you, but send it on the off chance.[38]

During his twelve-day stay, he also noted that porcupines and skunks had been diminished in the park. "Apparently there are no gray wolves," he commented, but found ample evidence of a mountain lion killing a bull elk, where previously he noted they attacked only yearlings and cows. "The water ouzel stays here all winter, as do many ducks, geese, and swans. I have heard it [water ouzel] sing beautifully this time, and also the solitaire," he wrote.[39]

In a letter to his youngest son, Quentin, he sent a drawing of a pack mule, which he said carried his clothes and other items. "There are about twenty mules in the pack train," he noted. "They all follow one another in single file up and down the mountain paths and across the streams."[40] Despite his whirlwind schedule, Theodore wrote individual letters to each of his children, an effort he would continue throughout their adulthoods.

Major Pitcher kept brief notes of each day's activities, which give more insight into what Theodore and John Burroughs did on this trip.

April 9—Left the post at 9 a.m. and arrived at the camp on the Yellowstone river about 1:30 p.m. At night a large campfire was lighted near the president's tent and after dinner the party sat around it and told hunting stories until bedtime. This was almost a nightly performance.

April 10—Before starting out, the president announced that under no circumstances would he fire a shot in the park, even if tempted to do so by a mountain lion up a tree, lest he should give people ground for criticism. Rode up the river [Yellowstone] as far as Hell Roaring. Saw a number of deer and elk and also saw an eagle attack a band of elk. Had lunch at Hell Roaring creek, consisting of hardtack and sardines.

April 11—Rode about 24 miles and got in among a band of nearly 2,000 elk. One band followed the party for over a mile.

April 12—As this was [Easter] Sunday the president decided he would take a walk alone. He tramped about 20 miles and spent the time among the elk.

April 13—Started for camp on Slew creek [Slough creek], rode slowly and watched the game. Much snow was encountered and Slew [Slough] creek was entirely frozen over, so could do no fishing.

April 14—Out looking for game. Found large herd of elk and the president took Mr. Burroughs among them. Arrived at Tower Creek Falls camp at 1 p.m.

April 15—President took a long walk alone and saw some mountain sheep.

April 16—Broke camp at Tower Falls and returned to Fort Yellowstone. Much game encountered.

April 17—Left Fort Yellowstone for Norris Basin. At Modern Gate the horses were abandoned for sleigh, and though the snow was four or five feet deep, the trip was made without trouble. Stopped for the night at Norris hotel.

April 18—Breakfast at 6 o'clock and a start made for the fountain, 20 miles distant; arrived there at 1 p.m. Snow very deep, but hard enough to bear the party. President spent afternoon at the geysers.

April 19 (Sunday)—Visited Upper Geyser Basin and saw Old faithful play.

April 20—Rode to Norris.

April 21—Started for canyon at 7 o'clock a.m.; snow very deep and soft in places, but got through with little difficulty. Visited canyon on skis. President showed skill on snowshoes and Mr. Burroughs proved himself an apt scholar.

April 22—Breakfast at 4 a.m.; left at 5 a.m. for post, which was reached at 1 p.m.[41]

While they were on skis, Burroughs "soon came to grief." As he was making his way, the snow under him gave way and he wound up going headfirst into the snow with his legs and skis in the air. He was quickly extricated and put on the right path. As they were going down an incline, Burroughs noticed from the corner of his eye Theodore taking a plunge. He was "pretty well buried" in snow, but managed to get back on his feet quickly, "shaking off the snow with a boy's laughter." Burroughs kidded him about "the downfall of the administration," before they resumed their downhill trek. A few minutes later it was Burroughs's turn to take another header into the snow.[42]

"Who's laughing now, Oom John?" Theodore said after pulling his friend out. Burroughs wrote that "the spirit of the boy was in the air of the Cañon of Yellowstone, and the biggest boy of us all was President Roosevelt."[43]

⚊ ⚊

A crowd of nearly four thousand people gathered in Gardiner, most brought in by train, where the cornerstone was to be laid for the archway that would lead people into Yellowstone Park. Newspaper reporters were anxious to cover the story after days of cooling their heels.

A line of carriages, each pulled by four horses, came up from Fort Yellowstone, carrying members of the president's party. Each time a carriage appeared, the anxious crowd began to cheer, thinking Theodore was on board. The area where the cornerstone was to be placed was roped off, with soldiers carefully positioned around the stone. The stone itself was held aloft, suspended by a crane, while a troop of cavalry lined the road from the stone to the speaker's stand. A band kept the crowd occupied while they waited for the event to begin. Several Mason members were in attendance and stood on the raised platform. (Theodore was a Mason.) Shortly after four o'clock, a group of riders appeared from around the bend of the road. Theodore and Major Pitcher were in the lead with a few other officers following, all "at a sweeping gallop." As they approached the dedication site, the band began to play "Hail Columbia," as the crowd gave "a mighty cheer of welcome." Dismounting, he raised his hat to acknowledge the crowd's laudation as he was led to the cornerstone.[44]

In the cornerstone was a box that held a record of the proceedings of the Mason's grand lodge meeting, the Mason's code of law, several coins, a bible, articles by Cornelius Hedges (an advocate for the creation of Yellowstone Park), photographs of the park, a photograph of Theodore, and copies of the *Montana Daily Record*, *Livingston Enterprise*, *Livingston Post*, and the *Gardiner Wonderland* newspapers. After Theodore spread the cement, the stone was lowered into place, and he returned to the speaker's stand. Although he held his speech in his hand, a reporter noted that "he did not refer to it often."[45]

> The Yellowstone Park is something absolutely unique in the world, so far as I know. Nowhere else in any civilized country is there to be found such a tract of veritable wonderland made accessible to all visitors, where at the same time not only the scenery of the wilderness, but the wild creatures of the Park are scrupulously preserved . . . its beauties can be seen with great comfort in a short space of time and at an astoundingly small cost, and with the sense on the part of every visitor that it is in part his property, that it is the property of Uncle Sam and therefore of all of us.
>
> The only way that the people as a whole can secure to themselves and their children the enjoyment in perpetuity of what the Yellowstone Park has to give is by assuming the ownership in the name of the nation and by jealously safeguarding and preserving the scenery, the forests, and the wild creatures. . . . The geysers, the extraordinary hot springs, the lakes, the mountains, the canyons, and cataracts unite to make this region something not wholly to be paralleled elsewhere on the globe.[46]

After a brief informal reception on his train, the Roosevelt Special left Gardiner at six o'clock for Livingston. It was there that Theodore reluctantly bade farewell to his friend John Burroughs. The naturalist would travel to Washington, parts of Montana, and Idaho before returning to his home in Peekskill, New York. Reflecting on his trip a few years later, Burroughs stated that he had "glimpses of the great, optimistic, sunshiny West that I shall not soon forget."

Heading East in the West:
Montana to Iowa

No law we ever devised will make a coward brave, or a fool wise, or a weakling strong.

"THE NEXT THREE DAYS AFTER LEAVING WYOMING WERE VERY HARD and rather monotonous. I went through Nebraska, Iowa, and northeastern Missouri. I spoke at dozens of prosperous towns, in each case to many thousands of the most friendly and often enthusiastic citizens. I genuinely like and respected them all. I admired the thrift and indeed the beauty both of the country and the towns—and I could not, to save my neck, differentiate one town from another or one crowd from another," Theodore wrote to John Hay. "Moreover, much though I liked them and though I was to see them, it was inevitable that I should begin repeating myself unless I wished to become merely fatuous."[1]

After two weeks of enjoying himself in Yellowstone, Theodore was back to the grind of the tour. It was true he was beginning to repeat himself in his speeches, continually citing the need for good citizenship, good leadership of elected officials, good character, honesty, decency, and common sense. Whenever he began a speech, he *always* acknowledged the Civil War and Spanish-American War veterans in the audience first. He was very proud of them and of how they considered him "one of their own." Despite the repetitiveness of his subject matter, the people wanted to hear their president speak. It didn't matter to them if he said the same thing to the people of Madison, Wisconsin, or Medora, North

Dakota. What mattered was that he was speaking only to them at that moment. He was sharing with the citizens of a town or city what he felt was important. They felt included by his speech, no matter the length. He always addressed his speeches by acknowledging the state he was in, complimenting them on their prosperity and fortitude. Theodore's speeches became very personal to the people who heard him.

He was *their* president.

Leaving Livingston, Montana, on the way to Gillette, there was some excitement for the Secret Service agents. A tramp was discovered riding the train, sitting on the outside vestibule between the baggage car and the club car. "One of the agents raised the window in front of the club car and started to grab the man when the tramp aimed a blow at him through the glass, shattering it," reported the *New York Times*. The Secret Service agent grabbed the man's leg and managed to drag him into the club car, where he was overpowered and put in handcuffs. He was identified as Edward Russell, a member of the Sailors' Union in San Francisco. When the train pulled into Billings, Montana, he was turned over to local police. When asked by a reporter why he was on the train, Russell replied that he was trying to reach his mother in St. Paul, Minnesota.[2]

In New Castle, Wyoming, Theodore stressed to his audience the virtues of the people behind the law and its administration.

> We must have clean and decent government; we must have good laws; we must have decent officials to make and to execute the laws. If we do not it is your own fault. It is a republic; it is a democracy; and it is our own fault if we do not get decent laws and decent administration of laws. But all that a good law can do, all that a good administration of the law can do is to give each man the chance to show the good stuff there is in him. No law we ever devised will make a coward brave, or a fool wise, or a weakling strong.[3]

Traveling south along the borders of Wyoming and South Dakota, his train stopped in Edgemont, South Dakota, where Theodore was treated to a "cowboy show" arranged by the Society of Black Hills Pioneers. When his train pulled into the depot, numerous cowboys yelled a hearty hello, a band broke into a song, and a cannon fired a salute in his honor.

Speaking to the crowd, Theodore paid tribute to the pioneers who first blazed a pathway through "the shaggy wilderness" and to the cowpunchers who drove the cattle to this region "making ready the way for civilization." Recognizing that the pioneer days had passed, he stressed that the virtues of the pioneer spirit were still alive. "You won, and you could only win because you had in you the stuff out of which strong men are made," he noted.[4]

With his speech concluded, Theodore shared a lunch at a nearby mess wagon while watching several cowboys demonstrate their skills on horseback. The only disappointment of the day was when a prized bucking horse with a nasty reputation for throwing riders proved to be quite gentle, causing a reporter to note that "a greenhorn would not have had much trouble in keeping on his back." The cowboys provided an escort to bring Theodore to his train, and as the "Roosevelt Special" left the station, the cowboys "dashed alongside the President's car and he shook hands with many of them from the window."[5]

After a brief stop in Ardmore, Theodore's train entered the state of Nebraska, making its first stop in the town of Crawford, where the Tenth U.S. Cavalry saluted him with drawn sabers and a local band played "Hail to the Chief." The next stop, Alliance, attracted people from miles around, coming by wagon, buckboard, buggies, or horseback to hear his brief speech. A reporter for the *Alliance Herald* commented that "Teddy" looked like his usual self, "glasses, teeth, smile and all," adding that he showed the dividend of his recent outing in Yellowstone.[6]

Sunday found him in Grand Island, where he once again requested that the local committee members shun any formal parade or greetings. Theodore and his party remained on their train during the morning, and then went to St. Stephen's Episcopal Church for Sunday services. Throughout the day, the local fire department watered the ground around Theodore's train in an effort to keep the dust to a minimum due to the windy conditions. Later in the day, he went for a twenty-five-mile horseback ride to Taylor Ranch. Theodore requested that he and his party be driven in carriages to the edge of town, where they would mount their horses in order to avoid making any display on Sunday. The ride took them past the original German settlement that was founded in 1857. Not far from that site, Theodore stopped at the farm of one of the original settlers, William Stolley, speaking with him for a few minutes before resuming his ride.

Arriving at Taylor Ranch, Theodore washed up and requested a whisk broom to clean his jacket before sitting down to lunch. The meal consisted of cream and bread, cold lamb and ham, olives, pickles, coffee, and strawberries with whipped cream. Returning to town, he paid a brief visit to the Old Soldiers Home, where the residents formed a line. Theodore shook each soldier's hand with "a cordial grasp and a word of greeting."[7]

That evening Theodore dashed off a letter to Seth Bullock, who had left his train when it arrived in Alliance. He asked if Seth, "without serious detriment to the public business," could join him in Butte, Montana, on May 27. "I feel that it would be of real advantage to me to have you go from Butte at least through Cheyenne with me. I would like to have you along when I ride from Laramie to Cheyenne, and there are reasons why I think, on account of your connection with the regiment and with Montana, it would be a wise thing for me to have you at Butte."[8] Seth set aside his duties as a U.S. marshal to respond to his friend's request, showing up in Helena when the Roosevelt Special pulled into the depot.

On Monday morning, there was an official parade in Theodore's honor, and then he laid the cornerstone for the new Carnegie Library before giving a brief speech at the public school. "Your forefathers came into this country and as pioneers carved the prairie into fertile farms. You have had in the past to face hardships and disaster. The work of taming the new country is a rough one. You not only have to tame it, but you have to find out what can be done with it, and the penalty of trying to do the wrong thing is sometimes heavy. You have succeeded," he told the audience.

As his train headed to Hastings, it slowed down as it approached the small depot of Doniphan, where a crowd had gathered. Both Theodore and Nebraska governor John Mickey stood on the rear platform to wave at the people as the train rolled on. Arriving in Hastings at 10:15 in the morning, Theodore spoke to the assembled crowd during a "Nebraska zephyr." The reception committee had sent to Chicago for a large quantity of ribbons and other materials for decoration, only to see them blow away in the windstorm. Complimenting the people for their efforts in planting trees throughout the state, he also stated that the recent irrigation bill would be a boon for the state's farmers. Again, he advised the children in the crowd to play hard, but when it came time to work, they should not play at all. Theodore also relapsed into his familiar standard that a society can have good laws and good administrators, but in truth, one must rely on an individual's character. He then went to the site of another Carnegie Library, where he used a spade (no shovel could be found) to break the ground of the future book repository. With that task completed, he returned to his train, which left immediately for Lincoln.

Unfortunately, while Theodore was speaking about character, a group of pickpockets were busy working the crowd. One man was relieved of $35, and a bank manager had his diamond shirt stud taken, reportedly worth $200. Regrettably, Father McDonald of St. Celia's Catholic Church became a victim as well. He had recently officiated at the funeral of James Stack and was carrying endorsed checks to be dispersed to Stack's relatives when the pickpockets struck. His loss was $500, and all banks were notified to stop payment on those checks. The criminals were never caught.[9]

A chorus of factory whistles and church bells announced the arrival of Theodore's train in Lincoln. Everywhere one looked, businesses and homes were lavishly decorated in red, white, and blue. The Farmers and Merchants building boasted five hundred small flags over the front of the structure, and a large picture of Theodore draped with two large flags and the shield of the United States hung in the main entrance. The parsonage of St. Paul United Methodist Church was hidden behind "the national colors and a likeness of Mr. Roosevelt looking out at the procession from every window." Petery's Bakery not only decorated the front of the store, but the delivery wagon and horse were also properly attired. Hi Fung, a Chinese laundryman, hung a flag outside his business, which he closed "to all customers in honor of the occasion." Several boys decorated themselves with pieces of bunting, and dogs displayed silk ribbons tied to their tails.[10]

All of this for a thirty-minute visit from the president of the United States.

After the customary parade through a portion of the town, Theodore made a speech at the state capitol building. He once again spoke on several subjects he had covered in previous speeches: good laws and good citizenship. He stressed that the same qualities that made a good father, husband, neighbor, and worker were the same qualities that made a man a good citizen in his community and in the state. He once again stressed that honesty, courage, and common sense were necessary for any man to be worthy as a citizen. "Shame to any man who treats another with arrogance because he is less well-off, or with envy and hatred and malice because he is better off. Either feeling is a contemptable feeling for an American freeman to have," he stated.[11]

During his speech, a young woman fainted in the crowd and was carried away by two men. The good Samaritans fanned her with their hats until she revived. After assuring them she was all right, she disappeared into the crowd. The two men realized a short time later that they were victims of "The Fainting Bertha" game. The woman was a pickpocket, and while the two men helped her, she stole their wallets. Although the young woman escaped, eight other suspected pickpockets were arrested by local police.[12]

Leaving the capitol building, Theodore noticed a soldier dressed in his faded Spanish-American War uniform standing on crutches. Leaning forward, he looked directly at the veteran and made a motion of a hand clasp. No words were needed between them.[13]

The rain that had been beating down on Omaha let up shortly before Theodore's train pulled into the city's depot. Despite the downpour, a large crowd greeted the train with an enthusiastic cheer, waving small American flags. The decorations that hadn't been blown away by the wind were now soaked, but it mattered little to the people of Omaha.

Before he left the train, Theodore summoned the train engineer, fireman, and all other crew members to his car, where he thanked them for their efforts. Stepping out onto the depot platform, he was greeted with "a pandemonium of human voices and shrieking whistles" from the people who jammed the depot and surrounding streets. Acknowledging the accolades, Theodore tipped his top hat, bowed to the people, and smiled as he strode to his carriage. It was estimated that more than one hundred thousand people had come to Omaha to see Theodore.[14]

When his carriage turned off Sixteenth Street, "an aged veteran hobbled to the edge of the crowd and gave a cheer that was all his own." Theodore had just sat down in the carriage when he saw and heard the veteran. He quickly stood up and tipped his hat to "that poor shadow of a fading glory." Farther down the street, a young farmer raised his baby girl and yelled, "Here's my start, Mr. President!" Theodore laughed at the proud comment and waved to the man, who exclaimed to everyone around him, "He noticed my baby!" His carriage arrived at the Omaha Club, where Theodore was led to a private room where he washed away "traces of the day's journey" and spent time reading the city's evening newspaper until it was time for dinner.[15]

The banquet hall was elegantly decorated. Instead of the typical flag scheme, Stewart Pryor chose to use small incandescent globes in red, white, and blue attached to cables bound in green. The cables were hung diagonally across the entire room, corner to corner. Similar strands were found in the center of each table, with the incandescent bulbs "protruding above a tiny bank of asparagus sprengeri," which were given color by white and pink carnations. In front of the president's table was a mirror lake with a diminutive schooner, whose rigging was hung with Asparagus plumosus, while the tiny lake was rimmed with gallax leaves. Each table had a cannon with the carriage made of pink carnations and the barrel made of white carnations. Sideboards were surmounted by vases of white carnations banked by Farleyense and maidenhair ferns. When dessert had been served, Theodore called Stewart Pryor over, complimenting him that he had "never eaten a better dinner nor seen prettier decorations."[16]

As Theodore was leaving the Omaha Club, he was presented with a resolution embossed on leather and signed by thirty prominent members of the "colored citizens of Omaha." The resolution read

Whereas, Theodore Roosevelt, president of the United States, has by word and deed shown himself to be the president of the whole people of the United States and has decided that character and ability shall determine the eligibility of American citizens for political advancement and that race or color shall not debar them from such; and whereas, his public acts and utterances, while meaning much to all American citizens, have been of infinite value to holding open the door of hope and opportunity to negro American citizenship.

Therefore, be it Resolved, that we, as representatives of this class of American citizenship resident of Omaha and Nebraska, hereby express our gratitude to President Roosevelt for his manly and statesmanlike stand for right, assuring him of our confidence and pledging him our hearty co-operation for his future endeavors.[17]

Though pressed for time, Theodore lifted "his hat and shook hands with the colored men," expressing that this resolution touched him deeply. He was also given "an elaborate bridle" from the group.

The doors of the coliseum opened at seven o'clock and the huge crowd flowed in. The manager of the exhibition hall did his best to keep the reserved seats open, but after a few minutes all hope was lost, and the manager opened every available seat to the public. When Theodore entered the hall at 8:30, the crowd erupted into wild cheers and whistles. Charles Manderson, the state's former senator and Civil War general, spoke to the crowd with an unusual introduction. "Now, every mother's son and daughter of you sit down. It is my intention to turn this unruly mob over to the man who took the coal strike in the grip of his hand and settled it. I think our honored guest can command silence by his august presence as well as by reason of being the president of a great republic."[18]

"A gang of hoodlums" had worked their way into the hall, causing an uproar with "catcalls and insulting shouts" as Manderson made his introduction. Efforts by the police were unsuccessful, as the trouble-makers moved through the crowd evading them. Exasperated by their actions, Theodore yelled "Sit down!" with a tone that was "vehement" and "brought out with a power of enunciation which rang through the great coliseum and resounded against the rafters."[19] Order was returned when

Theodore stood at the podium. Observing that he was speaking on the anniversary of President Grant's birthday, Theodore stated that it was a good thing that citizens pay homage to the "illustrious dead," adding that citizens need to keep in mind what "we owe to the memories of Washington and his fellows who founded this mighty Republic." He also noted the need to recognize Lincoln (Theodore's favorite president), Grant, and others who saved the Union. But, he also reminded the audience, "it is a far better thing to pay the homage that counts—the homage of our lives and our deeds." He stated that exalted memories of our nation's past can become "curses if they serve the men of the Nation at present as excuses for shirking the problems of the day." But those memories can become a blessing if they serve as a catalyst for a person to "act as well in their time as the men of yesterday did in theirs." Theodore noted that each generation had its own peculiar problems, with each generation having certain tasks it must do. "Shame to it if it treats the glorious deeds of a generation that went before as an excuse for its own failure to do the peculiar task it finds ready to hand. Upon the way in which we solve our problems will depend whether our children and our children's children shall look back or shall not look back to us with the veneration which we feel for the men of the mighty years of the Civil War. Our task is a lighter one than theirs, but it is an important one, and do it we must, if we wish to rise level to the standard set us by our forefathers," he observed.[20]

Shenandoah, Clarinda, Van Wert, Osceola. The stops as he entered Iowa were brief, no longer than ten minutes. (In Crete, Nebraska, he gave a two-minute speech at the depot.) Rain clouds followed his train as it traveled through Iowa. Shenandoah had light sprinkles, but in Clarinda "the rain was coming down profusely." Yet Theodore carried on, including a carriage ride through the streets. An attempt was made to pull the top up to shield the president from the rain, but he refused. "If all you people can stand out here in the rain, I can ride through it!" he told the crowd.[21]

"The president's five speeches [in Iowa] were not of political affairs nor specific public questions and policies. In this, perhaps, the people found their sole criticism on his visit. Public men, especially, had hoped from him a definite discussion, in brief, of some of the questions of the day. Unfortunately, his time was too limited for this sort of thing, and he contented himself with general remarks upon the need of good citizenship and the hope of the land lying in the cultivation of a high public moral standard," commented the *Des Moines Register.*[22]

From the start of this tour, Theodore was adamant about avoiding political or partisan speeches. Though he did everything to avoid being dragged into a discussion of national or world events, one event was shaping up to become a war.

Russia had only one warm-water port, Vladivostok, on the Pacific Ocean; however, the port could operate only during summer months. Along the coast of China's Manchuria was Port Arthur (as it was known then), which remained open all year long to shipping traffic. Russia viewed Port Arthur as a strategic base for its merchant and military ships and struck a deal to lease the entire Laiodong Peninsula from China. (Some historians state that Russia intimidated China into the agreement.) Japan had held onto the Laiodong area after the First Sino-Japanese War in 1894; however, the country was forced by Russia, Germany, and France to relinquish the area (as well as Taiwan) in 1895. Japan lacked the ability to fight the three countries at once, and it was a humiliation the country would not forget. When Russia took up residence in Port Arthur, Japan realized it would not stop there. An attempt to negotiate an agreement with Russia failed, as Tsar Nicholas II regarded Japan as an insignificant country compared to his empire. This dismissive attitude would prove costly to Russia and to Nicholas II in the future.

Newspapers printed stories from China in columns next to reports of Theodore's tour. It was hinted that Theodore would convene a meeting of his cabinet to discuss the problems in Manchuria when he arrived in St. Louis. There is no evidence any of the reporters attempted to ask the president his opinions about conditions in China, and any inquiries relating to the issue would likely have been quickly dismissed.

The showers that had followed him since entering Iowa gave way to a cloudless, sunny sky in Des Moines as the Roosevelt Special pulled into the depot at 2:20.

Near the train station, an elderly Civil War veteran dashed out from the crowd toward Theodore's carriage. He managed to elude the police officer who attempted to stop him by grabbing his coat sleeve. Theodore witnessed the man deflecting the officer's grasp and leaned over the carriage, his hand outstretched toward the veteran. He "shook it with the grasp that showed he appreciated the efforts of the old veteran who had such a hard time reaching him." As Theodore's carriage made its way to the downtown section, a young woman on horseback ("a spirited horse" observed the newspaper) rode up to Theodore's carriage and extended her hand to him. Theodore "gracefully lifted his hat" to the woman and clasped her hand as both the carriage and rider moved forward. Along the route, he stopped the carriage at the home of Mr. and Mrs. W. L. Morris, where he shook hands with a group of ladies and even kissed a baby. "The only one kissed in all the city—perhaps in the state," gushed the *Des Moines Register*. The front yard of the home belonging to a Dr. Laird had been decorated with a tent and signage reading "Rough Rider's Camp." As Theodore passed by, he waved to the doctor and a group of children, shouting to them, "This is the title I most like to be known by!"[23]

He gave two speeches in town; one was a three-minute address at a high school auditorium, where he met Eugene Waterbury, a former corporal in Company B of the Rough Riders. Theodore recognized the man at once, clasping his hand and shaking it as if working a water pump. "Waterbury, I am mighty, mighty glad to see you, old man," he said. The two men talked for several minutes, with Theodore asking what the man had been doing since Kettle Hill in Cuba. Another person, a "little ragged urchin with a couple of copies of the afternoon papers under his arm" pushed his way through the crowd in an attempt to meet the president. A newspaperman stopped him, but when the boy explained his mission, the reporter took him to Theodore's carriage and provided an introduction. "How are you, my little man?" Theodore asked, taking his hat off and bowing to the boy before breaking into a hearty laugh as he shook hands.[24]

Arriving in Oskaloosa at 6:30 in the evening, Theodore was taken to the newly built YMCA building, which he dedicated. "We cannot afford to have our civilization go on without united and ordered effort on the part of decent people to see that the forces of decency have the upper hand. We do not need to bother about the weeds, they will grow anyhow; but the grain needs some careful tending and nothing augurs better for the future of this country than the way in which efforts are made, such as this, which has resulted in the erection of this association building here," he stated at the dedication. "Nature abhors a vacuum, and if you leave a young man's time when he is at liberty absolutely vacant he will fill it; and it is liable with what is not best worth having in it. Give him occupation; give him the chance to improve himself; make the path fairly easy that leads to clean living and decent work and you will help him up more than you will by a hundred mere preachings; you will give him the chance to be decent. More and more the Young Men's Christian Association has tended to do good throughout the nation because it has proceeded in so sane a spirit; a spirit which seeks not to dwarf or suppress healthy instincts, but to get them to turn in the right direction, because, like all true educational institutions, it recognizes what an education must mean."[25]

As his train began to depart the Des Moines depot, a young man climbed halfway onto the rear platform and extended his left hand to Theodore. "It's my left hand, Mister President, but it's the one closest to my heart." A reporter noted the president gave a hearty handshake and the young man jumped off the platform, swallowed up into the crowd.[26]

For two miles past the train station, large groups of people waved at the train, and Theodore, standing on the rear platform, returned the gesture until the crowd disappeared into the Iowa landscape.

Louisiana Purchase Centennial: St. Louis

We should be a great expanding Nation instead of a relatively small and stationary one.

On April 30, 1803, the United States purchased 530 million acres of land from France for the inconceivable price of $15 million. (In today's economy, it would be near $1.2 trillion.) For that price, the United States doubled its size, with land that today includes fifteen states.[1] Shortly after the purchase was completed, President Thomas Jefferson approved the funding of an expedition that would map and explore the area, as well as establish a presence on the western coast of the North American continent before Britain (or any other European country) could claim it. Jefferson appointed U.S. Army captain Meriwether Lewis and Lieutenant William Clark to command the Corps of Discovery expedition (also known as the Louisiana Purchase expedition). The group of thirty-one men left Camp Dubois (near present-day Wood River, Illinois) on May 14, 1803, and returned to St. Louis on September 23, 1805.

To commemorate the centennial of the Louisiana Purchase, an exposition was dedicated in St. Louis, with Theodore and former president Grover Cleveland as special guests for the opening day events.[2] Arriving in St. Louis on Wednesday, April 29, Theodore's two-day schedule was a strenuous one, with his first stop at the Odeon Hall, where he spoke to the Good Roads Convention. The Good Roads Movement began in 1880, with the rise in popularity of the bicycle, and worked to improve city and county roads. Many of the roads throughout the country were either dirt or gravel, making them dusty in the summer and muddy in the winter. Theodore believed that the nation had the right to demand quality roads, both in the city and the country, especially since automobiles were beginning to be more popular than bicycles.

> The faculty, the art, the habit of road building marks in a nation those solid, stable qualities which tell for permanent greatness. . . . Of course, during the last century there has been an altogether phenomenal growth of one kind of road wholly unknown to the people of an earlier period—the iron road. The railroad is, of course, something purely modern. A great many excellent people have proceeded upon the assumption that somehow or other having good railways should be a substitute for having good highways, good ordinary roads. A more untenable position cannot be imagined. What the railway does is to develop the country; and of course, its development implies that the developed country will need more and better roads. A few years ago, it was a matter of humiliation that there should be so little attention paid to our roads; that there should be a willingness not merely to refrain from making good roads, but to let the roads that were in existence become worse. . . . It is a fine thing to see our cities built up, but not at the expense of the country districts. The healthy thing to see is that the building up of both country and city go hand in hand.[3]

Theodore then went to St. Louis University, where he witnessed "the most stupendous intellectual feat" ever to take place in the city. The "Grand Act" was a theological defense of Catholic Church doctrines by Jesuit priest Father Joachim Villalonga. The priest argued "theology with all comers," believers and nonbelievers of any race or religion.[4] Theodore arrived in time to hear the concluding portion of Father Villalonga's presentation. From there, he went to the home of David R. Francis, former mayor of St. Louis and governor of Missouri, where he and Grover Cleveland would be guests for the next two days.

As Theodore started up the steps to the house, Cleveland greeted him, "Delighted to meet you here, Mr. President." The men were no strangers to one another, as Cleveland had served as governor of New York when Theodore entered the political arena as an assemblyman. Cleveland once stated that Theodore was "the most perfectly equipped and the most effective politician thus far seen in the Presidency."[5] Although they were members of opposing parties, Theodore was impressed with Cleveland's "high standard of official conduct and his rugged strength of character." However, with the 1904 presidential election looming on the horizon, there were growing concerns that Cleveland would make another run for president on the Democratic ticket. Cleveland, the only president to serve two separate presidential terms (1885–1889; 1893–1897), was giving serious consideration to the idea when he and Theodore met in St. Louis. (He would ultimately decline.)[6]

"There is a great wave of Cleveland sentiment among the Democrats and Independents," Theodore confided to his longtime friend, Senator Henry Cabot Lodge. "I think his nomination far from impossible and I believe he would be a formidable candidate. At the same time, we are as a whole in good shape as a party, and unless events work against us we should be able to carry the country next year."[7]

Whatever doubt he had about winning the election in 1904, Theodore showed nothing but confidence to the public, reporters, and Grover Cleveland. The schedule for the next day, April 30, had him up at seven o'clock, posing for photographs with Cleveland and Francis at quarter after eight, followed by breakfast and a reception at the St. Louis Club. At ten o'clock, he dutifully took his place in the lead carriage for the parade that would take him to the reviewing stand at the fairgrounds. Theodore officially dedicated the opening of the exposition at three in the afternoon, then attended a formal dinner at six, followed by a display of fireworks. Afterward, he would retire to his train, which was set to leave at twenty to eleven.

"Imagine a more disagreeable day," one newspaper reported. The weather turned chilly, causing many female guests in the reviewing stand to shiver until army blankets were handed out. This caused one lady to comment that they looked more like an "encampment of Indians in December." If the temperature wasn't uncomfortable enough ("sought the marrow and generally reached it"), the wind kicked up, blowing dust along the parade ground. (It was said Theodore could not see the marching troops across the street because of the blowing dust.)

As the parade went on and on, the lunch hour came and went. Distinguished visitors, mostly diplomats and their wives, began to complain. An "unknown person" (as described by the *St. Louis Republic*) informed them that there were "goodies" in a tent at the rear of the reviewing stand. (The tent had been set up for Theodore, Grover Cleveland, Cardinal Gibbons, and their guests to have "an elaborate luncheon" after the conclusion of the parade.) "An invasion of the President's luncheon place followed with astonishing rapidity," and the provisions, "unable to withstand such a fierce onslaught, evaporated and the damage was done," a reporter noted. The chef "nearly dropped in his tracks" when he realized that Theodore and the others had not eaten, stammering his apology. Theodore "laughed down the dismay" and requested anything that was left. A few sandwiches and cold coffee were served to the distinguished guests.[8]

Though Theodore publicly assured reporters that he was well treated, privately he told John Hay that "the arrangements at the Fair itself represented confusion worse confounded."[9] New York's *Sun* reported in its May 1 edition that Theodore stated Kansas City was "like an oasis in a desert," but visiting the exposition left him and his party with "nothing fit to eat" and he did not receive "decent treatment."[10] A day later, as the story was carried in several newspapers, assistant Benjamin Barnes stated "there was absolutely no truth" to the story. Whether or not Theodore made those comments mattered little since newspaper reporters were quick to point out the exposition's faults. W. W. Jermane of the *Minneapolis Journal* stated the exposition was "one grand mix-up from start to date." The treatment of the president and other distinguished guests "amounted almost to discourtesy" by forcing Theodore to stand at "a sloppy joe counter, running with spilled coffee, jostled by a miscellaneous crowd" as he ate a cold sandwich and drank even colder coffee. Jermane attacked the local committee for "trying to shirk the blame," noting that both the diplomats and President Roosevelt "fared hungrily, roughly and coldly." In addition, the reporter stated that transportation for the exposition was incompetent, sporadic, and expensive, and the entertainment listed in the program was "dismally futile." Allowing that the missteps could be a "good lesson" that could result in "reforms before the big game opens next year," Jermane concluded, "the exposition will fall many paces short of the Chicago standard" if it did not.[11]

"I will go and see my newspaper friends for a time and take a little rest," Theodore stated after finishing his cold meal, and retired to the newspaper reporters' lodgings. In the dormitory for the ink slingers, he took an hour's nap before delivering his dedication speech at the liberal arts building.

When the public was admitted to the building, there was a "woeful lack" of management of the crowd, who, the *Sun* observed, proceeded "stampeding up and down the aisles like a herd of Texas steers surrounded by a pack of ravenous wolves." Ushers were "conspicuous for their incompetency," and people who had priority tickets for seats found them occupied by those who held general admission passes. The crowd packed the building to "suffocation," crowding those who had seats.[12]

Audience capacity for the building was twenty-six thousand, but reporters estimated the crowd closer to fifty thousand.

As Theodore entered the building, the crowd roared with approval for several minutes before David Francis could officially declare the exposition opened. The location of the speaker's platform made it difficult for the majority of the audience to see, let alone hear anything. When it came time for Theodore to speak, he jumped up on a shelf that surrounded his presidential box, allowing the people to see him as he began his speech.

We have met here to-day to commemorate the hundredth anniversary of the event which more than any other, after the foundation of the Government and always excepting its preservation, determined the character of our national life—determined that we should be a great expanding Nation instead of a relatively small and stationary one.... When we acquired it, we made evident once and for all that consciously and of set purpose we had embarked on a career of expansion, that we had taken our place among those daring and hardy nations who risk much with the hope and desire of winning high position among the great powers of the earth. As is so often the case in nature, the law of development of a living organism showed itself in its actual workings to be wiser than the wisdom of the wisest. . . . Never before had the world seen the kind of national expansion which gave our people all that part of the American continent lying west of the thirteen original States; the greatest landmark in which was the Louisiana Purchase. . . . The acquisition of the territory is a credit to the broad and far-sighted statesmanship of the great statesmen to whom it was immediately due, and above all to the aggressive and masterful character of the hardy pioneer folk to whose restless energy these statesmen gave expression and direction, whom they followed rather than led.[13]

Ruffians and Jayhawkers:
Missouri and Kansas

Let us think carefully before, by any act of folly, we destroy what has thus so marvelously been built up.

LEAVING BEHIND THE FIASCO OF THE EXPOSITION, THE ROOSEVELT Special arrived in Kansas City, Missouri, on May 1 at nine in the morning. Once again, Theodore was greeted by local dignitaries, a band, and hundreds of well-wishers. Schools were closed, businesses suspended operation, and the city's mayor declared a local holiday. Residences and businesses were festooned with red, white, and blue bunting and American flags. Children stood "seven-deep" to see Theodore pass by, waving small flags and cheering the man who waved back at them.

A combination detachment of mounted police and Missouri National Guard accompanied the president's carriage along the five-mile route, which included a stop at Scarritt Point overlooking the Missouri River two hundred feet below. Arriving at the Convention Hall, a crowd of eighteen thousand greeted him, with sixty Harvard graduates launching into their college cry, which ended with "Roosevelt!" Five hundred Union and Confederate war veterans were part of the crowd and sat in a special section near the speaker's stand.[1]

After acknowledging the rousing greeting from his "college mates," Theodore launched into his speech, focusing on the Civil War veterans before him.

I do not usually say anything about our being a reunited country, because it is unnecessary. Of course, we are reunited, and in every northern audience, wherever I see a group of men wearing the button of the Grand Army of the Republic, I am certain to find a group of men prompt to cheer every allusion to the gallantry of the men who wore the blue and the gray. . . . And you, by your lives, by what you did, taught us lessons, not merely of war, but of peace. Never before in the history of this world has any country been so fortunate as to see two great armies disband after so gigantic a struggle and instantly every man turn his attention to working as hard in peace as he had fought hard in war. You left us, you men of those two armies, not only the right to glory in the courage and to glory in the faith, but in the valor and the steadfast devotion of each to the right as God gave you to see the right . . . the lessons you learned then teach us now the lesson we need most to apply: the lesson of sincere devotion to a lofty idea; the lesson of facing each task as it comes, with the world old virtues needed throughout the ages by every people, which is to work out successfully its problems in the world's history. . . .

That war could not have been fought as it was, it could not have left us such deathless memories; memories of the valor shown by each side; it could not have done that had you been riven among yourselves by any artificial distinctions, and if we of today let any divisions creep in among us, whether of creed against creed, race against race, or rich man against poor man, it will go evil with us in the future. . . .

Always, in any government, among any people, there are certain forces for evil that take many shapes, but which are rooted in the same base and evil characteristics of the human soul, in the evil of arrogance, of jealousy, envy, hatred; and to certain people the appeal is made to yield to one set of evil forces. To some it is made to yield to another set, and the result is equally bad in each case. The vice of arrogance, of hard and brutal indifference on the part of those with wealth toward those who have not, is a shameful and dreadful vice. It is not one whit worse than the rancorous hatred and jealousy of those who are not well off for those who are. The man, who, either by practice or precept, seeks to give to any man or withhold from him any advantage in law or society or in the workings of society or business because of wealth or poverty, is false to the traditions of this republic. . . .

Let us think carefully before, by any act of folly, we destroy what has thus so marvelously been built up. It is easy to pull down but not so easy to rebuild or to replace, and let us take serious thought from the history of the republics of old and avoid the rocks on which they foundered and the chief rock—the chief danger in the path of each of the old republics of antiquity of the middle ages. This chief danger came from the growth and encouragement of anything in the nature of class hostility. It will be an evil day for us when we try to make this a government especially designed to help any one class, save as that class includes honest, fearless, upright, hard-working citizens. And it will be only a less evil day when any considerable proportion of our people fail to remember that it is the duty of the government not to favor the rich man or to discriminate against him; or to favor the poor man or discriminate against him, but to favor every man, rich or poor, if he but behaves himself and does his duty to the state and to his neighbors.[2]

With his speech concluded, Theodore was escorted to the Hotel Baltimore for a luncheon with the Commercial Club of Kansas City. Speaking briefly to those gathered, Theodore noted that he was the eighth generation born in New York City and that Kansas City used to be referred to as the West many generations ago, but is now "in the middle." Observing that the West was "purely a relative term," you would have to locate a man's individual abode before you knew what he meant by it. Theodore related a story in which one of his cowboys at his ranch in the Dakota Territory had requested his money early because he was "going to spend the winter in the Far East." Enquiring if the cowboy meant he was going to Norway or Nubia, the cowboy retorted, "No. Duluth."[3]

Theodore was then "delivered into the hands" of the Mercantile Club of Kansas City, Kansas, crossing the state line. Captain Tyree Rivers, who served with Theodore in Cuba, commanded the Fourth U.S.

Cavalry Company, which escorted him across the state line. When the party passed the bluffs, a cannon fired a salute. The cannon's boom signaled every whistle and church bell in the city to announce the president's arrival. Before returning to the train station, Theodore stopped to view a demonstration at the Live Stock Exchange, which reminded him of his days in the Dakotas. A delegation of students from Kansas City University presented him with a gold badge set with pearls and diamonds as well as an honorary membership in the University Library Association.[4]

Leaving Kansas City, Kansas, at four o'clock, Theodore traveled to the town of Lawrence, where a short carriage ride through town allowed him to be greeted by the local citizens, neighboring towns, and "every farm house almost in the county." Within a half hour, the train was on its way to Topeka, where it would stay overnight. As his train pulled into the station, cannons fired a twenty-one-gun salute, and despite a chill wind that "rooted like a rock on the spot," the crowd was "packed like sardines in a box when tin is high and fish are cheap." One man stood on a ladder against a telephone pole for more than an hour in hopes of getting a snapshot of the president.[5]

Theodore's first order of business was to lay the cornerstone of the new YMCA building. In order to do this, he was made an honorary member of the International Order of Bricklayers and, presented with a silver trowel, "the President got busy." Loading the hod with mortar, he smoothed the layer down as the crowd good-naturedly joked with him. One man near the cornerstone shouted, "More mud, Teddy!" Theodore laughingly replied that he needed a shovel. "He worried around the cornerstone like a hen around her brood, exchanging repartee with the crowd," a newspaper reported.[6]

As he was driven to the governor's mansion, a man attempted to get on the president's carriage but was knocked off by a mounted policeman. The man, named Murphy, then jumped up on one of the steps of the carriage, stating, "I guess I'll ride here." A Secret Service agent riding in Theodore's carriage turned and threw "a well-aimed blow" that knocked the man to the gutter. The man, unarmed, was arrested, and his actions were attributed to a "spirit of bravado."[7]

During dinner at Governor Willis Bailey's residence, it was reported that Theodore "did most of the talking." Senator Joseph Burton relayed a story of a recently appointed U.S. marshal who had a reputation as "something of a hard character" before pinning on the badge. Many "bad men" in the district expected they would have an easy time of things with the new marshal but quickly realized their mistake as he made them "eat dirt." Theodore, impressed with the story, stated, "Senator, telegraph that man tomorrow that I want to see him."

Before leaving for the local auditorium, Theodore spoke to one of the mounted officers. "Haven't I seen you before—weren't you at Santiago with the regulars?" he asked. The officer, C. C. McIntosh, told the president he was correct, adding he carried many messages to him during their time in Cuba. "I thought so," Theodore smiled.[8]

Addressing the auditorium audience, Theodore mentioned that he needed "no urging" to speak about the YMCA, as the organization "exemplifies in practice just exactly what I like to preach"—the combination of "efficiency with decent living and high ideals." Theodore again cited the need for good character and decency in private life, commenting that he had "a great deal of faith" in the average citizen. "I think he is a pretty good fellow, and I think he can generally get on with the other average American citizen if he will only know him," he remarked. However, he cautioned, if a person does not know another man, he is apt to make "him a monster in his mind" and they will not get along. Should one "take the trouble" to know the other, understanding "he is a being just like himself" with the same instincts, purposes, tendencies, shortcomings, and desires for good, "you can get the two together with an honest desire for each to try not only to help himself but to help the other, [and] most of our problems will be solved."[9]

The following morning, a crowd gathered at the train depot waiting to see the president off. Before leaving, Theodore stepped out on the rear platform, commenting to the crowd about the previous night's incident in which the man tried to ride in his carriage. He described the carriage ride as "about the liveliest gait of the trip, and I don't think I ever saw such fast running policemen as you have here in Topeka." Leaning over the railing, Theodore extended his hand to a black policeman, stating he wanted "to shake hands with one of the sprinters." The officer "showed his delight with a broad smile."[10]

The rest of the day was filled with brief stops, most lasting no longer than ten to twenty minutes, with some as brief as three minutes. In Manhattan, Theodore told the crowd that the two things necessary for success were opportunity and "the power to take advantage of that opportunity." In Junction City, a crowd estimated between five and six thousand braved a "raw, cold day" to hear Theodore speak. Arrangements were made for children from city and county schools to have the "best position for seeing and hearing" the president. The local newspaper urged its citizens to see that Theodore's "only remembrance" of the town was of "the most pleasant character."[11] Stopping in Chapman for water, Theodore was given a football "that had seen hard service" and during the ride to Abilene, Theodore and his party "enjoyed playing football in the car." The Union Pacific engine pulling the president's train had been painted by the company's "most skilled painters" with designs of a sunflower and an American flag. At the depot in Abilene, a "magnificent arch," twenty feet high and wide, stood on the depot platform, adorned with red, white, and blue bunting, flags, and Theodore's picture in the center surrounded by a large eagle. "No city in the West has had a more beautiful greeting," boasted the *Abilene Daily Reflector.*[12]

Although no stop was planned for the town of Solomon, the train slowed as it approached the train depot, where two hundred people waited to see the president. Theodore stepped out on the rear platform and waved to the crowd as the train moved on. The train made a twenty-minute stop in Salina, where it was greeted by a group of college boys "exercising their lungs." Theodore told the young men, "I feel like I have been at a football game." As he spoke, he noticed a group of young cadets who stood with their hats off. "Put on your hats, boys," he told them. "I am old and tough myself." Reminding the crowd that football was like the great game of life, he noted, "The same rule applies to both. Don't flinch, don't follow and hit the line hard. This counts in life just as it does in sport. Don't sit at home and wonder why the world doesn't appreciate you."[13]

His ten-minute speech in Ellsworth was "straight from the shoulder to all Kansasans." (A train conductor stood behind him, carefully eyeing his pocket watch as Theodore spoke.) Passing through Wilson, the *Wilson World* noted that the people of the town and surrounding county had "a rare opportunity of looking upon one of the greatest of living men." Although the train did not make a stop, it slowed down to allow Theodore to step out onto the rear platform and wave to the people, "smiling that inimitable smile of his."[14] In Russell, he made a twenty-minute speech, and when informed it was time to leave, Theodore kept talking. A reporter commented that his voice "was not in the best form," but noted that no voice would be in the best of shape after a month of speaking. The crowd was "impressed with the simplicity of the President's manner, with the modesty of his attire and general good sense which he displayed." The reporter also complimented the residents of Russell and Russell County, who behaved in a "orderly, decent way. The general intelligence shown, the lack of rowdyism, the absence of people of the 'Rube' order" were a credit to the good name of the town and county.[15] In Hays, local millenary Sara Ryan placed a newspaper ad advising that ladies and girls should "look their prettiest . . . a real May flower," and was preparing hats for Theodore's visit that were "low in price." Theodore's visit lasted only five minutes, and reporters traveling with the president felt the town was "frosty" in its reception, whereas the *Hays Free Press* reporter stated that the crowd was simply respectful and not "rip-roaring."[16]

The ten-minute stop in WaKeeney allowed for a brief speech about which a reporter noted that "only once or twice" did Theodore's voice give any signs of failing. "The president's talk showed that he understands and appreciates western people and the conditions under which they are working. He was complimentary without using flattery," the reporter discerned. The train, making its way to Sharon Springs, would pass the small town of Collyer. A stop was not planned, but the train needed to take on water, and while doing so, Theodore stepped out onto the rear platform and spoke to the people and shook hands.[17]

—◦—

Theodore's train arrived in Sharon Springs on Saturday evening, May 2, at 8:30.[18] Once the well-wishers had dispersed from the depot, he slipped out for a walk "on the prairie sod" with Doctors Rixley and Butler and

Senators Long and Burton. Leading the party at "a swift pace," Theodore shared his knowledge of the sounds heard on the prairie, including the howl from a coyote and the hoot of a prairie owl. As the walk continued for nearly an hour, Senator Long remarked to Theodore that he hadn't been feeling strong for some time. "This walk is just the thing for you! It will do you good," Theodore stated as he continued on. (Long was forty-three at the time, two years younger than Theodore.) Returning to the train after their two-hour walk, Senator Long estimated that they had walked at least ten miles, but Senator Burton corrected him, stating it was more like twenty.

"About five, I would say," commented Theodore.[19]

Overnight, the town's population rose from 170 to more than 2,000 as people from surrounding areas came to see the president. As he had requested in the previous towns visited on a Sunday, the fanfare was kept to a discreet minimum. Town leaders had sent to Topeka for a large tent that would accommodate one thousand people for Sunday's religious services, but Theodore vetoed this idea, wanting to avoid any "Sunday program which savored of a circus." The tent was sent back to Topeka, and Theodore attended services at the Methodist Church not far from the train depot.[20]

In typical fashion, Theodore briskly walked in the cool morning air to the church. Six pews had been set aside for the president's party, with newspaper reporters sitting in the first row, members of the Grand Army of the Republic in the second pew, and the rest of Theodore's party taking up the last rows. Sitting on the aisle, he watched as two young girls, Myrtle Coates and Anna Bracken, came into the church looking for a place to sit. Theodore invited them to sit with him, sharing the hymnbook and singing along with the choir. Though it was noted that Anna was a bit shy when it came to singing, Theodore "sang lustily in a high tenor voice."[21]

Theodore told John Hay that Sharon Springs was similar to Medora, "a regular town of the cow country."

> It rejoiced in a church, although not in a preacher. The lack of one was supplied by draining the country for a hundred miles east and producing a Presbyterian, a Methodist and a dear old German Lutheran. I think every ranch within a radius of forty or

fifty miles sent its occupants to church that day, and the church was jammed. My own pew was the only one that did not bulge with occupants.

There were two very nice little girls standing in the aisle beside me. I invited them in and we all three sang out of the same hymn book. They were in their Sunday best and their brown sunburned little arms and faces had been scrubbed till they almost shone.

It was a very kindly, homely country congregation, all the people of a type I knew well and all of them looking well-to-do and prosperous in a way hardly warranted as it seemed to me by the eaten-off, wire-fence-enclosed, shortgrass ranges of the dry plains roundabout. When church was over I shook hands with the three preachers and all the congregation, whose buggies, ranch wagons, and dispirited-looking saddle ponies were tied to everything available in the village.[22]

While shaking hands with the congregation, a member of Theodore's party suggested that he should return to his train. Theodore refused. "No, these are my sort of people," he stated. One elderly man who shook his hand commented that "forty years ago today I was in Chancellorsville." Impressed, Theodore stated he wanted to shake his hand again and chatted with the veteran for a few moments, treating him like an old friend.[23] When he did return to his train, he remained outside talking to more people for a half hour before taking lunch.

After lunch, Theodore went for a horseback ride. He was accompanied by Dr. Rixley, N. H. Loomis (a Union Pacific Railroad executive), and Senators Long and Burton. Both senators had been practicing horseback riding for several weeks before Theodore's arrival. The ride lasted three hours, and the only one who kept up with Theodore was his doctor, Marion Rixley. Riding a chestnut sorrel mare, the owner, S. A. Chisum, told reporters that the president "did not ride her hard" when he returned the horse.[24] (In truth, Theodore did ride the horse very hard.)[25]

Back at his train, a group of people stood nearby, hoping for another glimpse of Theodore. One of them was young Pearl Gorsuch, who asked him if he'd like a baby badger. Not wanting to disappoint the child, Theodore said he would, which sent her father on a six-mile round trip to their ranch to obtain the creature. Handing the animal to Theodore, she told him that her brother Josiah had caught him in the morning. Delighted with the gift, he promptly named the badger after the girl's brother. In return, Theodore gifted the young girl with a gold and silver locket. Theodore later commented that Josiah reminded him of "a small mattress with a leg at each corner," but he quickly took a liking to him, often sitting in his car hand-feeding him as the landscape rolled on. Writing a letter to his son Kermit, he told him about the badger. "I named him Josiah, and he is now called Josh for short. He is very cunning and I hold him in my arms and pet him. I hope he will grow up friendly."[26] Josiah "became an intimate of the train until my return home, when he received a somewhat stormy welcome from the children, and is now one of the household."[27]

Five other girls stood near Pearl Gorsuch, hanging around the rear of Theodore's private car, "all in clean starched Sunday clothes and ribbon-tied pigtails." One of the girls was the daughter of the town sheriff, who kept nudging her father to make a request. The man motioned her to stop, which Theodore noticed. They were "exceedingly anxious to see the inside of my car," and he invited them in.

> The interior arrangements struck them as being literally palatial—magnificent. The whole population of the plains now looks upon the Pullman sleepers and dining cars just as Mark Twain describes people along the banks of the Mississippi as formerly looking at the Mississippi steamers, and for the same reasons.
>
> I liked the little girls so much that I regretted having nothing to give them but flowers; and they reciprocated my liking with warm western enthusiasm, for they hung about the car until it grew dark, either waving their hands to me, or kissing their hands to me whenever I appeared at the window.[28]

The following morning, before Theodore's train left for Colorado, he told the local citizens, "I had a corking good time."[29]

A Cowboy Breakfast: Colorado

I would not have missed this for anything. It reminds me of old times.

THE PEOPLE OF HUGO, COLORADO, WOULD NOT TAKE NO FOR AN ANSWER. Even from President Theodore Roosevelt.

As early as April 2, the *St. Paul Globe* carried the story that the Lincoln County Cattle Growers Association of eastern Colorado planned to arrange a "cowboy breakfast" for the president when his train came into the hamlet of Hugo. Two hundred "cowboys in range regalia" planned to salute him, as well as stockmen's families and guests.

Although his train would stop to briefly pick up Colorado governor James Peabody and Adjutant General Sherman Bell (who had served in Theodore's Rough Rider regiment in Cuba), Theodore let it be known that there simply wasn't enough time in his tight schedule to stop and have a breakfast, but the citizens of Hugo would not be discouraged. Ordering bunting in the national colors, they carried on with their plans and decorated the small depot and nearby buildings and homes.

Then they called in their ace in the hole: the cowboys.

The Bar O Z was about to start its spring roundup, and the citizens convinced the ranch's foreman, S. G. Sherman, to set up the ranch's chuck wagon near the depot. The foreman and the Bar O Z cowboys were only too happy to help.

Chuck wagons had been an essential part of cattle drives and ranch roundups for more than forty years. It was a commissary on wheels, nicknamed the "growler" or "camp wagon" by cowboys. It was an invention of legendary Texas rancher Charles Goodnight, who added a "chuck box" to the rear of a common, canvas-topped wagon. The chuck box held tin dishes, Dutch ovens, a kettle, and a large coffee pot and had several drawers containing the various staples a cook would need, including coffee (a coffee grinder was attached to the box), flour, beans, sugar, and even a bottle of whiskey for medicinal purposes. A folding board that attached to the bottom of the chuck box could be pulled up when the wagon was on the move and served as a preparation area for meals while in camp. Two water barrels were attached on either side of the wagon along with an axe, saw, and other tools, as well as an extra wagon wheel. Behind the chuck box was room for the cowboys to throw their bedrolls, while underneath the wagon was a canvas sling (called a "bitch" or "caboose") that held extra wood or buffalo chips picked up along the way for future use as firewood.

The stockmen chose Jack Keppel, a veteran cook of many cattle drives and now a rancher himself, who was "quite proud" to be chosen to handle the cowboy breakfast. Keppel brought along John Heyman, "as good a camp man that ever drew a breath," for assistance. On Friday, May 1, Keppel and Heyman arrived in Hugo to "get everything shipshape."

On that evening we swung the pot rack and cleared a space about the rear end of the chuck wagon and on Saturday we unpacked the provisions and laid in butter and such things as had been overlooked.

On Sunday, just to get my hand in and have things in working order, I cooked a big dinner for 150 natives and a couple of dozen "rawhides" from Denver.[1] I hadn't done any cooking for five years, and I was a little shaky about the job I had ahead of me, but the way those people ate and ate and came back for more convinced me that John and I could do the big stunt as well as anybody.

A few hours later I was wooling [roughly shaking] John Heyman to get him awake and beating around with a club to find daylight in the dark. The first thing I did after making up my fire was to put the beans back on. John and I then made twelve gallons of coffee in three big pots and got the French fried potatoes ready. The next thing was to make the biscuits and put them in the Dutch oven ready to bake. I made eight dozen of these and patted them out round and smooth. It's quite a job to make good biscuits, and you bet I was very particular with these. I wanted to have 'em just ready when the President came, so I went over to the depot and found out from the telegraph operator the exact moment when he would arrive. . . . When the President's train hove in sight we got pretty excited around that camp fire, I can tell you. I had picked out a big T-bone steak, the finest one I ever saw, for the President. As the train was slowing up I nodded to John Heyman to drop the big steak onto the hot surface of the oven, which was on the rack, and heated up just right. By this time the biscuits were done to a turn and everything was ready.

I had heard discouraging reports that President Roosevelt would not be allowed time enough at Hugo for him to get off and eat, but I knew if I could once get him in range of that beefsteak where he could get a whiff of that steak he would have to stay and eat.[2]

When his train came to a stop, Theodore greeted his old friend Sherman Bell and Governor Peabody, as well as the cowboys and citizens of the town who crowded around the train's rear platform. Theodore expressed his regrets that he could not stay and share breakfast due to an extremely tight schedule.

One of the mounted cowboys spoke up. "The chuck wagon is waiting, Mr. President, and breakfast is ready," he stated.

Looking from the platform, Theodore saw the chuck wagon. The smell of the coffee, beans, and steak wafted in the air luring him like a sailor to a mermaid.

"Now I'll have to go and eat something," Theodore replied. He quickly stepped down and in his typical lively gait was on his way to the chuck wagon. As the cowboys followed him, yelling their approval, Peabody and Bell, as well as the Secret Service detail, were left unaware. They quickly got off the train to catch up with him.[3]

The crowd at the depot, forced to stand behind a rope line, cheered the president. Theodore later commented, "It seemed absurd to get off and eat at a tail end of a chuck wagon in a top hat and frock coat, but they were so heartbroken by my refusal that I finally did."[4]

No doubt memories of his days in Dakota during spring and fall roundups came rushing back. As he approached the wagon, Theodore's smile grew bigger. Like a child looking at the presents under the family Christmas tree, he was heard to say, "This reminds me of the old times," and "by George, Dutch ovens!"

Before he shook hands with the president, Jack Keppel poured a cup of hot coffee, placing it on the folding board that would serve as Theodore's table. Next to the coffee was a tin plate and a can of sugar. Theodore heartily shook hands with Keppel and Heyman before picking up his plate to help himself to beans, a biscuit, and his T-bone steak.

Washing down a bite of his steak with the coffee, he looked around at the men gathered by the wagon. "This is bully!" Theodore smiled, cutting another slice from the steak. "I would not have missed this for anything. It reminds me of old times. I have been here before, boys—this is great!"[5]

Between mouthfuls, Theodore would shake hands with the cowboys, telling them how happy he was to see them. This wasn't political hyperbole; Theodore was speaking from his heart. He related to the cowboys, having lived and ridden with men of this ilk. Together, they had chewed dust, stopped stampedes, seen seasons change, and taken meals from a chuck wagon. Despite wearing a silk top hat and frock coat, on the inside, he was like them in so many ways.

Foreman S. G. Sherman, "dressed for the work ahead," was introduced to the president. Indicating Adjutant General Sherman Bell, Theodore remarked that the two men had the same name. Pointing to Bell, Theodore called him "one of my boys." (He used this sobriquet when referring to any of his Rough Riders.) "When this Sherman first came to us—when I first saw him," Theodore told foreman Sherman, pointing to Bell's dress uniform, "he was not wearing any better clothes than you have on now."[6]

Finishing up his meal, Theodore said he wished he could "drop off here and ride the line for a day or two with you boys." One cowboy offered to loan him his horse, but he reluctantly declined.

Turning to the foreman, Theodore thanked him, shaking his hand. "This has been a real treat—I thank you heartily," he said. Theodore then thanked Keppel and Heyman for the meal, laughing at their invitation to "come again."[7] As he made his way to the train, many cowboys followed, offering eager hands, which Theodore happily shook.

Standing on the rear platform as his train pulled out, he waved to the crowd. Several mounted cowboys began to shout and wave their hats as they raced the departing train. Beaming with delight, Theodore waved and watched them until the train gained speed.

"Well, I have cooked many a steak," Jack Keppel recalled, "but I was certainly more proud of that one than of any I ever turned out. It was a regular 'beaut,' and when Teddy cut into it and munched the first mouthful and I saw the tickled expression of his face I was so proud—well, I just had to swing my hat and holler."[8]

The engineer was making up for lost time, but the train had to make two stops along the way to take on water. In Deer Trail, forty-three miles east of Denver, more than two dozen people had shown up at the depot in hopes of getting a fleeting glimpse of the president. With the train taking on water for several minutes, Theodore ordered the rear platform lowered and he stepped off to shake hands with the people. The last one to greet him was a small boy on a white pony. As he shook hands, Theodore remarked, "There's a Rough Rider of the future." He laughed when the boy's pony crowded him against the train, although bystanders and his Secret Service agents did not share Theodore's delight.[9]

Like all other towns and cities that Theodore would visit during his tour, Denver was no different in its desire to display patriotic pride. Businesses and homes were decorated with the usual bunting and flags. The streets were swept clean, and the public was told that the depot would be closed to the public for Theodore's arrival. The day prior to Theodore's arrival, the *Denver Post* featured a front-page cartoon of a woman powdering her face in front of a mirror while wearing a hat labeled "Denver." In front of her on the vanity table was a framed photo of Theodore, captioned "He's Coming Tomorrow." The American Furniture Company announced that it would be giving away ten thousand photos of the president to all adult visitors. (Street vendors were selling the same photograph for eighty-five cents.)[10]

The Roosevelt Special arrived in Denver at 10:45 in the morning, having made up for the unexpected delay in Hugo. As always, Theodore made a point of thanking the train crew, which impressed one man who had been a supporter of William Jennings Bryan's failed run for the presidency in 1900. "Damned, if he don't get me," the man gushed.[11] The first man to greet Theodore at the depot was Father Robinet, who had been following Theodore's career long before he was in Washington. The priest had written long ago that before he died, he wanted to visit Theodore at the White House. The two men finally met in 1900 during Theodore's cross-country campaign trip as the vice presidential candidate. Shaking Father Robinet's hand, Theodore asked when he was going to come see him in Washington, and the priest promised he would visit later that summer.[12]

Once again, the familiar routine: a carriage ride through downtown Denver with hundreds of people waving flags and cheering. One uniquely noticeable noise from the crowd along the route was the "click-click" of hundreds of Kodak cameras snapping pictures of Theodore as he waved and bowed to the crowd on both sides of the street. (Throughout the carriage procession, he never once sat down.) At one point in the procession, a group of young girls stood alongside the street holding various bouquets of flowers. Theodore ordered the carriage to stop and invited the children over, taking the flowers and shaking each girl's hand before moving on.

For Harry Gasner, the day would not end well. Gasner, a butcher from Elyria, made "insulting noises" as the president passed along on Sixteenth Street. Those "within reach" hit him. Gasner hit back, and "in an instant there was a fight" in the alley off the street. Fourteen men were involved in the brawl, which was broken up when police officer McIntyre and Detective Loomis happened by. Three men, including Gasner, were arrested, while the others retreated to safer locations. All three men were taken to police headquarters and eventually released on their personal recognizance.[13]

When it came to a band of pickpockets, Denver police chief Armstrong vowed that the president would be back in Washington before these criminals got out of Denver. "I'm going to have these fellows vagged, put a ball and chain on 'em and make every mother's son of 'em work on the jail lawn for ninety days," he stated of those that were arrested. A gang of thirty pickpockets had been following the presidential tour since it began, but only about eight were arrested. Detectives were watching passengers disembarking the trains at Union Station, while other detectives boarded the trains as they approached the station and searched the cars, making arrests. One man, James Logan, tried to escape by breaking through a vestibule and jumping from the moving train. The fall "knocked him senseless and tore his face very badly." Treated by a doctor, he was then taken to jail.[14]

The west side of Colorado's state capitol building featured a speaker's platform, and the entire area was swarming with people, including boys—and even some men—who climbed trees to better hear Theodore's speech. At one point, as he was about to speak, the crowd began to push their way forward into the platform. Theodore promptly brought the situation under control when he pointed his finger to the group and ordered them not to push. Declaring that there was "plenty of room," he reminded the crowd that young children could get hurt. The crowd quickly stopped pushing.

Addressing the crowd about the recent irrigation law, Theodore declared it was "one of the best pieces of legislation put upon the statute books." Noting that some people would be disappointed, having built up their hopes "without a quite sufficient warranty of fact," Theodore was certain that "good will surely will come at once and well-nigh immeasurable good in the future from the policy" once it was in action. He reminded the citizens that two-thirds of their products came from irrigated farms, and "four years ago those products had already surpassed fifteen million dollars." The law, he observed, was to provide small irrigated farms, ordinary settlers and homemakers with those individuals repaying the cost of bringing water to their lands in ten annual payments. The law, Theodore noted, banned furnishing water to large tracts of land in order to prevent the acquisition of rights for speculative purposes, thereby preventing any chance of a landowner creating a monopoly or large-scale speculation project. This law would turn land with "waters now wasted" into prosperous land for homes "where twenty years ago it would have seemed impossible that a man could live." Theodore noted that this new law would be a "great national benefit" for the whole community.[15]

For, my fellow-countrymen, you can never afford to forget for one moment that in the long run anything that is of benefit to one part of our Republic is of necessity of benefit to all the Republic. The creation of new homes upon desert lands means greater prosperity for Colorado and the Rocky Mountain States, and inevitably their greater prosperity means greater prosperity for Eastern manufacturers, for Southern cotton growers, for all our people throughout the Union.[16]

Theodore returned to the train station and, as he exited the carriage, he turned to the driver, Frank Hill, and extended his hand and congratulated him on the "way you handle a team." Hill, taken by surprise, thanked the president.[17]

The Midland band in Colorado Springs broke into "Hail to the Chief" as Theodore's train pulled into the Denver and Rio Grande station behind the fabled Antlers Hotel. Cheers erupted the moment the crowd spotted the steam engine transporting its famous passenger and continued as the president exited his car.

Outside of the depot, Theodore briefly reunited with four former Rough Riders (Sherman Bell, H. K. Devereux, P. A. Wickham, and George Sharland), spending a few minutes recalling their time in Cuba and Theodore's breakfast in Hugo. Turning to the men, he pointed to Sherman Bell and said, "And what do you think, there was old Sherman with all his gold lace and me with a top hat eating just like in the old days. I remember some breakfasts where we didn't have much to eat. Do you remember that morning when we couldn't even get beans? And I think Sherman became a Nebuchadnezzar and got after grass."[18]

A group of Grand Army of the Republic members and Colorado militia escorted Theodore to the Antlers Hotel, the crowd trailing behind. People shouted greetings along the way, and Theodore took off his top hat and bowed to them.

The Antlers Hotel was originally built in 1883 but was destroyed by fire in 1898. Construction was quickly undertaken on a newer, more elaborate version, which opened in 1901. A large veranda greeted the guests, with a statue of Zebulon Pike, the man who discovered Pike's Peak, in the front. The hotel had two tall spires on either side of the building, which framed Pike's Peak when viewed from Cascade Avenue and Pike's Peak Boulevard.[19]

The front of the hotel had a sweeping entry for carriages and two huge American flags, joined together, formed a large bunting banner at the hotel's entrance. The crowd was contained behind a rope, and only carriages were allowed admission through the front entrance. When Theodore emerged on the second-floor balcony and saw the people were held back, he ordered the carriages moved and the rope to be let down to allow the crowd to come closer.[20] In his speech Theodore once again pointed to the Civil War veterans' abilities to withstand hardships as a model for present-day citizens in the United States to aspire, as well as the virtues of honesty and decency. "Together with honesty and decency must go the spirit impelling us to go out and fight to make things a little better in the world.... We can win only by making up our minds that life is not an easy but hard thing, and glory comes, not in seeking to make the task easy, but to do the task well."[21]

While Theodore was making his way off the balcony after his speech, Mayor Ira Harris stopped him to introduce him to a committee representing the "colored residents of the city" who presented him with a "heavy silver plate in a neat case" to honor "the stand the president took on the race question." In addition, they conferred upon him a resolution, read by Reverend W. E. Gladden, which endorsed his administration "on account of the manly position that he, as our chief executive, has taken against raising the 'color line' in federal appointments." The resolution went on to explain that the silver medal was for to his "sterling qualities of head and heart [that] commend him to favorable consideration of his countrymen." One side of the plaque read "A friend to the friendless. President of the people." Theodore, visibly touched by the gift, replied, "The only thing to do is to do the square thing."[22]

During his carriage ride through the city, he passed the YMCA building at Bijou and Nevada Avenues. In 1901, Theodore helped to lay the cornerstone of the building, and now it was completed. A banner between the second-floor balconies read: "August 10, 1901, We Welcomed

Vice-President Roosevelt to lay the cornerstone of this building. May 4, 1903, We Welcome President Roosevelt to the completed building." As his carriage passed by, Theodore stood up in his carriage, removed his hat, and bowed in the direction of the YMCA.[23] (Theodore was greatly disappointed that he could not stop to see the inside of the building.) The procession returned to the train station, and after a few farewell handshakes, Theodore left Colorado Springs.

The *Colorado Springs Gazette* wistfully noted that not one baby in Colorado Springs had been kissed by the president.

Theodore's stop in Pueblo was only fifteen minutes, enough time for a brief carriage ride over a newly built bridge to a platform in front of Mineral Palace.[24] Theodore spoke to an estimated one hundred thousand people who had come from various towns in the Arkansas Valley.

A reporter covering Theodore's speech noted that "the last part of the address was especially earnest, expressing his trust in the ability of the people of the republic to overcome the difficulties and problems that arise, not by genius or brilliance, but by the exercise of plain good and practical common sense and an insistence upon genuine liberty and fair play for each individual."[25]

As his train left Pueblo, siren whistles from nearby smelters "sounded a deafening goodbye."

Despite his avowed rule of not making any speeches past ten o'clock in the evening, Theodore broke it in Trinidad. When his train made a brief stop to take on water at 11:40, he stepped out onto the rear platform and greeted nearly one thousand people who had assembled. Eight minutes later his train pulled out.

"Denver, Colorado Springs and Pueblo showed the usual features," Theodore recalled to John Hay. "Enormous crowds, processions, masses of school children, local Grand Army posts; sweating, bustling, self-conscious local committees; universal kindliness and friendliness; little girls dressed up as Goddesses of Liberty; misguided enthusiasts who nearly drove the horses mad by dumping huge baskets of flowers over them and us as we drove by favorable windows; other misguided enthusiasts who endeavored to head stampedes to shake my hand and felt deeply injured when repulsed by the secret service men and local policemen, etc., etc., etc. But in the evening when I had reached Trinidad I struck the wild country once more."[26]

John Burroughs observed that politicians found Theodore to be "a hard customer." The famed naturalist stated Theodore's "sense of right and duty was as inflexible as adamant." AUTHOR'S COLLECTION

The "Roosevelt Special" was pulled by various engines and coal cars. Many bore a photo of Theodore at the front of the engine. AUTHOR'S COLLECTION

THE PRESIDENT ENCOUNTERS A FEW BEARS.

Theodore's meeting with several chiefs from Indian tribes at the capitol in Bismarck, North Dakota, inspired this political cartoon from the Washington, DC, newspaper, *Evening Star*. "The President Encounters a Few Bears" was a reference to Theodore's 1902 black bear hunt in Mississippi. AUTHOR'S COLLECTION

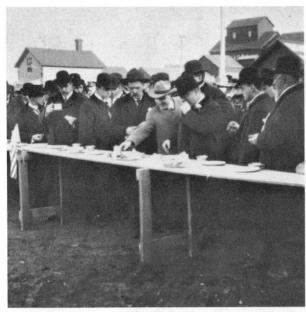

In Bismarck, North Dakota, Theodore (third from right) stops for a barbecue sandwich. His longtime friend Seth Bullock (second from Theodore's left) also sampled the food.
AUTHOR'S COLLECTION

Theodore and Major John Pickard took a ride around what was then known as Fort Yellowstone (now called Mammoth Hot Springs). Visitors can explore this area in Yellowstone National Park today but must remain on walkways to protect the delicate (and dangerous) landscape.
THEODORE ROOSEVELT COLLECTION, HOUGHTON LIBRARY, HARVARD UNIVERSITY

Theodore (center) stands with numerous friends in Medora's town hall. John Burroughs (right, with white beard) stands next to him. Owning two cattle ranches, Theodore spent nearly three years (on and off) in this town when it was part of the Dakota Territory. Although this visit was brief, he enjoyed himself immensely, sharing memories with many friends. THEODORE ROOSEVELT COLLECTION, HOUGHTON LIBRARY, HARVARD UNIVERSITY

On April 24, 1903, Theodore dedicated the cornerstone for the northern entrance to Yellowstone. Today, it is known as Roosevelt Arch. AUTHOR'S COLLECTION

During many stops on his two-month tour, Theodore gave speeches from many elaborate speaker's stands. This one, in Newcastle, Wyoming, was set up for Theodore's speech, which only lasted fifteen minutes. AUTHOR'S COLLECTION

Archie, Theodore's son, poses with Josiah the badger, a gift to his father from a little girl in Sharon Springs, Kansas. Unfortunately, Josiah's natural tendencies soon forced him to be relocated to the Bronx Zoo. THEODORE ROOSEVELT COLLECTION, HOUGHTON LIBRARY, HARVARD UNIVERSITY

In many cities and towns, it was not uncommon for Theodore to stand on a table or a chair so the large crowd could see and hear him. This was the case during his speech in Hannibal, Missouri. THEODORE ROOSEVELT COLLECTION, HOUGHTON LIBRARY, HARVARD UNIVERSITY

The Southwest: New Mexico

There can be no greater privilege than to meet a missionary who has done good work.

NEARLY THREE HUNDRED PEOPLE OF THE HAMLET MEADOW CITY rolled out of their beds in order to be at the depot at three-thirty in the morning. They were part of the New Mexico delegation that would accompany Theodore to his stops in Santa Fe and Albuquerque. "It is doubtful if there is another city of the size in the United States that would get three hundred citizens out of bed at three-thirty o'clock and send them a hundred miles to greet the president," commented a New Mexico newspaper.[1]

By the time the train arrived in Santa Fe, the sun and the president were up. "Musketry rolled, bells rang joyously, bands crashed martial music and thousands lifted their voices in hearty acclaim" noted the reporter for the *Las Vegas (NM) Daily Optic* of Theodore's arrival. "Never in its history has Santa Fe shown so enthusiastic and highly colored a scene," he added.[2]

At the train depot, the prerequisite greeting from the local committee and politicians took place before the procession made its way to the territory's capitol, where a speaker's podium was set up on the west side of the building.[3] Speaking to the audience, Theodore was careful not to express any support for New Mexico's admission to the Union. (New Mexico became a state in 1912, along with Arizona.) Instead, Theodore pointed out how the Rough Rider unit was a configuration of a "typical American regiment," bringing men from all areas of the country. The only rivalry in the regiment, he observed, was that each man desired to "do his duty a little better than anyone else."

He then turned to the current issues of the territory, acknowledging "all the difficulties under which you labor" and assuring that the future would "far make good the past." Noting the territory had come to "an era of fuller development," its evolution needed to take place "principally through the average of foresight, thrift, industry, energy and will of the citizens." Theodore praised the territory's bountiful land for grazing and requested the citizens' support for "preservation and proper shape of the forest reserves."

These forest reserves are created and are kept up in the interest of the home-maker. In many of them there is much natural pasturage. Where that is the case the object is to have that pasturage used by the settlers, by the people of the Territory, not eaten out so that nobody will have the benefit after three years. I want the land preserved so that the pasturage will do, not merely for a man who wants to make a good thing out of it for two or three years, but for the man who wishes to see it preserved for the use of his children and his children's children.

That is the way to use the resources of the land. I build no small hope upon the aid that under the wise law of Congress will ultimately be extended to this as to other States and Territories in the way of governmental aid to irrigation. Irrigation is of course to be in the future well-nigh the most potent factor in the agricultural development of this Territory and one of the factors which will do most toward bringing it up to Statehood. Nothing will count more than development of that kind in bringing the Territory in as a State. That is the kind of development which I am most anxious to see here the development that means permanent growth in the capacity of the land, not temporary, not the exploiting of the land for a year or two at the cost of its future impoverishment, but the building up of farm and ranch in such shape as to benefit the home-maker whose intention it is that this Territory of the present, this State of the future, shall be a great State in the American Union.[4]

Theodore believed one should care for the land for future generations, not just for a year or two. During his years as a rancher in Dakota

Territory, he had personally seen the damage caused from overgrazing by other stockmen eager only to make an immediate profit with little thought for the future. Theodore voiced his concerns about overgrazing to the Little Missouri Stockmen Association and the Montana Stockgrowers Association, but they rebuffed his warnings.[5]

The *Las Vegas Daily Optic* was quick to point out that "a vast majority" were disappointed with the president's speech, expecting him to support statehood. Despite the crowd's discouragement, his speech was received with "sufficient enthusiasm." The newspaper also noted "the president's opinion is important" and had he "been favorably inclined," New Mexico would have been given statehood. "New Mexico is not likely to come in [as a state] until the strenuous president thinks we are ready," the paper claimed. The *Daily Optic* offered two suggestions. The first was to "convince the strong-minded man that he is mistaken and the territory is ready now." The other option was "to get to work at once to bring ourselves up to the standard which he has made."[6]

The procession around the city stopped at the San Miguel Church, where the son of George W. Armijo was going to be baptized. Armijo had been a sergeant in Troop F of the Rough Riders who had remained in contact with Theodore ever since. When the former Rough Rider married his wife, Josefa, in 1902, Theodore sent a letter of congratulations.[7] Now Theodore would become the godfather of Armijo's child, Theodore Roosevelt Manderfield Armijo.

"Nothing would do but that I must stand sponsor for it [the baby's baptism]. He was a Catholic, but the Bishop made no objections, and accordingly, lighted taper in hand, I stood solemnly behind the father and mother while the baby was christened in the old adobe mission cathedral. His ancestors and mine had doubtless fought in the Netherlands in the days of Alva and Parma, just about the time this mission was built and before a Dutch or English colonist had set foot on American soil," Theodore later recalled.[8]

"No king, emperor, prince or any other potentate in ancient days of Rome and Greece ever received such an enthusiastic and hearty reception as President Roosevelt was given this afternoon," gushed the *Albuquerque Citizen*.[9]

Theodore's carriage made its way to the Alvarado Hotel, where he spoke to the people of Albuquerque. He stressed how impressed he was with "what you are doing with irrigation." There was a fenced platform in front of him that featured forty-five little girls in white dresses (representing the states of the Union).[10] On the steps of the platform was another girl in white (depicting the territory of New Mexico), waiting to be admitted to the union. Pointing to the young girl outside the fence, he said, "When we have been able to get on a little more with it [irrigation] there will not be the slightest difficulty with my poor little friend on the outside of the fence." Theodore noted that when irrigation is properly started, "even the rain is an insufficient substitute for it."[11]

Turning his attention to the children, who he referred to as "the future," he reminded parents that "school can only supplement the home, and you expect the school teachers to undo what you do if you do your part ill. Remember that you cannot unload everything on the school teacher. The father and the mother have got to do their part decently and fairly and conscientiously, and also not foolishly." He ended his speech reminding the crowd that "the west could never have been settled, could never have been brought up to what it is, if it had not been for the adventurous temper and the iron resolution of those who first tamed the shaggy wilderness and turned it into habitations for men."[12]

Theodore made two additional speeches, albeit brief. The first was to students of a Catholic school. "There can be no greater privilege than to meet a missionary who has done good work," he commented. "Of all the work that is done or that can be done for our country, the greatest is that of educating the body, the mind and above all the character, giving spiritual and moral training to those who in a few years are themselves to decide the destinies of the Nation." He also spoke to students of an Indian school, stating that if they work and do their duty, they can "stand on a par with any other American citizen. Of course, I will do as every President must do, I will stand for his rights with the same jealous eagerness that I would for the rights of any white man."[13]

The Albuquerque Commercial Club made Theodore an honorary member, giving him one of the most unique membership cards ever made. It was a saddle blanket created by Elle, a Navajo woman from the village of Ganado.[14] The *Albuquerque Citizen* had noted that Elle was the "most expert . . . for this line of work, and as long as she lives will be admired by the Indians for having woven a blanket for the 'Great White Father' in Washington." She had finished the blanket the evening before Theodore's arrival, and it was displayed in the window of the Harvey Curio Shop attracting "a constant throng of visitors" prior to its presentation.[15] The blanket measured fifty-three inches by twenty-nine inches, with a red background and a blue center running down the middle. In the center, in white letters, it read:

The President
Honorary Membership Card
Commercial Club
Albuquerque, New Mexico
May 5, 1903[16]

At the train station, Theodore met T. J. Shinick, who gave him one of his old business cards from when he and his partner had a carriage company in Oyster Bay in 1870. Theodore remembered the man and was "glad to see an Oyster Bay man out in this fine country."[17]

Though newspapers did not mention anyone attempting to publicly speak to Theodore about statehood, he could not miss several banners that citizens had erected along the route of his procession. "We want the right to vote for him!" one read; another stated, "We greet you, but can't vote for you." One banner had an ironic bite to it: "Our welcome is as cordial as though we lived in a state."

⁓

As the Roosevelt Special made its way across the desert in the later hours of the evening, residents of several hamlets gathered at depots as the train made water stops. Informed that Theodore had retired for the night, they were not to be dissuaded. They yelled and some even fired their pistols in the air, hoping to rouse the president from slumber.[18] In Gallup, New Mexico Territory, one man threatened to "explode a stick of dynamite under the train car" unless Theodore came out. Instead, the man compromised by shooting off a firecracker.[19]

"The secret service men on duty last night had an unhappy time," reported the *Arizona Daily Star*.[20]

The Big Ditch: Arizona

Leave it as it is. You cannot improve on it. The ages have been at work on it, and man can only mar it.

THE ELEMENTS HAVE BEEN AT WORK FOR MILLIONS OF YEARS. WIND, rain, and erosion were the sculpting tools that carved it. Its width ranges from 175 yards to 18 miles. Its depth is more than a mile, or six thousand feet. The deepest part of the canyon extends for 56 miles, whereas its entire length, along a winding course, is nearly 277 miles. The northern rim of the canyon stands at roughly 8,200 feet—a full 1,200 feet higher than the southern rim. The most obvious color of the land is red, but buff, gray, delicate green, pink, and, at its greatest depths, dark brown, slate gray, and violet are also visible. The silence is deafening and welcoming.

This is the Grand Canyon.

There is no other place on Earth that offers such a vast and significant record of our planet's geologic events. However, erosion has caused immense gaps in the stratum, translating to millions of years. The layers of stratum, which once were the Earth's surface, delineate the age of the canyon. The oldest layer, in the lowest part of the canyon, dates back more than 2.5 billion years. As the canyon walls rise, limestone, sandstone, and shale, dating back 540 million years, are revealed. The next gradation forms the majority of the canyon walls and dates to about 300 million years ago. Rocks from the Mesozoic era (250–65 million years ago) should be next, but this layer has disappeared due to erosion. Then there is the layer belonging to the Paleozoic era dating from 570 to 245 million years.[1]

The creation of the canyon is relatively new—in geologic terms— being only six million years old. The canyon was originally created by the flow of the Colorado River. The river's steep incline coupled with its velocity and volume chiseled and shaped the canyon we see today, and the river continues to shape the canyon, albeit at a lesser rate. The width of the canyon was created by a combination of rain, wind, temperature, and erosion over time, and just like the Colorado River, these elements continue to alter the canyon. One other very important factor in the creation of the Grand Canyon is the semiarid climate. Had it not been for this climate, rains would have eliminated the canyon walls, destroyed the distinctive sculpturing, and the various color hues would not exist.

The Grand Canyon was home to many pueblo and cliff-dwelling tribes, and their numerous ruins can be found throughout the canyon, many dating back to the prehistoric era. The first known sighting of the Grand Canyon by a European occurred in 1540, when Francisco Coronado explored the area. Two Spanish priests recorded their travels through the area in 1776, and many of the first trappers in the early 1800s were known to have camped in the area. However, it wasn't until 1857 when the first American was credited with reaching the river inside the canyon. U.S. Army lieutenant Joseph Ives traveled north into the canyon by river, and when his steamer crashed below Black Canyon (where Hoover Dam is situated today), he used a skiff to continue upriver for an additional thirty miles before making the rest of his journey on foot. Ives got as far as Diamond Creek before calling off his expedition.[2] Commenting in his report, Ives claimed the region was "valueless" and believed the area would be eternally vacant. Twelve years later, John Wesley Powell's expedition down the Colorado River and through the Grand Canyon caught the attention of the newspapers and their readers, including Theodore.[3]

The Grand Canyon also attracted entrepreneurs. Ralph Cameron quickly recognized the canyon as a potential tourist attraction and, with his brother Niles, constructed a hotel at the head of the Bright Angel Trail, which was possibly an old game trail. The Cameron brothers and their partner, Pete Berry, vastly improved the route, even filing paperwork to create a private toll road in 1891. However, within six years, the lack of foot traffic caused the trail to fall into disrepair.[4] Emery and Ellsworth

Kolb made a home at Grand Canyon with the 1904 opening of their photography studio on the edge of the canyon. The brothers took photographs of tourists on the mule train as they went down the canyon and developed and sold them upon their return. In addition, they photographed more remote areas that allowed the public to see places they would normally never visit, making the Grand Canyon even more popular.[5]

Unfortunately, the Grand Canyon was unprotected. Miners filed claims and dug holes in the walls to extract valuable minerals, and businessmen saw only profits with the area's growing popularity. No one cared how many animals were hunted, how many trees were cut down, or how many ancient ruins were desecrated.

All that changed when Theodore Roosevelt arrived.

At four in the morning, his train passed through Flagstaff in Arizona Territory, ignoring the large numbers of citizens who gathered in the chill before sunrise hoping to see the president. Making a brief stop to take on water, the train was gone before the sky showed any signs of gray. In Williams, the Roosevelt Special switched onto the rail line for the Grand Canyon and continued on.[6]

More than one thousand people came to the canyon to see Theodore, the majority of them traveling by train. (One newspaper claimed that "more white men than ever before assembled on the brink of that mighty chasm will bid him welcome.") The train pulled into the Grand Canyon station at 9:30, and as it came to a halt, people swarmed it. Cheers erupted as Theodore stepped off the rear platform in riding clothes and doffed his cowboy hat as he made his way to a string of saddled horses. "He is roughened and sunburned by his trip through the National Park, and his common place clothes and the old sombrero that he jams about with the abandon of a schoolboy gives him the ensemble of a rough and ready cowpuncher," commented the *Bisbee Daily Review*.[7] Another newspaper noted that his face was "brown as a brick." Several former Rough Riders gathered around him, forcing a delay as he took time to speak to his men.

In the crowd he spotted Ben Daniels, a former Rough Rider and friend. Daniels had been appointed by Theodore as U.S. marshal in Arizona Territory in late 1901. The man was given a positive recommendation by attorney general Philander Knox, despite stories about his background—real or imagined. Theodore stood by his friend, vouching for the man's honorable background before the Senate. However, by February 1903, newspapers revealed Daniels's criminal past and he was forced to resign. Daniels, who had worked cattle drives and hunted buffalo, was arrested along with other men in Montana Territory in 1879 for stealing government mules. While in custody, he managed to escape, but not before he shot an army officer and a soldier. (The officer, a lieutenant, later died.) In Dodge City, he was arrested by Bat Masterson (who later became a personal friend of Daniels and Theodore). Daniels was sentenced to three and a half years in prison, and upon his release, he pinned on a lawman's badge, working in Dodge City, Lamar, and Cripple Creek before joining the Rough Riders in 1898.

Speaking to a reporter at the Grand Canyon, Daniels expressed some trepidation about seeing Theodore, but he wanted "to show the president he was not afraid to meet him, notwithstanding the unpleasant experience following his Marshal appointment." To Ben's surprise, Theodore greeted him heartily. "Old man I am awfully glad to see you, by George! Get a horse and come with us, and ride with me on my train down the road tonight," he said to an astonished Daniels.[8]

As Theodore mounted his horse, the crowd from the train followed him and began to gather around his mount. Theodore, laughing with delight, warned them, "Look out for the business end of this horse!"[9] The group mounted and galloped off to Rowe's Point, three miles west of the station. (It is now known as Hopi Point.)[10]

"The immortal picture of the great Corsican at the pyramids, halting his legions before humanity's tremendous monuments, will be dimmed by the memory of a grander leader of the mightiest host of peace, gazing with rapt veneration upon God's most awful mundane manifestation," Joe Chisholm breathlessly penned for the opening of his *Bisbee Daily Review* story on Theodore's arrival to the Grand Canyon. "However, should he prove, as many affect to believe a placid politician, this will be remembered only as the date of a picturesque incident."[11]

Returning from his ride, Theodore addressed the crowd from the balcony of the Grand Canyon Hotel. He began his speech by mentioning how many men from the Arizona Territory had served in the Rough Riders. "As long as I live it will be to me an inspiration to have served with Bucky O'Neill.[12] I have met so many comrades whom I prize, for whom I feel respect and admiration and affection," he stated. Theodore then went on to discuss how the effects of irrigation would be of "greater consequence to all this region of country in the next fifty years than any other material movement whatsoever."[13]

He then turned his attention to the Grand Canyon. At this moment, Theodore would propose ideas that would continue to define his presidency for generations. He was about to take a major step in his conservation beliefs that would continue to affect and protect not just the Grand Canyon, but other wonders of nature.

In the Grand Canyon, Arizona has a natural wonder which, so far as I know, is in kind absolutely unparalleled throughout the rest of the world. I want to ask you to do one thing in connection with it in your own interest and in the interest of the country to keep this great wonder of nature as it now is. . . . I was delighted to learn of the wisdom of the Santa Fe railroad people in deciding not to build their hotel on the brink of the canyon. I hope you will not have a building of any kind, not a summer cottage, a hotel, or anything else, to mar the wonderful grandeur, the sublimity, the great loneliness and beauty of the canyon.

Leave it as it is. You cannot improve on it. The ages have been at work on it, and man can only mar it. What you can do is to keep it for your children, your children's children, and for all who come after you, as one of the great sights which every American if he can travel at all should see.

We have gotten past the stage, my fellow-citizens, when we are to be pardoned if we treat any part of our country as something to be skinned for two or three years for the use of the present generation, whether it is the forest, the water, the scenery.

Whatever it is, handle it so that your children's children will get the benefit of it. If you deal with irrigation, apply it under circumstances that will make it of benefit, not to the speculator who hopes to get profit out of it for two or three years, but handle it so that it will be of use to the home-maker, to the man who comes to live here, and to have his children stay after him. Keep the forests in the same way. Preserve the forests by use; preserve them for the ranchman and the stockman, for the people of the Territory, for the people of the region round about. Preserve them for that use, but use them so that they will not be squandered, that they will not be wasted, so that they will be of benefit to the Arizona of 1953 as well as the Arizona of 1903.[14]

———

After his speech, Theodore helped to hand out diplomas to the five graduating students from Flagstaff High School. *The Coconino Sun* commented, "It is not every graduate who is fortunate enough to have the chief magistrate of the nation as sponsor for the efficiency of the system of education as taught in our public schools as a weapon in the battle of life, and they should always bear in mind that they have a greater than ordinary incentive to right living and right doing."[15] The students, in turn, presented him with Navajo buckskin boots that were "handsomely and elaborately ornamented."

Dick Hartman, a Civil War veteran, was introduced to Theodore. Hartman had a unique claim: he had met every U.S. president since James Buchanan (1857–1861). "Roosevelt seized both of Hartman's hands, fervently assuring him that he considered the meeting an honor," a reporter noted. Hartman gave Theodore "an old ballot that was voted for Abraham Lincoln in Placer County, California, in 1864" by Tom Tracy, a friend who now lived in Bisbee, Arizona. He also gave the president a photo of a bear that had been captured in Bisbee. He told Theodore, "Mr. President, here is a paper bear, but you will get the real article when you get back to Washington." Theodore remarked that the bear was a beauty and asked if it was gentle. Hartman assured him the bear was that, as well as trained to box and wrestle. "Is that so?" Theodore remarked. "The boys will be tickled when they get him." Hartman and others had tried to transport the cub, named "Teddy," to the Grand Canyon, but the railroad company could not "devise ways and means for transporting a bear through Arizona." It was announced in late May that "Teddy" would be sent by train to the Washington Zoo, where he would live out his days. It was expected that Theodore and his family would visit the cub upon his return home. A newspaper noted that "Teddy" weighed 125 pounds but is "very good-natured, but not so strenuous at present."[16]

Chief Ma-Na-Ka-Ja of the Havasupai Tribe was introduced to Theodore, who told the tribal leader, "I do not forget the Red Man. I will think of his welfare as well as that of the white man. If an Indian does wrong to the white man, I'll cinch him, and if a white man wrongs the Indian, I'll cinch him too. Live in harmony with each other, and advance together."[17] Theodore noted in his speech that there were many members of Indian tribes in the Rough Riders, noting they were "good enough to fight and die, and they are good enough to have me treat them exactly as square as any man." However, he noted that "we must save them from corruption and from brutality," adding, with regret, that at times "we must save them from unregulated Eastern philanthropy"[18]

Theodore and his group once again mounted horses and rode fourteen miles to Grandview Point, the southernmost point on the Grand Canyon's South Rim. Returning to his train, Theodore spent a half hour visiting with his former Rough Riders before departing at six in the evening for California.

—◆—

In a letter to his daughter Ethel, Theodore called the Grand Canyon "wonderful and beautiful beyond description. I could have sat and looked at it for days. It is a tremendous chasm, a mile deep and several miles wide, the cliffs carved into battlements, amphitheaters, towers and pinnacles, and the coloring wonderful, red and yellow and gray and green."[19]

In 1882, then-senator Benjamin Harrison introduced a bill to make the Grand Canyon the nation's second national park. The bill failed, as did two more attempts by Harrison in 1883 and 1886. As president, the best Harrison could do was to create the Grand Canyon Forest Reserve in 1893, providing some protection to the area, although mining and logging were still permitted.

After his visit to the Grand Canyon, Theodore encouraged Congress to designate the area as a national park. Timber and mining interests used their influence to delay and eventually kill any action. Twenty-one days after the passage of the Antiquities Act on June 8, 1906, Theodore used the new law to create the Grand Canyon Game Preserve to protect wild animals within the Grand Canyon Forest Reserve. Frustrated by the inaction of Congress, Theodore granted national monument status to the Grand Canyon on January 11, 1908. Three weeks after Theodore's death, the Grand Canyon received national park status on January 26, 1919.[20]

Today, the Grand Canyon hosts more than five million visitors yearly.

The Golden State: Southern California

We have passed the time when we could afford to let any man skin the country and leave it.

THEODORE'S TRAIN SLOWLY SNAKED THROUGH THE WESTERN END OF Arizona Territory and into the Mohave Desert of southern California as the sun began to show itself on the horizon. Of all the stops in the twenty-one states and two territories, California would be the most exhausting for Theodore. He would make fifty-two scheduled speeches in eleven days, and on his first day, May 7, he gave six in various locations.[1]

"This is the first time I have ever been to California," he stated to the crowd in Barstow, "and I cannot say to you how much I have looked forward to making the trip. I can tell you now with absolute certainty that I will have enjoyed it to the full when I get through."[2]

Members of the Rough Riders contingent living in Los Angeles learned that General C. F. A. Last, general of the California National Guard, chose men from his group to serve as the president's guard in Los Angeles. The former Rough Riders would be placed to the extreme outside, well behind Theodore's carriage. One former Rough Rider told a reporter, "We have been shamefully treated in this matter."[3] Taking a lesson from their former commander, they dispatched a small group to meet with Theodore in Redlands and informed him of their slight.

In Redlands, as his train pulled into the Santa Fe station, the crowd was treated to a surprise as the engine rolled to a stop. Theodore was sitting in the fireman's seat of the locomotive, grinning happily. His carriage made a brief procession through the town, and when he passed an assembly of fifteen hundred children, they started singing "America." He gracefully bowed to the large group. Another group of children, sitting in the stands across from the Casa Loma Hotel, began to shout, "There he is! There he is!" Turning in his carriage, Theodore stood up, removed his hat, and waved with both arms to the children, who were "wild with delight."[4]

Redlands, known as the "land of the flowers," was a shining example of Theodore's concept of irrigation turning barren countryside into a thriving land full of bountiful crops. The hot, dry climate, along with an ample supply of water, provided the necessary ingredients for citrus production. The Atchison, Topeka, and Santa Fe Railroad's arrival in the mid-1880s set off a land boom in the area that soon garnered the nickname "inland empire." The California citrus industry proved to be a profitable one for nearly ninety years. After World War II, urban growth soon replaced many of the citrus orchards.[5]

Prior to giving his speech from the Casa Loma Hotel, Theodore unveiled a memorial bust of President McKinley. McKinley was very popular in the area due to his vigilant tariffs that kept foreign citrus products out of the country.[6] Arriving at the hotel, Theodore climbed the stairs of the speaker's stand, and stated that he had rarely enjoyed a day as much as this one.

> I waked up coming through the Mojave Desert, and all that desert needs is water, and I believe you are going to get it. Then we came down into this wonderful garden spot, and though I had been told all about it, told about the fruits and the flowers, told of the wonderful fertility and thought I knew about it, it was not possible in advance to realize all the fertility, all the beauty, that I was to see.... Seeing what you have done makes me realize more and more how much this whole country should lay stress on what can be done by the wise use of water, and, therefore, the wise use of the forests on the mountains....
>
> The people of our country have grown to realize and are more and more in practice showing that they realize how indispensable it is to preserve the great forests on the mountains and to use aright the water supply that those forests conserve. This whole country here in Southern California shows what can be done by

irrigation, what can be done by settlers foresighted enough to use the resources in such way as to perpetuate and better, not exhaust, them. We have passed the time when we could afford to let any man skin the country and leave it. . . .

I think our citizens are more and more realizing that they wish to perpetuate the things that are of use and also the things that are of beauty. You in California are preserving your great natural scenery, your great objects of nature, your valleys, your giant trees. You are preserving them because you realize that beauty has its place as well as use, because you wish to make of this State even more than it now is the garden spot of the continent, the garden spot of the world. . . .

Do you know what strikes me most, as I meet you, the people of Southern California, representing a community which has drawn its numbers from all the civilized peoples of the globe, from all the States of the Union? What strikes me most is that good Americans are good Americans from one end of the Union to the other. . . . I firmly believe that your mighty future will make your past, great though your past is, seem small by comparison.[7]

After a lunch in the hotel dining room, Theodore returned to his train, which departed for San Bernardino. "After we got out of the Mojave Desert, with its burning plains and waterless mountains, its cactus and fantastic yucca trees," he wrote to John Hay, "we crossed the Cascades and came at once into that wonderful paradise of southern California—a veritable hotbed of fruits and flowers. The people were wildly enthusiastic of course, and I have literally never seen anything like the flowers. Wherever I went the roads were strewn with them, and generally a large proportion of the men, women and children were festooned with them."[8]

As his train passed through the Santa Fe rail yards toward the station, Theodore was on the rear platform, "his arms literally full of flowers, and himself half hid behind the mass of California roses. And the President was laughing, a regulation Roosevelt laugh," commented the *San Bernardino Daily Sun*.[9]

Theodore's procession made a stop at a local school where "the children took up the thunder . . . for the next five minutes . . . their class yells, cheers and shouts greeted the guest of the hour in one glad acclaim." Standing before the children, a reporter noted that it "required all the tact and authority" by the teachers to control the children's "almost irrepressible tendency to cheer again."[10] Speaking to the children, parents, and teachers, Theodore stated the most important duty was "taking care that the boys and girls are so trained as to make the highest type of men and women in the future." He added that this duty could not be "shirked by the home," reminding parents that teaching and training children cannot be put off "entirely upon the teachers." Acknowledging the teacher's efforts, he stated "they have done and are doing their duty so well entitles them in a peculiar degree to the gratitude of all Americans who understand the prime needs of the Republic."[11]

Waiting for the president's arrival at the town park, one man expressed surprise at seeing his friend, a Democrat, in the crowd. "I may be a Democrat," the man replied, "but Roosevelt is just as much my president as he is yours."[12]

As his procession made its way through town, Theodore was greeted by representatives of five Southern California Indian tribes: Auga Caliente, Coahuilla Valley, San Manuel, Potrero, and Indio. Greeting them, he stated he "would look out for their best interests." The tribal members later held a council and "expressed joy" for the attention Theodore had shown them.[13] When his carriage turned the corner at Third and E Streets, James Waters "let out a war whoop that would have done credit to a Comanche Indian." Hearing the yell, Theodore looked at Waters, who was waving his hat, and replied, "I thank you."[14]

The steps to the speaker's stand were carpeted with the national colors and flowers. Stretched across the side of a nearby building was a huge flag banked with palm leaves, with roses and entwined with roses to "relieve the monotonous tone of the greenery."[15] Greeted with cheers, Theodore wasted no time in launching into his speech.

> California and the region round-about have in the past fifty or sixty years traversed the distance that separates the founders of the civilization of Mesopotamia and Egypt from those who enjoy the

civilization of today. They have gone further than that. They have seen this country change from a wilderness into one of the most highly civilized regions on the world's surface. They have seen cities, farms, ranches, railroads grow up and transform the very face of nature. The changes have been so stupendous that in our eyes they have become commonplace. We fail to realize their immense, their tremendous importance. We fail entirely to realize what they mean. Only the older among you can remember the pioneer days, the early pioneer days, and yet today I have spoken to man after man yet in his prime who, when he first came to this country, warred against wild men and wild nature in the way in which that warfare was waged in the prehistoric days of the Old World. We have spanned in the single life—in less than the life of any man who reaches the age limit prescribed by the Psalmist—in less than that time we have gone over the whole space from savagery to barbarism, to semicivilization, to the civilization that stands two thousand years ahead of that of Rome and Greece in the days of their prime.

The old pioneer days have gone, but if we are to prove ourselves worthy sons of our sires we cannot afford to let the old pioneer virtues lapse. There is just the same need now that there was in '49 for the qualities that marked a mighty and masterful people. . . . No people can advance as far and as fast as we have advanced, no people can make such progress as we have made and expect to escape the penalties that go with such speed and progress. The growth and complexity of our civilization, the intensity of the movement of modern life, have meant that with the benefits have come certain disadvantages and certain perils. A great industrial civilization cannot be built up without a certain dislocation and certain disarrangement of the old conditions, and therefore the springing up of new problems. The problems are new, but the qualities needed to solve them are as old as history itself, and we shall solve them aright only on condition that we bring to the solution the same qualities of head and heart that have been brought to the solution of similar problems by every race that has ever conquered for itself a space in the annals of time.[16]

At his train in San Bernardino, Theodore shook hands with one of the leaders of "Teddy's Terrors," adding he would shake hands with all of them at that evening's dinner in Riverside. "I would like to join you on your train," Theodore stated, "but I must stay with my own party. I know I would have a better time with you." Before leaving San Bernardino, one of the members caught a pickpocket in the act and turned him over to police officers.[17]

On the way to the station in Riverside, Theodore's train stopped not far from the intersection of Victoria and Myrtle Avenues. There, he helped to plant a Mexican Fan Palm with a memorial marker that reads: "In remembrance of the constant friendship of Queen Victoria for the American Republic this memorial palm was started by Theodore Roosevelt, President of the United States of America, May 7, 1903, the gift of the son of the American Revolution of the sixth generation of American ancestry."[18]

Darkness fell on Riverside as Theodore's train arrived, but that did not stop the procession. Streets were illuminated with red, white, and blue incandescent lights, and all the businesses had their fronts decorated in the national colors. He was driven to the speaker's stand at Seventh and Main Streets, where Theodore told the onlookers that although he had read about California, he hadn't formed any idea of "the fertility of your soil, the beauty of your scenery, or the wonderful manner in which the full advantage of that soil had been taken by man." Turning to one of his favorite causes, he spoke highly of the community and its use of irrigation for growing crops. "In many other parts of the country I have had to preach irrigation. Here you practice it, and all I have to say here is that I earnestly wish that I could have many another community learn from you how you have handled your business," he commented. "Not only has it been useful, but it is astonishing to see with the use you have combined beauty. You have made of this city and its surroundings a veritable little paradise."[19]

If his traveling through California did nothing else, it certainly justified Theodore's belief in the recently passed irrigation law by seeing firsthand how irrigation had successfully worked in an arid climate. From that time on, whenever naysayers would rebuff his appeals for irrigation projects, he would proudly point to the successful citrus industry in California. With an intensity and passion that could only be his, he proved his point, which in turn led to the creation of more useful farmland that had once been dry and parched.

Theodore stayed overnight at the Glenwood Mission Inn in Riverside, where a dinner was held in his honor. He invited the small group of Rough Riders to the event and later met with them in the hotel parlor, shaking each man's hand. The group informed their colonel about being denied the honor of escorting and guarding him—along with his usual Secret Service agents—in Los Angeles.

Theodore quickly solved the matter.

"You are my own boys," he told them, "and I know I can trust you. I want you to be next to me."

He turned to his secretary, William Loeb. "Telegraph that my boys must be my immediate body guards in Los Angeles. They are my boys, and I want them as close as I can get them."[20]

Before leaving Riverside the following morning, Theodore replanted one of the two original navel orange trees in front of the Glenwood Mission Inn.[21] At nine o'clock, he arrived in Claremont to speak at the college. On the way to the university, the "presidential party was pelted with [rose] buds."

As he spoke to the students, Theodore acknowledged the Civil War veterans in the audience. "I always envy you men of the Grand Army because you do not have to preach; you practiced. All we have got to do is to try to come up to the standard in peace which you set alike in war and in peace." Noting that everyone had to have material prosperity "underlying our life," each individual still needed to pull his own weight, earn his own way, and not be a burden to the community. Theodore observed the individual who wants to "do a tremendous amount in life," yet will not start by earning his own way would be of little use in the world. He compared people like that to "those admirable creatures" in the Civil War who were "willing to begin as brigadier generals."[22]

We must have first the desire to do well in the day of small things, the day through which all of us must pass, the day which lasts very long with most of us. We must have the desire and the power to do well industrially as a community, as individuals. Before we can do anything with the higher life, before we can have the higher thinking, there must be enough of material comfort to allow for at least plain living. We have got to have that first before we can do the high thinking; but if we are to count in the long run we must have built upon the material prosperity the power and desire to give to our lives other than a merely material side. It would be a poor thing for this State and for this country if, no matter how great our success in business, in agriculture, in all that pertains to the body, we had not provided for our children and those that come after us, to get what is good alike for the soul and the mind.[23]

—◦—

"It is expected that the front of every residence will be as attractive as it is possible to make it. The weeds between the curbs and gutters should also be thoroughly removed," read a notice in the *Pasadena Daily News*. The Board of Directors of Trade also suggested residents along the selected parade route be urged to see that their "lawns and sidewalks are cleaned and trimmed for this occasion at least."[24]

The Roosevelt Special arrived at the Pasadena station five minutes later than scheduled. People were straining at the rope barrier to get a glimpse of the president, and several local residents thought the train carrying the famous passenger was "anything but attractive in its exterior appearances." Some residents mistook it for a tourist train until they saw the swarm of reporters gather around the rear platform. Two hundred members of the Grand Army of the Republic served as his escort to the carriages parked in front of the station and Hotel Green Park. R. R. Bain carried a snare drum that had belonged to his great-great-grandfather, who had taken it from the Hessians in the 1777 Battle of Saratoga. (Bain and his brother used the same drum during the Civil War.) "Right cheerily its notes rang out today," the local newspaper commented.[25]

Those citizens waiting at the train station let out a loud, synchronized cheer when they spotted Theodore as he made his way to his carriage. Crowds lined the streets waving small American flags, bunting hung from every office window, and the air was filled with hoots, hollers, and cheers as his carriage began its procession. A group of students from Throop Polytechnic Institute (known today as CalTech) hollered out their own yell in the president's honor.

What's the matter with Roosevelt?
He's all right!
Who is Roosevelt?
He's a lolla, he's a lulu.
He's just all right!
Who is? Roosevelt!

Clicking sounds of cameras, "from the Brownie kodak of the novice, to the great massive affair of the professional" composed their own melody as the procession moved along. The exterior of the local Elks Club featured a large photo of Theodore with a banner reading, "Welcome, B.P.O.E." (Benevolent and Protective Order of the Elks), its members leaning out every available window shouting, "Welcome to Pasadena!"[26]

"We speak often of the old pioneer days, and of the wonderful feats of our countrymen in those days, but we are living right in the middle of them now, only we are living under pleasanter auspices," he told the crowd at Wilson High School. Theodore noted how this region in twenty years went from being a sheep pasture to a fertile irrigated region, building up the community yet "preserv[ing] all the charm, all the refinement, of the oldest civilizations." Having traveled through "literally a garden of the Lord," he never dreamed that "the rose could blossom" until his arrival in California.[27]

Admitting the problems facing the citizens of 1903 may well be different than those facing citizens of 1860, Theodore urged them to adopt the spirit of perseverance the men displayed in fighting for the Union in the Civil War. He noted that should any man claim that there can be liberty "in spite of and against the law" that individual was simply asserting that "anarchy is liberty." Theodore observed that from the beginning of time, anarchy, in all its forms, "has been the hand-maiden, the harbinger, of despotism and tyranny." Warning that the clearest way to invalidate "republican institutions" and destroy "the essential democratic liberty that we enjoy" was to allow anyone, under any excuse, to place "the gratification of his passions over the law." Theodore exhorted that the "supreme law of the land" had to be complied with "by every man, rich or poor, alike."[28]

Reminding the crowd that "new problems come up all the time," the tremendous growth of "our complex industrialism" assured new conditions and difficulties would have to be faced. However, he cautioned, "any man who says that by following him, that by invoking some specific remedy, all injustice, and all evil, and all suffering will be done away with, misleads himself and you."

> There is not a man of us here who does not at times need a helping hand to be stretched out to him, and then shame upon him who will not stretch out the helping hand to his brother. While we must remember that—remember that every man at times stumbles and must be helped up, if he lies down you cannot carry him. He has got to be willing to walk. You can help him in but one way, the only way in which any man can be helped permanently—help him to help himself.[29]

After his speech and a drive through a portion of the city, Theodore paid a visit to Lucretia Garfield, the widow of President James Garfield, at her residence, "chatting for fifteen minutes." In her home, the widow proposed a toast to the president, but Theodore declined, instead saying, "No! We pledge you, Mrs. Garfield." Although the visit was brief, Theodore confessed, "It was hard to leave that dear old lady."[30] Pasadena mayor William Vedder then escorted the president to see the Arroyo View. Impressed with the expansive view, Theodore urged Mayor Vedder, "Don't you ever let them change it—not even a shrub or a tree—make them leave it in its natural state if you can. What a grand natural park Pasadena could have right here at its door."[31]

It all started because of the railroads.

November 9, 1885, the first train from Chicago arrived in Los Angeles. People from the eastern states had been bombarded with pamphlets,
newspaper stories, and photographs extolling the bountiful sunshine,
fresh air, and fertile land for growing to be found in Los Angeles. A new
group of *snowbirds* had been born.[32] Those with health issues found the
dry climate beneficial, whereas others saw the opportunity to accumulate
wealth. Like those in 1849 who clambered farther north to the gold fields,
Southern California was amid a new rush—land.

To help matters, both the Atchison, Topeka, and Santa Fe (ATSF) and
Southern Pacific Railroads engaged in a rate war, challenging one another
to grow the most business. A typical fare from Chicago to Los Angeles
in 1885 was about $125, but ATSF dropped its prices to as low as $25,
resulting in more than two hundred thousand visitors to Los Angeles in
1887 alone. Real estate prices leaped upward—two to three times—from
the previous year. New towns in surrounding areas were organized literally overnight.[33] Like any endeavor promising easy money, the land boom
burst in 1888. Los Angeles, licking its wounds, found the real estate bubble
quickly turned into a public relations debacle for the city. Tourism dropped
off, but the city continued to expand, albeit slowly. A new sewer system
and an electric trolley were added, and the dirt streets were paved. The
city's chamber of commerce went to work to bring back the tourist trade.

California's reimaging began by publicizing one of the state's most
prolific products—citrus. Citrus fairs were held in various areas, touting
navel oranges, lemons, and grapefruits. The fairs were not limited only to
the state: California citrus products were soon traveling across the country to be shown in various exhibitions and fairs. California citrus became
a leading attraction, along with promotion of California's mild winter
climate. It was an offer too good to pass up for easterners braving snowy,
damp winters.

Businessmen in Los Angeles realized they needed more than citrus to
attract tourists. Together with the railroads, they once again began to pro-
mote California as a Garden of Eden, a place like nowhere else.[34] In 1893,
Max Meyberg, a local merchant, came up with the idea of a festival, the
Fiesta de Los Angeles. That April, seven thousand people lined Spring
Street to watch a parade and later attend a celebration ball. The entire

event lasted four days, with various parades acknowledging everything from early California history to current successful businesses. Every year the festival took place, except in 1898, due to the Spanish-American War, and 1900. In 1901, it resumed under a new name, La Fiesta de las Flores (fiesta of flowers). That year, President McKinley, during his West Coast trip, was the guest of honor.[35]

On May 8, 1903, festival leaders had arranged the opening of the four-day event to coincide with Theodore's arrival in Los Angeles.

"All ladies and gentlemen desiring to be properly costumed for the occasion should get a tailor-made gown or suit," announced an ad two days earlier from J. Korn Ladies and Gentlemen's Tailor. Banks notified customers that they would close at noon on May 8, and Los Angeles police chief Charles Elton declared that a "police dragnet" was "now at work" to "gather in crooks that expect to reap a Fiesta Harvest." Elton stated that anyone who "doesn't look good" was going to be "gathered in by the police until after the Fiesta celebration."[36]

One person who was swept up quickly by the police was John Czolgosz, the brother of Leon Czolgosz, who assassinated President McKinley. At three o'clock in the afternoon on May 8, two detectives from the Los Angeles Police Department showed up at the XLNT Tamale factory and questioned him. He originally gave his name as Joe Hoffman, but the detectives pressed him and he finally admitted his real name. They told him they needed to ask him some questions at police headquarters, which would take about a half hour. "Instead of releasing me, they placed me in jail," he told a reporter. When he asked why he was locked up, the only answer was that he'd be "let out in a short time." Czolgosz was not released until the following morning, long after Theodore's train had left the city. He also complained to the reporter that he nearly starved while in jail, stating that the two meals a day they served were "nothing fit to eat." He claimed he had to quarrel to get a blanket to sleep on in his cell. The reporter, who described him as having "shifty grey eyes" and walking "stoop-shouldered" noted that Czolgosz flatly denied wanting to harm the president and was not responsible for the actions of his brother. He also told the reporter that if he could find "a good lawyer to take my case," he would sue the city and the police department for keeping him in jail without filing any charges against him. (He never found a lawyer to take his case.)[37]

Given the events in Buffalo, New York, in 1901, the Secret Service and local police were taking no chances. In Redlands, the police detained a man who sent threatening letters to President McKinley in 1901 and had recently sent similar letters to Theodore. (He was also released after Theodore left the city.) Another man, Otto Heim, was arrested in Chicago on May 1 for writing "rambling and threatening letters" to the president. In a letter addressed to the American people, Heim claimed, "You will never, if I can help it, drive me insane, but I will drive insane T. Roosevelt, and with him the American people." He was held for a sanity hearing and later instutionalized.[38]

As Theodore exited his train at the Los Angeles station, his fellow Rough Riders formed a pathway to his carriage. As he got in, Theodore stood up and looked at his boys. "My boys once, my boys now!" he said. He also told them they all looked splendid, which elicited a reply from one man, "You're not looking quite natural, yourself." Laughing, Theodore replied, "I'm not living on embalmed beef anymore."[39] The procession made its way through the city streets to the Westminster Hotel at Fourth and Main Streets, where Theodore had lunch with the reception committee members and various local and state politicians.

Leaving the dining room, former Rough Riders crowded around their colonel, ignoring the elderly lady seated in a chair just outside the room who unsuccessfully attempted to get the president's attention. Mayor Snyder stepped up to Theodore and announced that the lady's son had served with him and had recently died. Theodore made his way to her and asked about her son. The woman, who had traveled from England, corrected the story, saying her son was not dead, but living here in California. She had come to see him, as well as Theodore, with "whom he would die to serve, if necessary." Relieved to hear her son was still alive, he spent a few moments speaking to her before retiring to his hotel room. Within a half hour, Theodore arrived at the reviewing stand in front of city hall on Broadway near Third Street. While waiting for the parade to begin, he chatted "gleefully" with various people around him. Across the street was a group of Rough Riders, who occasionally became "very noisy." Theodore placed his hands around his mouth and yelled they were "all right!" which made them cheer.[40]

As the parade began, Theodore was taken with many of the floats, but more than anything, he admired the riders on horseback. As one young Mexican girl rode by on a pony, Theodore commented to Mayor Snyder, "that girl knows how to ride all right!" A reporter for the *Los Angeles Times* noted that Theodore's eyes were "gleaming" as floats and bands passed by. However, it wasn't the Chinese dragon that delighted him, nor the many pretty girls on floats that caught his attention, but a horse attempting to buck off its rider, a vaquero. Theodore was taken by the horse's efforts and the rider's laughter in response to his mount's action.[41] No doubt it brought back memories for the president.

At the end of the parade, Theodore's carriage took him to Central Park, at Sixth and Hill Streets, where he spoke to a large crowd. Commenting on the Fiesta Parade, Theodore said he did not recall "ever seeing quite the parallel to the procession I have just witnessed." Declaring that "this country is one of the great leading nations of mankind and is bound to become ever greater as the years roll by," Theodore demanded that the United States "must have a navy corresponding to its position." In addition, he added, with two great oceans on either side of the country, the need for a navy "capable of asserting our position" was necessary. Acknowledging that the completion of the Panama Canal would be important commercially, he noted that it would also be vital if the country ever became involved in a war. "I want to see the American Republic with a fighting navy," he explained, "because I never wish to see us take a position that we cannot maintain. I do not believe in a bluff. I feel about a nation as we all feel about a man; let him not say anything that he cannot make good, and having said it, let him make it good."[42]

Theodore added that he believed in doing "all we can to avoid a quarrel," to speak courteously to "all the other peoples of mankind," and to carefully refrain from wronging anyone; in turn, he expected that "they do not wrong us." Observing that the nation was "growing by leaps and by bounds" and the country's various interests were advancing with great rapidity, he said that it was incumbent that "the growth of the navy takes place with equal rapidity with the growth of the interests that it is to protect."

Turning his attention to the preservation of forests and water, Theodore remarked, "I only have to appeal to your own knowledge, to your experience. I have been passing through a veritable garden of the earth yesterday and today, here in the southern half of California, and it has been made such by the honesty and wisdom of your people, and by the way in which you have preserved your waters and utilized them. I ask that you simply keep on as you have begun, and that you let the rest of the nation follow suit. We must preserve the forests to preserve the waters, which are themselves preserved by the forests, if we wish to make this country as a whole blossom as you have made this part of California blossom."[43]

Theodore had to cut short the processional drive through the city, much to his regret, in order to return to his hotel room to attend to some "Business of State."[44] After attending to business, Theodore dressed for dinner at the hotel and then took his carriage to view the Night Pageant Parade. The parade down Broadway consisted of fifteen floats illuminated by electric lights. Each float was named for a flower and designed as a fanciful rendition of each blossom. Theodore was thoroughly impressed with the parade, even though the long day was beginning to tire him. At the parade's conclusion, he returned to his train for a night's sleep.

A newspaper reporter asked Bubber, a newsboy, his opinion of the parade. "Bully!" he replied.[45]

Theodore's train left Los Angeles just as the sun was breaking over the horizon. By eight in the morning, his train stopped in Oxnard, where he was given a quick tour of a sugar beet factory by one of the Oxnard brothers, founders of the town. Speaking to a group gathered outside the factory, Theodore stated how impressed he was "to see the tangible evidence of the extraordinary industry" that had started only five years earlier. He added that he was not surprised by the success, "because the last two days in California have taught me not to be surprised at anything."[46] Arriving in Ventura less than an hour later, Theodore had his very first view of the Pacific Ocean. He then went to visit the old mission church, Santa Buenaventura, with Father O'Riley, even climbing into the belfry to ring the ancient wooden bell. At the town's plaza, he commented to the assembled group, "I have been, of course, amazed at the yield of your soil, treated as it has been with such wisdom and industry by those who have tilled it, showing especially the amount that can be done by irrigation, the amount that can be done by a combination of scientific and practical agriculture, at your oranges, at the growth of the beet-sugar industries, at all your fruit products, at all your agricultural products."[47]

Theodore's train stopped in Montecito, three miles south of Santa Barbara. The four-mile carriage ride took him past lemon orchards, many beautiful homes, and views of the Channel Islands. In the Santa Barbara harbor was the training ship *Alert*, which used its signal flags to spell out "Welcome to the President of the United States." As Theodore stood on the speaker's platform in the Plaza del Mar, the naval ship fired a twenty-one-gun salute in his honor.[48] Standing before the residents of Santa Barbara, he told them this was his first time seeing the mighty Pacific Ocean. He noted that an older civilization had inhabited this region "three-quarters of a century before the first hardy people of the new stock crossed the desert, crossed the mountain chains, or came by ships up from the Isthmus." Theodore congratulated them on keeping a "continuity of historic interests" with memorials. He was also pleased to see the architecture of new buildings, as well as the older ones; they were "keeping the touch and flavor of the older civilization." It gave a "peculiar flavor to our own new civilization, and in an age when the tendency is a trifle toward too great uniformity." He asked the crowd if they truly appreciated how beautiful their country is. "Sometimes people grow so familiar with their surroundings that they fail entirely to appreciate them," Theodore said. "I had read and heard of the marvelous beauty of Southern California, the beauty of your climate, the wonderful fertility of your soil, but I had not realized it; I could not realize it until I saw it. It seems to me as though there could not be another spot on the world's surface blessed in quite the same way that this has been blessed."[49]

Theodore toured the Santa Barbara Mission, visiting with the Franciscan fathers and viewing the sacred burial ground of several old padres from the last century and a quarter. Before boarding his train, he took a moment to praise the work of the forest rangers, who had escorted him in this area.

> I am, as you gentlemen probably know, exceedingly interested in the question of forestry preservation. I think our people are growing more and more to understand that in reference to the forests and the wild creatures of the wilderness our aim should be not to destroy them simply for the selfish pleasure of one generation, but to keep them for our children and our children's children. I wish you, the Forest Rangers, and also all the others, to protect the game and wild creatures, and of course in California, where the water supply is a matter of such vital moment, the preservation of the forests for the merely utilitarian side is of the utmost, of the highest possible consequence; and there are no members of our body politic who are doing better work than those who are engaged in the preservation of the forests, the keeping of nature as it is for the sake of its use and for the sake of its beauty.[50]

The Golden State: Northern California

I have never seen anything like the flowers and fruits of this region.

"If I were President, they couldn't get me to go through that sort of penance if I never received a nomination or a vote," stated Edward H. Hamilton, a reporter covering Theodore's visit in California for the *San Francisco Examiner*. "But Theodore Roosevelt acts as if he enjoyed it all. His laugh is very quick at everything that is laughable, his speeches are different from time to time, and I should say that he made a good deal of a hit with the crushing throngs which make the streets of Los Angeles ways of perspiration and profanity."[1]

Theodore's train made its way up the coast of California after leaving Santa Barbara, making a brief stop and an equally succinct speech in the coastal town of Surf before traveling to San Luis Obispo, where he visited another mission church. Theodore complimented the farmers of the region who grew large vegetables and fruits and had won several prizes from various eastern agricultural producers. "I know of one Eastern producer who said that the products of this county would have to be barred, because he had already spent five-hundred dollars in prizes to the county and had gotten back but fourteen dollars for seeds," he commented. He added that he knew the largest pumpkin, watermelon, and onion came from this county and "your agricultural products have made a name for themselves to be feared."[2] There was another brief stop and speech in Paso Robles, before his train arrived in Del Monte shortly after midnight. Theodore remained on his train for the evening but took a room at the Hotel Del Monte the following morning. Like other Sundays on the tour, Theodore would spend this one quietly, keeping events to a minimum.[3]

Theodore began his Sunday with a horseback ride, leaving the California welcoming committee literally in the dust. He requested that only a few from his party accompany him on the seventeen-mile ride over Cypress Point. At three o'clock he attended Episcopal church services and then took a walk around the grounds of the hotel. Among the trees, he heard the vocal notes of a thrush and would not leave the area until he was able to observe it. While he was on his walk, his secretary, William Loeb, was working out details of Theodore's three-day visit to San Francisco, Oakland, and Berkeley. Viewing the crammed schedule, Loeb quickly vetoed several things and began working on a more practicable itinerary.[4]

His day of rest also found Theodore catching up on his correspondence to his children. To his daughter, Ethel, he described his horseback ride that morning. "My horse was a beauty, spirited, swift, surefooted and enduring," he noted. "As is usually the case here they had a great deal of silver on the bridle and headstall, and much carving on the saddle. We had some splendid gallops. By the way, tell mother that everywhere out here, from the Mississippi to the Pacific, I have seen most of the girls riding astride, and most of the grown-up women. I must say I think it very much better for the horses' backs. I think by the time that you are an old lady the side-saddle will almost have vanished—I am sure I hope so." In a letter to Archie, he told of riding down the beach: "the surf was beating on the rocks in one place and right between two of the rocks where I really did not see how anything could swim a seal appeared and stood up on his tail half out of the foaming water and flapped his flippers, and was as much at home as anything could be." He also said that Josh, the badger, was well and "we took him out and gave him a run on the sand today."[5]

The Roosevelt Special left Del Monte at eight o'clock on Monday morning, May 11. Fifty minutes later, there was a ten-minute stop in Pajaro before heading to Santa Cruz, where the president was escorted to a narrow-gauge train on the South Pacific Coast Railroad. The train took him to Big Groves Station, then he was escorted to the Big Tree Grove (known today as Henry Cowell Redwoods State Park) where he enjoyed a steak breakfast and spoke to eighty people. During this brief part of his visit to the trees, he was escorted by navy militia. Taking advantage of their presence, Theodore once again spoke of the importance of naval superiority. "We must have a first-class navy," he declared. "A nation like ours, with the unique position of fronting at once on the Atlantic and the Pacific, a nation forced by the mere fact of destiny to play a great, mighty, and masterful part in the world cannot afford to neglect its navy, cannot afford to fail to insist upon the building up of its navy." Noting that the country's naval force was "wonderfully good," he urged that "we must strive to make it better."[6]

He went on to congratulate the people of the county and the state in their drive to preserve the grove of redwood trees. "Cut down one of these giants and you cannot fill its place," he warned. Stressing those trees must be preserved for future generations, he applauded the state for being "thoroughly awake" in preserving monuments of the past—human and natural. He observed "no man for speculative purposes or for mere temporary use" should exploit the redwood groves, and if associations and individuals could not preserve them, then the state or, if necessary, the nation should step in. "We should keep the trees as we should keep great stretches of the wildernesses, as a heritage for our children and our children's children," Theodore proclaimed. "Our aim should be to preserve them for use, to preserve them for beauty, for the sake of the nation hereafter."[7]

There is a photograph of Theodore standing in front of a huge redwood tree with a sign on it that reads "General." He is wearing his top hat and a long overcoat, his left hand in the coat pocket, while his right hand held at his side appears to be making a fist. There is a stern look on his face, his jaw and lips are tightly set, the usual wide, teeth-baring smile is absent. In spite of the grandeur of the great trees, he looks unhappy, even angry.

He was angry.

Arriving at the grove, the sheer size and beauty of the trees left him speechless. The sun's rays shining through the branches to the ground were, to him, another version of paradise. Then he saw *those signs*. Nailed to each tree was a sign with a name, such as "Giant" or "Old Fremont." To make matters even more unpleasant, the "scarred and hollowed trunk" of one the "Three Sisters" had business cards tacked to it. (It was common practice for visitors to stroll by this trunk and stick their cards onto it.)

Speaking to the assembled audience, Theodore wasted no time in letting his displeasure be known—and outlining what needed to be done.

> All of us ought to want to see nature preserved. Take a big tree whose architect has been the ages; anything that man does toward it may hurt it and cannot help it. Above all, the rash creature who wishes to leave his name to mar the beauties of nature should be sternly discouraged.
>
> Those cards pinned up on that tree give an air of the ridiculous to this solemn and majestic grove. To pin those cards up there is as much out of place as if you tacked so many tin cans up there. I mean that literally. You should save the people whose names are there from the reprobation of every one by taking down the cards at the earliest possible moment; and do keep these trees, keep all the wonderful scenery of this wonderful State unmarred by the vandalism or the folly of man. Remember that we have to contend not merely with knavery, but with folly; and see to it that you by your actions create the kind of public opinion which will put a stop to any destruction of or any marring of the wonderful and beautiful gifts that you have received from nature, that you ought to hand on as a precious heritage to your children and your children's children. I am, oh, so glad to be here, to be in this majestic and beautiful grove, to see the wonderful redwoods, and thank you for giving me the chance, and I do hope that it will be your object to preserve them as nature made them and left them, for the future.[8]

Theodore then waved off anyone accompanying him as he walked into the forest. The huge trees, measuring nearly three hundred feet in height and sixteen feet in width, are found in a forty-square mile grove, with some trees being over 1,400 years old. While he was enjoying the trees, staff members were quick to remove the cards from the trunk as well as the trees' nameplates. When he returned, Theodore agreed to have a tree named for him with one strict proviso: the tree would never have a sign posted on it or near it bearing his name.[9]

Reluctantly, Theodore left the redwoods behind and traveled on to San Jose, where, as *San Francisco Examiner* reporter Edward H. Hamilton noted, "Nothing seemed to go just right here in San Jose." The location of the speaker's stand at the train station proved a hardship for Theodore when—not once, but twice—his words were drowned out by two "shrill blasts" from a locomotive, quickly followed by the clanging of another train's bell. A third train, within two hundred feet of the stand, was backing up, its smokestack puffing heavy clouds of smoke. "Mr. Roosevelt pulled through without any show of annoyance or temper," the reporter observed. After the speech, the president and his party were "put to the torture" of a two-hour drive in thick dust. "Evidentially the local committee thought that as the President had been a Rough Rider he would enjoy a rough ride. They gave it to him," Hamilton commented. Despite Theodore being "fairly distinguishable" in spite of the dirt, others in his party who followed the president's carriage were "ludicrously incognito" thanks to layers of soil. One member of Theodore's party later joked that if one wanted to prevent a man from getting any presidential appointment, all that was needed was to state that he was on the committee that arranged the San Jose drive.[10]

After staying overnight in San Jose, Theodore's next stop was Palo Alto, where he spoke to the students of Stanford University. "America, the Republic of the United States, is, of course, in a peculiar sense typical of the present age," Theodore stated. "We represent the fullest development of the democratic spirit acting on the extraordinary and highly complex industrial growth of the last half century. It behooves us to justify by our acts the claims made for that political and economic progress." However, he cautioned, if our only homage is "lip loyalty," the enormous deeds in the time of Washington and Lincoln, the men who fought for our independence and to keep the union together "will simply arise to shame us." The only true way, he advised, to honor those who came before us was by rising to the standards they set. "There are plenty of tendencies for evil in what we see round about us," Theodore commented. "Thank heaven, there are an even greater number of tendencies for good."[11]

He then turned his attention to the redwoods he had just visited. "If the students of this institution have not by the mere fact of their surroundings learned to appreciate beauty, then the fault is in you and not in the surroundings," he told them. Acknowledging that they had some of the greatest "wonders of the world" and "singularly majestic scenery," Theodore emphasized the need for preserving them for those who come after them. Talking about the grove of trees he visited the previous day, he felt "most emphatically" that those giants "which were old when the first Egyptian conqueror penetrated to the valley of the Euphrates," should not be turned into roof shingles. "That, you may say, is not looking at the matter from the practical standpoint," he acknowledged. "There is nothing more practical in the end than the preservation of beauty, than the preservation of anything that appeals to the higher emotions in mankind."[12]

"I am now on my way to San Francisco which will be a hard and tiring experience," he wrote to Henry Cabot Lodge. "Then I shall be four days in the Yosemite, with John Muir. I am in pretty fair shape and my voice has held out astonishingly. Seemingly I have been received with great enthusiasm. I have never seen anything like the flowers and fruits of this region."[13]

The next three days would certainly test his "strenuous life" theory. He would give six speeches in San Francisco, three in Oakland, and one at the University of California in Berkeley. There would be procession after procession, the ever-ambitious politicians and never-ending welcoming committees pushing to have a personal moment with the president, not to mention the ever-important photo opportunities.

Arriving in San Francisco, Theodore was welcomed by the usual groups of politicians and welcoming committee members, as well as British Navy admiral Andrew Bickford, who stated, "I am here, sir, by express command of His Majesty the King to congratulate you on your safe arrival and to welcome you, sir, to the shores of the Pacific."[14] (Bickford was commander in chief of the British Navy Pacific Station, and his flagship, HMS *Grafton*, was visiting San Francisco.) After greeting U.S.

Navy admiral Henry Glass and U.S. Army major general Arthur MacArthur (father of future five-star general Douglas MacArthur), Theodore thanked the train engineer and fireman before taking a processional ride through the city's streets. As his carriage passed McNutt Hospital, a group of nurses, in their white dresses and caps, stood on the hospital balcony and waved. Theodore, in turn, bowed to the ladies. Another young woman proved to be an accurate pitcher when she threw a bouquet of flowers to his carriage, knocking Theodore's top hat off. He turned around, grinning, and bowed to the girl.

At four o'clock, he was delivered to the YMCA hall to witness the burning of the mortgage ($115,250) and the dedication of its new building. (The San Francisco Fire Department detailed four men to stand by in case of an accident.) The hall was "packed to the ceiling, and of course there was no getting along the street outside without a scrimmage," the *San Francisco Examiner* noted.[15]

After the burning of the mortgage, Theodore commented, "It would be hard to overestimate the amount of good work done by the Young Men's Christian Associations." He added that human nature would not be improved if "you attempt to take the bad out of it, by leaving a vacuum, for that vacuum is going to be filled with something, and if you do not fill it with what is good it will be filled with what is evil." Theodore complemented the YMCA and all its branches for its "civic and social righteousness, for decency, for good citizenship."[16]

Theodore attended an "informal, friendly, and essentially bohemian" reception at the San Francisco Press Club. Walking past the club's vast library room, he paused. "Here's where I revel," he said. During the reception, he was given an honorary membership and signed the club's register book.

The evening was devoted to a dinner given by the citizens of San Francisco at the Palace Hotel, where Theodore stayed while in the city. The big room sported "flowers in profusion" strewn around the tables, and a big sign in electric lights reading, "The land of sunshine, fruit and flowers greets our President." Speaking to the audience, Theodore noted that he was not "by inheritance a Puritan," although he acquired the belief that when one was having "a good time, it is not quite right." He was enjoying himself so much in California that "I have had a slight feeling that maybe I was not quite doing my duty. But I cannot say that I am penitent about it."[17]

———

Theodore's day on May 13 began at eight in the morning when he left the Palace Hotel for a reception given by the Native Sons of the Golden State and Old California Pioneers at their hall. His escort this morning included members of the Ninth Cavalry, an all-black troop that fought alongside Theodore in Cuba. Former mayor James Phelan presented Theodore with a gold sculpture of a bear hunt, *The Bear Fight*. Accepting the gift, Theodore noted, "I am deeply touched by the beautiful gift you have given me, and you see this shows that even a President can be a successful bear hunter. I had begun to think that my acquaintance with that noble animal must cease."[18]

Sixty thousand schoolchildren lined both sides of Van Ness Avenue from Market Street to Pacific Avenue waiting for Theodore's carriage. "A large detail of policemen worried themselves into old age endeavoring to hold in check the youngsters and keep them lined up in such shape as to avoid being run over by the Presidential entourage," reported a local newspaper. Theodore instructed his driver to go past the children slowly so those on one side of the street had a chance to see him before his carriage turned around and went down the other side of the street. The entire time, he stood up, tipped his hat and bowed to the youngsters, many of whom wore handmade Rough Rider hats in his honor.[19]

Riding to the Presidio, Theodore viewed the barracks before heading to the golf links where a military review would be given. Exchanging his carriage for a horse, Theodore and his group rode "at a brisk trot" to review the troops before taking his seat in the stands, where he received a twenty-one-gun salute. Infantry, cavalry, and light artillery passed in review. The caissons of the light artillery went past the reviewing stand three different times: at a walk, a trot, and a "terrific gallop."[20] Leaving the Presidio, his carriage took him through Golden Gate Park and along the beach to Cliff House, where he attended a luncheon in his honor. "The President was very hungry," observed the reporter for the *San Francisco Chronicle*.

"He had scarcely seated himself before he began to munch on the salted almonds, and when the oysters were served, he consumed them with an avidity that would have done justice to the heartiest of rough riders."[21]

Riding back through Golden Gate Park, Theodore attended the groundbreaking ceremony for a President McKinley memorial near the Baker Street entrance to the park. With a bronze shovel, he was asked to turn the first piece of soil for the statue. As he was shoveling the dirt, he spotted a quizzical look from one person in the crowd. He admitted that he was "working overtime," which brought a reply from one man, "Have you got a union card?" Theodore laughed in reply before speaking about the late president.

Many veterans from the Civil War and the Spanish-American War were in attendance, and a group of Rough Riders presented Theodore with a silver canteen. Private George King, who had served directly under Theodore, was chosen to give the canteen to his former colonel. He said that this wasn't given to him as the nation's president; "it springs from the hearts of all soldiers." One reporter observed that this occasion was a "particularly happy" one for Theodore, as he got to rub shoulders with veterans from the Civil War and his Rough Riders. Mr. Roosevelt never looked so happy as when he is talking fight," the newspaper stated. At that moment he was not the president of the United States, but the colonel of the Rough Riders. "He looked upon the faces before him and saw they were beaming with friendliness, and the sight gave him courage, so that he made a heart-to-heart talk, rather than a set speech," commented the *San Francisco Examiner*.[22]

Anything "his boys" did for him touched his heart. When they mustered out after the war, they presented him a bronze work by Frederick Remington called The Bronc Buster. The gesture moved him nearly to tears. This time was no different.

> Now, comrades, I guess you do not wonder that I am fond of the men of my regiment. In receiving this beautiful canteen, I want to say that I shall prize it even more than the old one, and all of us know how we prize the old one. I want to thank you and my comrades of the Spanish-American War from my heart; and I do

not have to say to you of the old war *[Civil War]* that there is no other bond that can unite men quite so closely together as the bond of having in actual service drunk out of the same canteen.

I want to say to you a word about Mr. King. The only time I ever saw him nervous was just now. He was not only a first-class soldier, but I am sure that all of you will understand me when I say that in the field he was also a first-class cook. I shall never forget one day right after the San Juan fight when I had lived sumptuously for thirty-six hours on two hard-tacks, Comrade King, somehow or other, had evolved the ingredients of a first-class stew, and with an affection which was mighty real in its results to me at that moment, brought some of it to me. And I have never tasted, not even at the wonderful banquet that I have attended in San Francisco, anything quite so good.[23]

That evening he was given a dinner at the home of the head of the reception committee, M. H. DeYoung. The dinner was limited to fourteen guests who dined in a room with American Beauty roses placed in a low basket at the center of the table, giving it "a picturesque effect." A society reporter noted that the "white silk shades of the candelabra were very pretty with the exquisite damask, pink Venetian glass and silver. Beauty of Blazewood roses were arranged in handsome vases about the room."[24]

While Theodore was attending the dinner, ten thousand people filed into Mechanics Pavilion to get a seat to hear the president's speech. Within one hour the pavilion was filled to capacity, and red, white, and blue bunting, along with some "cavalry yellow," hung from the rafters. Several flags were strung across the hall giving "the interior a picturesque appearance." Garlands, entwined with roses, were suspended in every direction, and replicas of bears and eagles were attached to the balcony. "San Francisco greets our President" was brightly illuminated behind the speaker's platform. A forty-piece orchestra conducted by Paul Steindoff gave a concert for nearly an hour before Theodore arrived at nine o'clock. As he entered the room, Theodore received a five-minute standing ovation. "The roar that filled the structure sounded like waves breaking on the shore on a stormy day," commented the reporter for the *San Francisco Call*.[25]

"Before I came to the Pacific Slope, I was an expansionist, and after having been here I fail to understand how any man, convinced of his country's greatness and glad that his country should challenge with proud confidence its mighty future, can be anything but an expansionist," Theodore told his audience. The century that had just begun would soon see commerce from the Pacific Ocean become a major component in history. "The seat of power ever shifts from land to land, from sea to sea," he observed. Theodore pointed out areas in the Pacific region that were coming into their own, noting how Australia "has sprung into being," while Japan was "shaking off the lethargy of centuries" and taking her place "among civilized, modern powers." Many European nations were now seating themselves along the eastern coast of Asia, "while China by her misfortunes has given us an object-lesson in the utter folly of attempting to exist as a nation at all if both rich and defenseless."

With the nation now stretching from the Atlantic to the Pacific Oceans, Theodore stressed that the country "holds an extent of coast line which makes it of necessity a power of the first class in the Pacific." That extension of "America's geographical position on the Pacific is such as to ensure our peaceful domination of its waters in the future if only we grasp with sufficient resolution the advantages of that position," he commented. The country was taking major steps by laying cables across the ocean; steamships "larger than any freight carriers that have previously existed" and the completion of the Panama Canal would be an "incalculable benefit to our mercantile navy, and above all to our military navy in the event of war."

I most earnestly hope that this work will ever be of a peaceful character. We infinitely desire peace, and the surest way of obtaining it is to show that we are not afraid of war. We should deal in a spirit of justice and fairness with weaker nations, and we should show to the strongest that we are able to maintain our rights. Such showing cannot be made by bluster; for bluster merely invites contempt. Let us speak courteously, deal fairly, and keep ourselves armed and ready. If we do these things, we can count on the peace that comes to the just man armed, to the just man who neither fears nor inflicts wrong. We must keep on building and maintaining a thoroughly efficient navy, with plenty of the best and most formidable ships, with an ample supply of officers and men, and with those officers and men trained in the most efficient fashion to perform their duties. Only thus can we assure our position in the world at large. It behooves all men of lofty soul fit and proud to belong to a mighty nation to see to it that we keep our position in the world; for our proper place is with the great expanding peoples, with the peoples that dare to be great, that accept with confidence a place of leadership in the world. . . .

I ask that this generation and future generations strive in the spirit of those who strove to found the Republic, of those who strove to save and perpetuate it. I ask that this Nation shape its policy in a spirit of justice toward all, a spirit of resolute endeavor to accept each duty as the duty comes, and to rest ill-content until that duty is done. I ask that we meet the many problems with which we are confronted from without and from within, not in the spirit that seeks to purchase present peace by the certainty of future disaster, but with a wise, a fearless, and a resolute desire to make of this Nation in the end, as the centuries go by, the example for all the nations of the earth, to make of it a nation in which we shall see the spirit of peace and of justice incarnate, but in which also we shall see incarnate the spirit of courage, of hardihood, the spirit which while refusing to wrong the weak is incapable of flinching from the strong.[26]

"I want you all to draw a practical lesson from this commemoration," Theodore stated from the speaker's stand in Union Square. "We today dedicate this monument because those who went before us had the wisdom to make ready for the victory." The dedication was a monument to Admiral George Dewey and his victory over the Spanish fleet in Manila Bay in 1898. Theodore stressed the success of Dewey's mission in the Philippines was due to having a naval fleet ready for the challenge. "To dedicate the monument would be an empty and foolish thing if we accompanied it by an abandonment of our national policy of building up the navy," he added. "And good though it is to erect this monument, it is better still to go on with the building up of the navy which gave the monument to us, and which, if we ever give it a fair chance, can be relied upon to rise level to our needs." Theodore noted once a war has begun, "it is too late to improvise a navy." Any naval war, he stated, was "two-thirds settled in advance" because of preparation that was done years earlier. "In 1882 our navy was a shame and a disgrace to the country in point of material. The personnel contained as fine material as there was to be found in the world but the ships and the guns were antiquated, and it would have been a wicked absurdity to have sent them against the ships of any good power. Then we began to build up the navy. Every ship that fought under Dewey had been built between 1883 and 1896," he noted.[27] Theodore, while he was assistant naval secretary, had helped in that matter, ordering new ships to be built, along with additional training for the sailors. Naval superiority was something Theodore knew well, as his first major book, *The Naval War of 1812*, was required reading at the Naval Academy and every U.S. naval vessel was required to have a copy in the ship's library.

"We come here as patriots remembering that our party lines stop at the water's edge," he stressed. The reason Dewey's fleet was successful in 1898, he reminded the audience, was due to the cooperation of both parties under previous administrations and Congress, which formed a "resolute effort to build adequate ships." Theodore observed that the country could not have fought the Battle of Manila Bay if it "had not been for so many years making ready the navy." He also declared that even the best ships and guns will not count unless they are "handled aright and aimed aright" with proper training and practice for the sailors. "The shots that count in battle are the shots that hit," Theodore stressed. Concluding his speech, he told the audience to "applaud the navy and what it has done. That is first-class. But make your applause count by seeing that the good work goes on. Besides applauding now see to it that the navy is so built up that the men of the next generation will have something to applaud also."[28]

Leaving Union Square, Theodore's carriage went to the transport dock at the end of Folsom Street. Before he boarded the cutter *Golden Gate*, he inspected a transport ship, the *Logan*, which was making preparations for sea. The *San Francisco Call* noted he made a "very rapid trip through the vessel, and paid particular attention to the quarters of the men." Remembering how the military's plans failed in transporting his Rough Riders and regular army units to Cuba, Theodore's interest in upgrades to this ship were of paramount importance. As the cutter pulled out of San Francisco Bay, several naval ships fired a twenty-one-gun salute. Landing at the docks in Oakland, he boarded his train for Berkeley and gave the commencement speech at the university.

Despite the president's brief tour of Berkeley, the citizens raised five hundred dollars to decorate the path of his carriage. Wire netting was stretched along the sidewalks and filled with cut flowers to a height of six feet on each side of the street, literally "a wall of flowers." Schoolchildren lining each side of the street gave him a "lusty welcome" as he went by.

At the commencement exercise, university president Benjamin Wheeler called Theodore to the stand and conferred on him a degree of doctor of laws. "You have shown how the highest intellectual ideals can be carried out in action. You are an inspiration to the youth of the land over which you have been chosen to preside. With this handclasp I admit you to the ranks of the University of California."[29]

"Fellow members of the University of California," Theodore began, causing the audience to erupt into applause and laughter.

> Much though I have been interested in the wonderful physical beauty of this wonderful State, I have been infinitely more interested in its citizenship, and perhaps most in its citizenship in the making. . . . We talk a good deal about what the widespread education of this country means; I question if many of us deeply consider its meaning. From the lowest grade of the public school to the highest form of university training, education in this country is at the disposal of every man, every woman, who chooses to work for and obtain it. . . . Where the State has bestowed education the man who accepts it must be content to accept it merely as a charity unless he returns it to the State in full, in the shape of good citizenship. I do not ask of you, men and women here today, good citizenship as a favor to the State. I demand it of you

as a right, and hold you recreant to your duty if you fail to give it. ... From all our citizens we have a right to expect good citizenship; but most of all from those who have received most; most of all from those who have had the training of body, of mind, of soul, which comes from association in and with a great university. From those to whom much has been given we have Biblical authority to expect and demand much in return; and the most that can be given to any man is education. I expect and demand in the name of the Nation much more from you who have had training of the mind than from those of mere wealth. To the man of means much has been given, too, and much will be expected from him, and ought to be, but not as much as from you, because your possession is more valuable than his. If you envy him, I think poorly of you. Envy is merely the meanest form of admiration, and a man who envies another admits thereby his own inferiority.

We have a right to expect from the college bred man, the college bred woman, a proper sense of proportion, a proper sense of perspective, which will enable him or her to see things in their right relation one to another, and when thus seen while wealth will have a proper place, a just place, as an instrument for achieving happiness and power, for conferring happiness and power, it will not stand as high as much else in our national life. ... Every man, every woman here should feel it incumbent upon him or her to welcome with joy the chance to render service to the country, service to our people at large, and to accept the rendering of the service as in itself ample repayment therefore. Do not misunderstand me. The average man, the average woman must earn his or her living in one way or another, and I most emphatically do not advise anyone to decline to do the humdrum, every-day duties because there may come a chance for the display of heroism. I ask of you the straightforward, earnest performance of duty in all the little things that come up day by day in business, in domestic life, in every way, and then when the opportunity comes, if you have thus done your duty in the lesser things, I know you will rise level to the heroic needs.[30]

After a luncheon at the university president's residence, Theodore's train took him to Oakland for a brief visit. The plans for his time in the city had been longer, but William Loeb ordered them reduced for the sake of Theodore's stamina. He was escorted by a detachment of army and navy personnel, where he gave a speech to more than ten thousand people "fairly packed into Lafayette Park." Theodore told the citizens he did not have much to say because since his arrival in the state he "felt a good deal more like learning than teaching." He admitted that the only thing that "marred my visit" was having to speak. "I have come from the East through the West," he said, "beyond the West, to California; for California stands by itself; and from one end of this country to the other, addressing any audience, I have felt absolutely at home; I have felt that I was speaking to men and women who felt as I did and thought as I did, to whom I could appeal with the certainty of being understood; because wherever I have spoken I have addressed audiences like this, audiences composed of Americans and nothing else."[31]

Returning to the dock to board the cutter, Theodore ordered his carriage to stop twice. The first time was to briefly thank "his boys," Spanish-American War veterans. "Afloat and ashore, nothing could have pleased me more than to have you turn out to be my escort today; to see that familiar gray hat, blue shirt, khaki trousers and leggings, I feel as if I was at home with you." Before bidding them goodbye, he asked them to join him in resolving to "do our part" in that the "standard of citizenship is kept up" and to see the average American citizen "understands what a good man our brother, the army and the navy man, officer and enlisted man of the regular service, was and is." He then stopped at the dock to thank several Civil War veterans for the privilege to see and speak to them. Noting their example of service "we endeavored to follow" and the memories of their deeds must "forever be to all Americans a source of inspiration to duty, whether it be in war or in peace."[32]

Taking the cutter across the bay, he went to the town of Vallejo, where the St. Vincent school band played "Hail to the Chief." Theodore promptly went to work laying the cornerstone for the YMCA auxiliary clubhouse. He was presented with a golden trowel to commemorate the clubhouse for "the bluejackets and marines of the United States Navy."

From there he returned to the wharf to go to Mare Island to view the naval yard with Secretary of the Navy William Moody.

Back at the Palace Hotel, Theodore prepared for his last event in the city, a dinner given by the Union League. He kept the assembled diners waiting twenty minutes as "he lingered in his apartments to use the first available moments in a long and busy day to write his regular daily letter to his wife."

Entering the room, he was given a hearty welcome by the four hundred guests. When seated at his table the orchestra began to play "God Save the King" in honor of British admiral Bickford. Mistaking the song for "My Country 'Tis of Thee," the audience began to sing the American version of the tune until Theodore stopped them. "With a warning movement of his head and a suggestive spread of his hands the President checked the song and turned with a gentle nod toward the British Admiral, who was a guest of honor, and out of respect to the Admiral's presence, the President very pleasantly indicated the tune to be restarted. It was a passing incident, but it showed the alertness of the Chief Executive," reported the *San Francisco Chronicle*.[33]

"It is absolutely essential if we are to have the proper standard of public life that promise shall be square with performance," Theodore reminded the audience. "A lie is no more to be excused in politics than out of politics. A promise is as binding on the stump as off the stump; and there are two facets to that crystal. In the first place, the man who makes a promise which he does not intend to keep and does not try to keep should rightly be adjudged to have forfeited in some degree what should be every man's most precious possession—his honor. On the other hand, the public that exacts a promise which ought not to be kept, or which cannot be kept, is by just so much forfeiting its right to self-government. There is no surer way of destroying the capacity for self-government in a people than to accustom that people to demanding the impossible or the improper from its public men. No man fit to be a public man will promise either the impossible or the improper; and if the demand is made that he shall do so it means putting a premium upon the unfit in public life. There is the same sound reason for distrusting the man who promises too much in public that there is for distrusting the man who promises too much in private business. If you meet a doctor who asserts that he has a specific remedy that will cure all the ills to which human flesh is heir, distrust him. He hasn't got it. If you meet a businessman who vociferates that he is always selling everything to you at a loss, and you continue to deal with him, I am glad if you suffer for it."[34]

With his speech concluded, Theodore changed in his hotel room and left for his train. As his carriage arrived at the ferry dock, Theodore requested the four mounted San Francisco police officers to come see him. He delayed the ferry until he had the chance to express his thanks to the four men. "I want to commend you for your good horsemanship and to also thank you for the manner in which you have escorted me through the streets of San Francisco," he stated, shaking their hands.[35] With that, the carriage boarded the ferry to cross over to Oakland. His train left twenty-five minutes after midnight.

Theodore was on his way to Yosemite.

Tramping with Muir: Yosemite

It was so reviving to be so close to nature in this magnificent forest.

IN 1903, THE ONLY WAY A PERSON COULD VISIT YOSEMITE WAS TO TAKE a train to the small hamlet of Raymond, the closest railroad depot. From there a visitor would have to endure a twelve-hour, sixty-seven-mile ride on a stagecoach before reaching the southern entrance near the Wawona Hotel.[1]

John Muir arrived in Oakland on May 14 and took the ferry across the bay to see Theodore at his hotel. The president was amid his final dinner banquet in the city, so Muir briefly viewed Market Street before deciding to return to the train to sleep. After breakfast the following morning, May 15, he and Theodore officially met in his private car and talked until they arrived in Raymond.

Theodore's train pulled into the small depot at eight o'clock, greeted by a receptive crowd of nearly fifteen hundred people. Already dressed in his camping clothes, he had no intention of making a speech and told the reception committee that he had not been given any previous notice. He also added that he would have to change into a suit in order to address the crowd. The committee members assured him the crowd wanted to hear from him and his clothing was just fine. A platform was set up on the porch of Bowen's Hotel, where he spoke briefly to the people.[2]

"I did not realize that I was to meet you today, still less to address an audience such as this and I had only come prepared to go into the Yosemite with John Muir, so I must ask you to excuse my costume," he said. "I have enjoyed so much seeing Southern California and San Francisco that

I felt my trip would be incomplete if I did not get up into your beautiful country and then see the Yosemite. Before I came on this trip I was inclined to grumble because I found we were giving relatively four times as much time to California as to any other State. Now I feel that we did not give it half enough. It ought to have been eight times instead of four times."[3]

With the short speech concluded, Theodore boarded a stagecoach driven by Tom Gordon. He sat next to the driver while Muir sat behind him, pointing out sights and trees along the way. A second stagecoach carrying other members of the president's party and Secret Service agents followed, and a thirty-man detachment of U.S. Cavalry provided an escort. The party stopped for lunch at Awahnee Tavern, eighteen miles north of Raymond. Theodore's stagecoach arrived at the Mariposa Grove of Big Trees late in the afternoon, and photographs were taken in front of the Grizzly Giant (which had no signs on it) and the Wawona Tunnel Tree.[4] Theodore then bade farewell to everyone, including members of his party and Secret Service agents. (They would stay at the Wawona Hotel.) The Yosemite Park Commission had planned an elaborate dinner at the hotel (including a fireworks display rumored to cost $400) without Theodore's knowledge or approval.[5] Theodore, who had tired of the bright city lights and twenty-one-gun salutes, wanted only to camp out in the open, see the trees, hear the birds, and talk with John Muir. Charlie Leidig and Archie Leonard would be his guides, along with a member of the U.S. Army, Jack Alder, serving as a packer. Four mules would haul all the needed equipment for the trip, with Leidig also handling the cooking cores.

Theodore and Muir took a walk among the sequoias. Amazed at their height and beauty, he could not help but to tell Muir that it was the greatest forest site he had ever laid eyes on. After walking among the trees, they returned to camp, where Theodore requested that Leidig not "let anybody disturb me, because I am tired and want to rest and sleep." The guide assured him that he would see to it that he wasn't bothered and proceeded to cook a dinner of fried chicken, beefsteak, and plenty of hot coffee. After talking for a while, the party settled down for a good night's sleep under the Grizzly Giant tree.[6] In his autobiography, Theodore recounted that the night was clear as they laid down in the grove.

"The majestic trunks, beautiful in color and in symmetry, rose around us like the pillars of a mightier cathedral than ever was conceived even by the fervor of the Middle Ages."[7] (It is estimated the Grizzly Giant is between 1,900 and 2,400 years old.)

Breaking camp before sunrise, they were in the saddle by 6:30, leaving the Mariposa Grove behind. Theodore asked Leidig to "outskirt and keep away from civilization" as they made their way to Glacier Point. Leading the party, Leidig took them down "a narrow defile known as the Lightning Trail." They avoided all main roads with one exception—a bridge near the Wawona Hotel where they were "compelled to cross the South Fork of the Merced River." Guests at the hotel had expected the party to pass in front of the hotel, but Leidig had them hugging the riverbank and they passed unnoticed, even though they were "within 100 yards of the place."[8]

Switching to the Empire Meadows Trail, they made their way to a ridge east of Empire Meadows where they stopped for a cold lunch. They encountered "a lot of snow as they crossed toward Sentinel Dome," with each member taking turns getting off his horse and breaking a trail. The "party plowed through" nearly five feet of snow in Bridalveil Meadows, and at one point, Theodore got "mired down" in the snow and Leidig had to use a log to get him out. ("It was snowing hard and the wind was blowing," recalled Leidig.) John Muir suggested they camp on the ridge just behind Sentinel Dome, but Leidig disagreed. He urged them to go down to "the approximate location of the present campgrounds at Glacier Point, since there was ample water and better camping conditions."[9] Theodore backed Leidig's suggestion.

As they approached Glacier Point, they were met with a "blinding snowstorm," which continued for several hours. With the camp set up and dinner eaten, Muir talked endlessly about his theory that glaciers formed the Yosemite Valley.[10] They also discussed conservation of the forests, including Yosemite. Muir told Theodore to watch as he grabbed a burning branch from the fire and lit a dead pine tree near the edge of the cliff. The lifeless tree was engulfed with flames while Muir danced. Theodore joined in, springing around the burning pine. He told Muir that it was a "candle that took five-hundred years to make!"[11]

During the night, the snowstorm continued and when they awoke well before the dawn, there was five feet of white powder covering the ground and, according to Leidig, "everything was frozen." The harsh conditions did not bother Theodore in the least; he reveled in them, using the light from the campfire to shave by.

With the sun up, everyone remained at Glacier Point as the photographer from Underwood and Underwood arrived to take the photographs that had been prearranged. Today, those pictures are some of the most iconic photos of Theodore, depicting his passion for conservation. Two were taken with Theodore alone. One photo has him standing near the cliff's edge, with Yosemite Valley behind him and Yosemite Falls in its full flowing beauty. Theodore, dressed in his Norfolk coat with a sweater over a rough shirt, his riding pants, leather leggings, a well-worn bandana around his neck, and his light western slouch hat, stands looking at the camera. His face wears the determined look of a man who has made a decision about which there will be no further discussion. His right hand is at his side, his left on his hip. It is not a pose of defiance, but one of conviction. It is pure Theodore Roosevelt.

In the second solo photograph of him, he is sitting on Overhanging Rock, his feet in front of him and his left arm again resting on his hip. That same look is on his face, as if it were carved from the granite rocks. Theodore and Muir posed together for a picture, with Theodore striking the same pose as he had for the one by himself, whereas Muir looks relaxed and contented, his arms clasped behind him. Just before this picture was taken, Theodore informed Muir that he wanted the Yosemite Valley below them to become part of Yosemite Park.[12]

This could explain the determined look on Theodore's face.

Departing Glacier Point, Theodore took the lead, followed by Leidig, Leonard, Muir, and Alder. Arriving in Little Yosemite Valley for lunch, they rested on the grass. Reaching Camp Curry at two o'clock in the afternoon, they found a big crowd forming a line across the road in an attempt to stop the president and shake his hand. (The Yosemite Park Commission had advertised Theodore's visit to the park days earlier.) Annoyed at the crowd trying to halt his travel, he asked Leidig what could be done. "Follow me," his guide said, nudging his spurs into his horse's flanks. The animal leaped and started off, quickly forcing the crowd to part. As Theodore passed the people, he waved his hat as he galloped on.[13]

At Sentinel Bridge, they met up with Theodore's party, as well as members of the Yosemite Park Commission, which was still anxious to hold a dinner in his honor. Theodore walked over to Chris Jorgensen's cabin and studio, where he was to stay during his visit, and apologized to the artist for the change in plans. Had the plans of the Yosemite Park Commission been carried out, Theodore would have had a chef brought in from San Francisco to cater his meals, but Theodore preferred the meals cooked by Charlie Leidig. Returning to the horses on the bridge, he was presented with the key to Yosemite (made from manzanita) by the park's guardian, John Stevens. Theodore told the group, pointing at Glacier Point, "Just think of where I was last night. Up there amid the pine and silver firs in the Sierrian solitude, in a snowstorm, too, and without a tent. I passed one of the most pleasant nights in my life. It was so reviving to be so close to nature in this magnificent forest."[14]

When Governor Pardee began talking about the evening banquet and fireworks display, Theodore cut him off abruptly. "We will pitch camp at Bridalveil!" he flatly stated. (John Muir had suggested the area for their next camp.) That put an end to discussions of any events planned in Theodore's honor.[15]

As they began to cross the bridge, a young boy greeted Theodore with, "Hello, Teddy!" Theodore stopped his horse, "a frown darkened his face." Guiding his horse over to the boy, he gave him a short lecture on manners "with father severity."[16] As he began to ride off, he spotted young Ellen Boysen standing with her mother, holding a flag in her small hands. He reached down and picked up the young girl, kissing her cheek. "God bless you, little angel," he said, returning her to her mother. With a wave of his hat to the child and parent, he galloped off into the valley of Yosemite.[17]

Arriving at Bridalveil Meadows, they were followed by a group of people. Once they set up their campsite, Theodore asked Leidig if he'd "get rid of them."[18] Walking out to the people, the guide explained that the president was very tired and wanted to get some rest and asked them to leave. The people obliged, including some who literally tiptoed away. Walking back to the camp, Theodore said, "Charlie, I'm as hungry as hell.

Cook anything you wish." After Leidig told him that dinner would be ready in thirty minutes, Theodore stretched out on some blankets and was soon fast asleep. He said Theodore's snoring was "so loud" that it could be heard "above the crackling of the campfire." After dinner, Theodore and Muir walked out into the meadow until darkness fell, returning to the campfire where they continued to talk about a variety of things.[19]

One problem, according to Leidig, was that both Theodore and Muir "wanted to do the talking." Theodore once stated that Muir was "able to influence contemporary thought and action on the subjects to which he devoted his life." He praised the naturalist as "a great factor in influencing" and being able to secure and preserve the natural phenomena that makes "California a veritable Garden of the Lord."[20] One thing about Muir that did surprise Theodore was his total lack of interest in birds and their songs. Muir knew very little about them, and cared even less, as it was the forest and the land that held his passion and interest. Despite the naturalist's lack of curiosity regarding fowl, Theodore stated that he was always glad to have visited Yosemite with Muir.[21]

Sunrise on May 18 was bittersweet for Theodore. After breakfast, the stagecoach arrived to take Theodore back to the Wawona Hotel and then to Raymond. As with Yellowstone, Theodore would have preferred to remain in Yosemite longer. Before taking his place alongside the coach driver, Theodore turned to Leidig, Leonard, and Alder and shook their hands. "Goodbye and God Bless you," he told them. After lunch at the Wawona Hotel, the entire party headed to Raymond and to Theodore's train. Stagecoach driver Tom Gordon set a record that day, which remained unbroken during the forty years that the stagecoach took passengers from Raymond to Yosemite. Gordon made the sixty-seven-mile ride in ten hours.[22]

Throughout his stagecoach ride to the train and for days later, all Theodore really cared to talk about was the wonders of Yosemite and the magnificent sequoias.

Leaving Raymond, Theodore's train made stops in Berenda, Merced, and Modesto as the evening's darkness fell. The following day he arrived in

Sacramento, where he spoke to five thousand students assembled in the Plaza. Theodore, greeted by "a chorus of cheers that fairly overwhelmed the President," paid tribute to the teachers. He declared, "There is no body of men and women in all our country to whom so much is owing as to those who are training the next generation, because it is the merest truism to say that the next generation determines the fate of this country." He added that a "peculiar debt" is owed to those "who are educating the boys and girls of today, who will be the men and women of tomorrow, and upon whom we must depend to keep alive the traditions of our citizenship."[23]

After a meal at the Sutter Club, Theodore spoke to a large crowd assembled outside the state capitol building. Praising California's rich agricultural business, he once again noted how irrigation was such an important factor in any crop's success. He stressed that the water supply needed for irrigation "cannot be preserved unless the forests are preserved." Theodore urged the citizens of the state to protect their forests, especially the sequoias:

> I want them preserved because they are the only things of their kind in the world. Lying out at night under those giant Sequoias was lying in a temple built by no hand of man, a temple grander than any human architect could by any possibility build, and I hope for the preservation of the groves of giant trees simply because it would be a shame to our civilization to let them disappear. They are monuments in themselves. I ask for the preservation of the other forests on grounds of wise and far-sighted economic policy. I do not ask that lumbering be stopped at all. On the contrary, I ask that the forests be kept for use in lumbering, only that they be so used that not only shall we here, this generation, get the benefit for the next few years, but that our children and our children's children shall get the benefit. In California I am impressed by how great the State is, but I am even more impressed by the immensely-greater greatness that lies in the future, and I ask that your marvelous natural resources be handed on unimpaired to your posterity. We are not building this

country of ours for a day. It is to last through the ages. We stand on the threshold of a new century. We look into the dim years that rise before us, knowing that if we are true the generations that succeed us here shall fall heir to a heritage such as has never been known before. I ask that we keep in mind not only our own interests, but the interests of our children. Any generation fit to do its work must work for the future, for the people of the future, as well as for itself. . . . I earnestly ask that you see to it that your resources, by use, are perpetuated for the use of the peoples yet unborn. Use them, but in using, keep and preserve them. Keep the waters; keep the forests; use your lands as you use your bays, your harbors, as you use the cities here, so that by the very fact of the use they will become more valuable as possessions.[24]

The Northwest: Oregon and Washington

If one is a good Westerner he is necessarily a good American.

"Had an order been given to Weather Forecaster Edward H. Beales, a better day could not have been supplied," commented the *Daily Oregon Statesman* regarding Theodore's arrival in Salem.[1]

Special trains carried "people from the country and neighboring towns" into the city in "a steady stream from all thoroughfares."[2] The Southern Pacific Railroad stopped all freight trains from passing through the area for twelve hours, and passenger trains were sidetracked for ten minutes prior to the arrival of Theodore's train. The Southern Pacific depot as well as the state capitol were "almost covered in National colors." (The city's decorating committee requested residents along the line of the processional march to decorate their houses, all of which happily complied.)

The crowd, estimated to be nearly forty-five thousand, was "a seething mass of humanity." People waved flags and cheered as Theodore's carriage made its required processional run through a portion of the city. All along the way, Theodore would stand up, wave his hat and bow to the appreciative crowd. As his carriage passed Willamette University, J. B. Tuthill gave out the Harvard cheer. This caught Theodore's attention, and he yelled, "What year?" "'87," replied Tuthill. Theodore waved his hat in reply. Passing a line of Grand Army of the Republic members, Theodore stood up in his carriage, removed his hat, and bowed his head.[3]

Arriving at Marion Square, Theodore mounted the speaker's platform and removed his hat when two thousand schoolchildren began to sing

"America"; he joined them in singing the chorus. In his speech to the children, Theodore once again spoke of the importance of both parents and teachers in educating "the smaller generation of men and women." He said he was glad to "see the elder folks, I am gladder to see the children. I have six myself, and I claim to be, in a certain sense, an expert in them."[4]

As his carriage left Marion Square, he noticed Constance Kanter, a five-year-old girl lying on a four-wheel carriage. (The young girl was undergoing surgeries to cure a spinal problem.) Theodore ordered his carriage to stop and walked up to the young girl. Bending down, he took her hand and quietly spoke to her before returning to his carriage. "Nothing could have been more unaffectedly simple and genuine through this impulsive act upon the President's part," commented the *Daily Oregon Statesman*.[5] No doubt the young girl's spinal issues brought to mind his older sister, Anna, who was forced to wear a back brace from her early years due to being dropped as a baby. Two weeks later, Theodore sent a letter to the young girl's father, stating how one of his sons suffered from water on the knee and "had to wear an instrument" for nearly two years. "This has brought home to me very keenly what it means for a child to suffer in this way, and still more to suffer as your dear little girl was evidentially suffering," he added. "I wish it had been in my power to do something that would have given her even a moment's real happiness."[6] (On December 19, 1903, Theodore replied to a letter sent by little Constance, addressing her as "my dear little Friend." Thanking her for her letter, he stated that "I shall always remember you" and enclosed a signed photo.)

Arriving at the capitol, Theodore happily shook hands with several Civil War veterans who lined the steps. Addressing the audience, Theodore noted that "if one is a good Westerner he is necessarily a good American." However, he warned his listeners the most "dangerous citizen" in the country was the one who would attempt to "persuade any sect of our people" that it is in their interests to "over-reach any other sect of our people." He noted that, fundamentally, "we shall go up, or go down together." Good times may come to some more than others, yet "they will come more or less to all." Adding that if the Lord's hand was "heavy upon us," suffering from floods, droughts, disease or "effects of our own folly," the suffering may not be equal to all but would be felt by all in some manner.[7]

"In no way is it possible permanently to help any of us by trampling down others," he stated. He observed that the rich man can be helped only if the conditions of the wage-worker are flourishing. Noting that if it were possible to "do away with all the wealth in this country" and take it away from the present owners, "the first and greatest sufferers" would be those who are "least well off in the world's goods." Following that line of thought, Theodore added that "the greatest danger in any republic" is the man who seeks to ignite the "spirit of envy, jealousy, or distrust as between one class and another" and urges them to "do wrong, or to follow him because it will be for their interests."[8]

He went on to tell the story of how he caught a ranch hand placing his brand on an unbranded calf (cowboys called unbranded cows "mavericks") from another ranch. He fired the man on the spot, noting that if he'd steal for him, it was only a matter of time before that man would steal from him. "It is the same thing," Theodore went on, "the same rule applies in civic life. A public man who seeks to persuade any of us to do wrong in our interests, will, whenever it becomes in his interest, do wrong to us, just as he seeks to do wrong on our behalf. There is but one safe rule to follow in public life, as in private life, and that is the old, old rule of treating your neighbor as you would like for your neighbor to treat you."[9]

※

"The guards and police had their hands full and the secret service men and detectives mingled with the people and kept sharp eyes out for suspicious characters" as Theodore arrived in Portland.[10] While law enforcement watched the crowd (estimated to be 150,000), Brown's Military Band played and two cannons fired a salute. Procession carriages were brightly decorated with flowers and draped over the rear of Theodore's carriage was an American flag, trailing "gracefully as the vehicle advanced." Members of the Grand Army of the Republic, marching in columns of two along both sides of his carriage escorted him to City Park. Theodore, along with the grandson of William Clark, laid the cornerstone for the Lewis and Clark monument.

"We come here today to lay a cornerstone of a monument that is to call to mind the greatest single pioneering feat on this continent," Theodore told the crowd, "the voyage across the continent by Lewis and Clark, which rounded out the ripe statesmanship of Jefferson and his fellows by giving to the United States all of the domain between the Mississippi and the Pacific." Theodore went on to recount the advent of the fur trade and the wagons that carried stalwart pioneers to their state in the 1840s.

> You have built up here this wonderful commonwealth, a commonwealth great in its past, and infinitely greater in its future.... We have met to commemorate a mighty pioneer feat, a feat of the old days, when men needed to call upon every ounce of courage and hardihood and manliness they possessed in order to make good our claim to this continent. Let us in our turn with equal courage, equal hardihood and manliness, carry on the task that our forefathers have entrusted to our hands; and let us resolve that we shall leave to our children and our children's children an even mightier heritage than we received in our turn.... I am confident that before this Republic there lies a future so brilliant that even the deeds of the past will seem dim in comparison.[11]

Theodore and his party stayed overnight at the Hotel Portland, taking up the entire east wing of the second floor. That evening he attended a dinner at the hotel but was assured he was not required to make any speech. Outside the hotel was a large American flag made entirely from red, white, and blue electric lights, "the finest ever seen in Portland" boasted the *Oregon Daily Journal*. Another flag on display was "mammoth but somewhat frayed and soiled." It was the first American flag to be hoisted in Manila after the surrender of Spain in the 1898 battle. The flag was originally made for the cruiser *Olympia*, but with Spain's defeat, Admiral Dewey sent it ashore so all could see the stars and stripes.[12]

Rising at 6:45 the following morning, Theodore looked over letters and dictated a few telegrams before leaving the hotel for his train. At the station, he personally thanked his carriage driver and the police officers who escorted him to the depot. Before leaving, Oregon National Guard sergeant E. E. Kimblin gave Theodore two Chinese pheasants, one for his daughter Alice and one for Theodore Junior. "Sergeant, those birds are splendid!" Theodore replied.[13] Shaking a few more hands, Theodore's train left Portland, heading to the state of Washington.

———

Theodore's visit to the state of Oregon was a pleasant venture, with one small exception.

Binger Hermann.

Hermann, whose parents immigrated to Oregon in 1859, held a seat in the state's House of Representatives (1866–1868) and was elected to the state Senate (1868–1870). He had served nearly twelve years in the U.S. House of Representatives (1885–1897) when President McKinley appointed him commissioner of the General Land Office (GLO). From the first time Theodore met Hermann, he did not care for the man. He believed Hermann was far more interested in obtaining river and harbor appropriations for the state than in protecting forests and other places, such as Crater Lake. (Theodore signed the bill to designate Crater Lake as a national park on May 22, 1903.)

The Holsinger Report was an investigation into a complex and large-scale land fraud happening in the Arizona Territory. The report named some very prominent and wealthy men who committed fraud against the U.S. government regarding hundreds of thousands of acres of the choicest lands. (Some believed that it was in the millions of acres.) A request by Secretary of the Interior Ethan Hitchcock to see the Holsinger Report spelled the end of Hermann's position at the GLO in December 1902. Examining the report, Hitchcock noticed that the date the GLO received it was nearly six weeks earlier. Demanding to know why the report was not forwarded to him, Hermann could offer only a weak excuse.[14] It was enough for Hitchcock, and more than enough for Theodore, who demanded Hermann's immediate resignation. Hermann's political supporters jumped to his defense but to no avail. He was forced to resign on February 1, 1903.

Fate stepped in for Hermann, ever the professional politician looking for the next step up the ladder. The death of Congressman Thomas Tongue in January 1903 opened a door for Hermann to restore his tarnished reputation. Naturally, a comment from President Theodore Roosevelt would be very beneficial to his campaign. It didn't matter that the president had demanded his resignation; this was just politics. Hermann's election committee went into overdrive before Theodore even set foot in Oregon. Using any and all political connections, Hermann and his party sought to get Theodore to shake hands with him in public, proving that Hermann was not damaged goods. Even better would be for the president to include him in a public speech in Salem or Portland. Any form of positive sentiment would help with his election to office.

Binger Hermann had a better chance of surviving a Dakota winter in a flimsy cabin than getting any notice from Theodore.

The *Eugene Guard* took note of Theodore's refusal to even acknowledge Hermann in his speech in Salem. This was so obvious to the newspaper reporter that some of his comments appeared completely in capital letters.

[T]he President omitted expressing any sentiment favorable to Mr. Hermann, IT BEING ESPECIALLY NOTICEABLE THAT HE DID NOT GREET HIM WITH THE USUAL WARMTH that former acquaintances would exhibit.... THERE WAS NO PERSONAL INDICATION IN HIS MANNER TOWARDS HERMANN BY THE PRESIDENT OF DESIRE FOR HIS SUCCESS is looked upon as demonstration of the President's unwillingness to go on the record for the man whom he forced out from the commissionership of the General Land Office.... The sum total of the incident has been to leave no doubt as to the President's frame of mind, and that frame of mind is of disgust at the bad taste and "nerve" of Mr. Hermann.[15]

Binger Hermann was not deterred. He followed Theodore's train to Portland. He even sought the help of the editors of the *Oregon Daily Journal*, which published "An Open Letter to the President" on the front page on May 20 in the hope that Theodore would read it. The editors asked the president to confirm "writing a few lines over your own signature" stating that Hermann was not discharged at "your instigation."[16] Theodore did not bother to reply. Binger Hermann followed Theodore to every city event. If Theodore smiled, so did Binger. When Theodore shook hands with people, Binger was right behind him offering both hands. If a camera was near the president, Binger was certain to get his face in the picture. One of his campaign managers explained Binger Hermann's omnipresence: "He has to make good, even if he had to be fired onto the President's platform by a mortar gun."[17]

Hermann won the election to finish out Tongue's term and won reelection in 1904. However, a grand jury in Portland indicted him in 1905 for destroying evidence and conspiracy to commit fraud. (He reportedly destroyed thirty-four books containing thousands of letters and papers relating to land fraud claims.) He was found not guilty but in 1910 was charged in another land fraud case in which the jury was hopelessly deadlocked.[18]

As he entered the Evergreen State of Washington, the tour was beginning to wear on Theodore. Though he had always led a strenuous life, the continual processional of parades and speeches was tiring. He thoroughly enjoyed meeting the people of the country, but the routine of the tour was quickly becoming a slog. It was also difficult to avoid repeating the same themes in his speeches, no matter how much he changed their structure.

The ever-present political hacks, looking for any opportunity to bend his ear and shake his hand like a water pump, also grew tiresome, especially after Binger Hermann's continual shadowing in Oregon. Having politicians ride a president's coattails was certainly nothing new nor was it limited to the man in the White House, as virtually any political office had its share of adulators. None of this was new to Theodore, as he would not suffer fools gladly. People for whom Theodore had little use or people who he did not respect would learn his feelings at once through his cold stare or icy reception.

While he was in San Francisco, Theodore sent a letter to Henry Cabot Lodge, noting that he had a "great reception" but had "literally been driven almost to the point of exhaustion; for the local committee is even worse than most local committees are in point of lack of consideration."[19] He went on to say that the previous evening he had attended a banquet that ended at one o'clock in the morning, and before eight the following morning "citizens of note had begun to arrive." The *Oregon Daily Journal* noted that Theodore "begins to look tired," stating "it is believed that he is growing weary of his journey, and he is not loath to say that he is happy that it is nearing the end."[20]

Another reason was a case of homesickness. Theodore missed his family, and not being able to share with them the Grand Canyon, Yellowstone, and Yosemite only amplified his longing. In a letter to his youngest child, Quentin, he said he was "very homesick for mother and you children." He added that whenever he sees a little boy, either brought to see him or passing by in a procession, "I think of you and Archie and feel very homesick. Sometimes little boys ride in the procession on their ponies, just like Archie on Algonquin."[21]

Soldiering on as he entered Washington, a stop in Kalama found him meeting "George Washington," a black bear cub that had been raised by saloon owner John Suber after he discovered its mother had died. "He looks just like the bear I have seen in some of the cartoons reflecting more or less upon my prowess as a hunter," Theodore commented.[22]

Heading northwest through the state, he made brief stops at Chehalis, Centralia, Olympia, and finally Tacoma, where he would stay overnight at the Tacoma Hotel. "There is a merry row on between Seattle and Tacoma over the visit of President Roosevelt," commented the *San Francisco Examiner* on May 10. Tacoma's welcoming committee had the understanding that it would be in charge of the presidential party from the moment the president entered the city until he arrived in Seattle on the steamship *Spokane*. Congressman William Humphrey and two members of the Seattle reception committee demanded they be given complete charge of the party from the moment Theodore stepped on the boat in Tacoma, but the former city committee remained firm in its plans. Humphrey, despite his blustering, could not show any documentation that gave him authority to make any demands. However, Tacoma's committee had numerous telegrams to and from the president's secretary, William Loeb, confirming the city's arrangements.

The hurt feelings in Seattle did not subside even with Theodore's visit. The *Seattle Star* could not resist one last jab at Tacoma as the president left town: "The only feature that has marred the plans of the committee from start to finish has been the jealous envy of the little village at the lower end of the bay, whose chief title to recognition is the genuine swinishness it has displayed in trying to hog everything in sight while the president was west of the Cascades."[23]

Arriving in Tacoma, Theodore's procession took him to Wright Park. Recalling the old western motto that a man should never draw unless he means to shoot, he also felt it was a sound policy for foreign affairs. "Do not threaten; do not bluster; above all, do not insult other people," he commented, "but when you make up your mind that the situation is such as to require you to take a given position, take it and keep it, and have it definitely understood that what you say you are ready to make good." Theodore stressed that he hoped the United States would always have peace with other powers, but peace does not come to the country "as a favor granted in contempt." Instead, he said, it should be the type of peace that comes to "the just man armed, the peace that we can claim as a matter of right." He observed that the best way to maintain any peace was to show the nation was not afraid of war if it was "unjustly treated or wronged." Theodore noted that the past few years illustrated that "whether we wish or not" the United States would have to play a larger role in world affairs. "It is not open to us to decide whether we will play it. All that is open to us to decide is whether we will play it well," he stated. He added that due to the country's interest in trade across the Pacific Ocean, the United States must have "a decisive say in its future matters." The only way that can be done, he said, was by building and maintaining an adequate navy. "If we fail to build an adequate Navy," he concluded, "then sometime some great power, throwing off the restraint of international morality, will take some step against us, relying upon the weakness of our Navy."[24]

Leaving the speaker's stand, Theodore noticed Otto Winter in the crowd. He quickly made his way over to the former Rough Rider and greeted him warmly. He invited Winter to ride with him to the hotel and be his guest the next day when he visited the naval yard in Bremerton.[25] He then laid the cornerstone of the city's Masonic temple before retiring to the Tacoma Hotel. The following morning his carriage took him to the wharf where he boarded the steamship *Spokane*. As the steamer pulled away from the dock, a band on the wharf played "A Hot Time in the Old Town Tonight" and the revenue cutter *McCullough* escorted the steamship across Commencement Bay and the Puget Sound. As the steamer made its way, Theodore had a perfect view of the snow-capped Olympic Mountains, while Mount Rainier was "shrouded in fleecy clouds."[26]

As Theodore arrived at the naval yard, he was greeted by a twenty-one-gun salute as the steamship was tied to the dock. He was then escorted to the nearby dry dock where he was to inspect a ship with Secretary of the Navy Moody and a company of marines and "Jack Tars."[27] The foreman of the yard presented Theodore with a small plate mounted in a rosewood case, which had been part of the keel of the battleship USS *Oregon*. "I want to thank you and through you your fellow workmen for this token. I also wish to repeat what I have said before, that the victories of Manila and Santiago reflect credit not merely upon those who fought, but upon every man who did his work in preparing the ships for battle," he stated. "Nothing could have pleased me more than to have received this gift from the men of the yard, and I appreciate it."[28]

The *Spokane* traveled to the Seattle side of Puget Sound with numerous boats and four revenue cutters serving as its escort. (It was fifty years to the day, May 23, that the city of Seattle was established.) The steamship landed at Arlington dock, and Theodore briskly walked down the gangplank to cheers and the waving of small American flags. Tipping his hat to the crowd, he made his way to the University of Washington. Passing Pioneer Square, "Nelson," the elderly chief of the Muckleshoot Tribe, was seated in front of a totem pole. The chief rose slowly and waved two American flags "with all possible energy" while Theodore returned a personal salute.

At the university, Theodore noticed audience members craning their necks to see and hear him. He grabbed a chair from behind him and stood on it, going on to praise the city's growth during the past fifty years. Theodore noted that no other body of water offers the commonwealth "the natural advantages that Puget Sound confers upon this State." Acknowledging that the state's growth had been phenomenal, he affirmed, "it has barely begun, and your growth in the half century now opening will dwarf absolutely even your growth in the immediate past." He went on to extoll the promise that the territory of Alaska would offer the United States, stating that he believed that within a century it would support a large population with its varied and boundless possibilities in agriculture, live-stock, lumber, and fishing industries. He closed his speech by stating that throughout his trip from the Atlantic to the Pacific, the one thing that "struck me the most is the reality of the unity of our people."[29]

Theodore then took a train, not the Roosevelt Special, to the city of Everett. Along the way, he stood on the rear platform waving to the people who lined the tracks to see him. "If these people have taken enough inter-est in me to come here from their homes, perhaps many miles away," he told a reporter, "I certainly feel enough interest in them to show myself."[30] The train arrived in Everett at six o'clock and took him through part of the industrial section of the city before a carriage processional escorted him to a park in the center of the city. Theodore noted the two great industries in Washington and Oregon were lumbering and fishing and urged the audience to carry on their work in these industries not only for themselves, but for their successors. Theodore stressed that the goal of both industries should not be to exhaust the state's resources but to utilize them to their fullest extent. However, he cautioned, they should be preserved so that those "who come after you shall share in the benefits." The country, he said, would no longer tolerate anyone "whose aim was to skin the country and get out."[31]

An equal concern facing the state was forestry. Noting that the lum-ber industry was the fourth largest business interest in the United States, wisdom should prevail in order to keep the business viable as a permanent industry. "Our aim should be to get the fullest use from the forest today, and yet to get that benefit in ways which will keep the forests for our children in the generations to come." Theodore observed that the state of Washington was blessed with climatic conditions that enabled the for-est to renew itself quickly, allowing the trees within a few short years to become "again a great mercantile and industrial asset." He concluded that the preservation of our forests depends chiefly upon the wisdom of the lumberman and the lumber industry working with "the men who have studied the scientific side of forestry; co-operation between them is the best and surest way of saving our forests."[32]

Returning to Seattle by way of the steamer *Spokane*, the ship stopped its engines as five Indian canoes raced on Puget Sound. Theodore took great interest in the race even though two canoes capsized, and as the rest neared the finish line, he yelled "like a baseball enthusiast at an 11-inning game."[33] Pulling into Seattle at eight o'clock, he was greeted by the city's lights blazing and with fireworks in the sky.

At the city's Grand Opera House, the audience had been patiently awaiting his arrival for more than an hour to present Theodore with a gold pan by the Artic Brotherhood. Theodore commented that our fate as a nation had driven "us forward toward greatness in spite of the protests" from those who were not as daring. When the Louisiana Purchase was completed, he said, "there were plenty of wise men" who believed the country was acquiring a desert or that the purchase was a violation of the Constitution. "And think how absolutely the event has falsified the predictions of those men," he retorted. Yet the same "bitter opposition" arose when the country bought Alaska from Russia in 1867. "And but five years ago there were excellent men who bemoaned the fact that we were obliged during the war with Spain to take possession of the Philippines and to show that we were hereafter to be one of the dominant powers of the Pacific," Theodore noted. Observing "the after events of history" proved predictions by those of little faith to be false, he scolded the critics, "so feeble and so timid," who slunk backward when the country asserted itself, daring to be great. Those who were critical of taking action always wanted to know what the cost would be and its ultimate meaning. "We do not know the cost, but we know it will be more than repaid ten times over by the result; and what it may ultimately mean we do not know, but we know what the present holds, what the present need demands, and we take the present and hold ourselves ready to abide the result of whatever the future may bring," he declared.[34]

Concluding his speech, a tired Theodore retreated to his room at the Washington Hotel, took a hot bath, and went to bed. He was so exhausted that he had forgotten that there was a banquet after his speech. Secretary of the Navy Moody went to his room and awakened Theodore, telling him the people expected an appearance by him. He quickly dressed in his evening clothes to make a quick appearance before returning to his room and to the arms of Morpheus.

Sunday morning was a bright, sunny day in which Theodore took a breakfast of cereal, fried chicken, potatoes, and hot coffee in his room. Heading to his carriage, he noticed the stuffed buffalo and caribou on display in the lobby and spent several minutes studying them. Theodore would not make any speeches nor participate in any processions today. He was driven back to the Grand Opera House, where he attended memorial services with members of the Grand Army of the Republic and Spanish-American War veterans presided over by Reverend J. M. Wilson.

A demonstration had been planned at the opera house in Theodore's honor, which he quickly put down. This was a problem he faced throughout his tour when it came to Sunday church services. Secretary Loeb or another member of the presidential party had to stress to the local church and minister that Theodore did not want in any way to be referred to in the pastor's sermon. Whereas a minister might feel it was incumbent upon him to make some sort of reference to the president, Theodore found it embarrassing; it did not follow normal church customs. He wanted nothing said or done that would not happen if he were not present.[35]

Theodore made a brief visit to Providence Hospital to see an old friend, Michael Meyendorff, who was recovering from an illness. After a lunch back at the hotel with Loeb and other members of his group, he spent some time reading. Midafternoon he left the hotel and, at the city's old cable railroad powerhouse, mounted a horse and rode off with Dr. Rixley, headed for Fort Lawton. The military installation was caught completely off-guard when the president of the United States rode into the fort grounds. He briefly visited with Captain H. G. Lyon before riding off. A group of soldiers were playing baseball, which Theodore stopped to watch. The soldiers quickly snapped to attention when they realized who was watching them. He waved off their official stance, saying, "Let me see you play." The next soldier at bat "swatted out a three-bagger." Returning to the city, Theodore and Rixley rode over Queen Anne Hill, taking in a spectacular view of the city and the Olympic Mountains. Back at the hotel, Theodore dined with members of his group and later met with representatives of the Harvard Club for a few minutes. By ten o'clock, he left for his train, which departed at midnight.[36]

❯❮

Ellensburg, Yakima, Pasco, and Wallula: each was a brief stop with an equally brief speech. In Walla Walla, his visit was a duplicate of others: large, appreciative crowds; cannons firing a salute; a processional parade; and a speech before leaving for the next town. Unbeknownst to Theodore or any others in his party, the stop here put his life in danger.

Joseph Barker was a butcher working at a meat market in Pendleton, Oregon.[37] A week before Theodore's arrival in Walla Walla, Barker made a comment to his boss, Patrick Kine, that he had two cartridges for his Winchester rifle, one for President Roosevelt and one for Emperor William (of Germany). A few days later, Barker quit his job, and, with rifle in hand, headed to Walla Walla. His comment set off a desperate search to find him.[38]

Believing that Barker actually planned to harm the president, Kine traveled to Walla Walla, where he alerted the local police department. He accompanied three officers as they scoured the town looking for Barker. They spotted him working in Chris Ennis's butcher shop, just four hours before Theodore's train was to arrive.

"He was arrested and sweated," noted one newspaper.[39]

Barker reportedly arrived in Walla Walla on Sunday in the early evening. He went to Farmer's Livery on Fifth Street, asking if he could leave his rifle there, adding he'd come back for it on Monday "as he had use for it." The livery was "a point of vantage along the route of the parade" where Theodore would pass, likely standing in his carriage and waving to the public. The following morning, May 25, Barker applied for a job at the Walla Walla Meat Market and was hired for the day due to increased business resulting from the influx of people who had come to see the president. A few employees of the meat market told a newspaper reporter that they noticed Barker acting "rather peculiarly," but due to the rush of business, they quickly forgot about him.

At the jail, Barker "appeared exceedingly angry" when detectives began to question him. He eventually admitted to having a rifle, which police discovered at Farmer's Livery, but denied any plans to kill the president. In a jailhouse interview with a newspaper reporter on May 26, Barker had "tears streaming down his face." He renounced being an anarchist, "but a second later made the statement that he was a socialist in the truest sense of the word." He was described in newspapers as being Swiss, short in stature, and "surly."[40]

"President Roosevelt would probably have been lying dead or desperately wounded tonight, ruthlessly shot down by an anarchist's hand, had not the clever work of the police force frustrated the alleged plot just in time," dramatically announced the *Butte Miner*. Newspapers did not run the story until Theodore was on his way to Idaho and out of harm's way.[41]

Barker was released from jail twenty-four hours after Theodore had left Walla Walla, with his rifle returned to him. This was not the first time Theodore's life was threatened during this tour.[42] Local police arrested anyone who made threats, often using the charge of vagrancy to hold them for twenty-four hours, until Theodore was no longer in the town or city. Suspects deemed real dangers to the president were turned over to federal authorities.

Newspapers described such people as "cranks."

In the Footsteps of Lewis and Clark:
Montana and Idaho

This beats embalmed beef, don't it?

THEODORE'S TOUR WAS NOW IN ITS LAST TEN DAYS, AS HIS TRAIN WOULD carry him to Wallace, Harrison, and Tekoa, Idaho, before doubling back to Spokane, Washington, all in one day: Tuesday, May 26. Theodore greeted well-wishers, shook hands with assorted politicians and welcoming committeemen, and gave speeches.

Before he arrived in Spokane, the carriage that would carry him through the streets was on display at the city's local Studebaker store. The Park Phaeton model, made of natural oak in a golden color, had been shipped to Spokane from Portland just for the day's events. "The seats are very high, so that everyone will have a good view of the president," noted the *Spokane Press*. Like other cities Theodore visited, red, white, and blue bunting adorned storefronts, buildings, and homes along the processional route. Spokane's dry goods stores ran out of bunting by noon the day before Theodore's arrival, and a hasty call was made to wholesale houses for additional material.[1]

As the city was busy decorating for the president's arrival, the police department was also very busy, giving "a thorough cleaning of disorderly and suspicious persons." Thirty-nine "bad characters" had been rounded up and held in jail until Theodore's train departed the city. Detectives and police officers from other nearby cities were brought in to assist Spokane's police force in maintaining order and attempting to deter pickpockets.

With the recent threat against Theodore's life in Walla Walla, no one was taking any chances, and any potential criminals were locked up.[2]

Theodore was greeted with a steady drizzle of rain as he stepped off his train at the depot on Hamilton Street. The ever-present politicians and committee members, eager for a moment in the spotlight, did not let the weather deter them. As his carriage made its tour of the city, the crowds also ignored the drizzle, giving the president a hearty welcome. At one point, Theodore ordered his carriage to stop because he had recognized a man in the crowd from his days in the Spanish-American War. He got out to shake hands with the man, identified only as Mr. Sanders, who had carried dispatches and orders for him.[3]

In his speech, which Theodore later considered his best,[4] he praised the state for playing its part in the great increase of trade with the Orient by use of railroads and shipping. He cited how the men who built the railroads and shipping companies helped the country by expanding trade with other nations. By either making or using their wealth, they created and developed great business enterprises that have benefitted the country and not harmed it. Theodore then turned his attention to the enforcement of the law for all people, rich or poor.

> No man is above it *[the law]* and no man is below it. The crime of cunning, the crime of greed, the crime of violence, are all equally crimes, and against them all alike the law must set its face. This is not and never shall be a government either of a plutocracy or of a mob. It is, it has been, and it will be, a government of the people; including alike the people of great wealth and of moderate wealth, the people who employ others, the people who are employed, the wage-worker, the lawyer, the mechanic, the banker, the farmer; including them all, protecting each and every one if he acts decently and squarely, and discriminating against any one of them, no matter from what class he comes, if he does not act squarely and fairly, if he does not obey the law.
>
> While all people are foolish if they violate or rail against the law—wicked as well as foolish, but all foolish—yet the most foolish man in this Republic is the man of wealth who complains because the law is administered with impartial justice against or

for him. His folly is greater than the folly of any other man who so complains; for he lives and moves and has his being because the law does in fact protect him and his property.

We have the right to ask every decent American citizen to rally to the support of the law if it is ever broken against the interest of the rich man; and we have the same right to ask that rich man cheerfully and gladly to acquiesce in the enforcement against his seeming interest of the law, if it is the law. Incidentally, whether he acquiesces or not, the law will be enforced, and thus whoever he may be, great or small, and at whichever end of the social scale he may be.

I ask that we see to it in our country that the line of division in the deeper matters of our citizenship be drawn, never between section and section, never between creed and creed, never, thrice never, between class and class; but that the line be drawn on the line of conduct, cutting through sections, cutting through creeds, cutting through classes; the line that divides the honest from the dishonest, the line that divides good citizenship from bad citizenship, the line that declares a man a good citizen only if, and always if, he acts in accordance with the immutable law of righteousness, which has been the same from the beginning of history to the present moment, and which will be the same from now until the end of recorded time.[5]

Before arriving in Spokane, secretary Loeb informed the reception committee that the president would make only one of two scheduled speeches "due to weariness." Spokane's committee had planned for Theodore to speak briefly to a large group of schoolchildren and then to break ground for the Salvation Army Athletic Club and give another speech. After receiving Loeb's statement, the local committeemen made the decision that Theodore would not speak to the children nor break ground for the club. The children and Salvation Army members were left waiting at their appointed positions only to see Theodore's carriage whisk by. This decision caused many hurt feelings and led to finger-pointing and heated censure from the *Spokane Press*. "There is constant buzz and murmur of discontent throughout the city at the bungles made by those in charge of the Roosevelt reception and the manner in which the entire celebration was handled," the newspaper commented. It went on to state that although Patsy Clark loaned his team of horses to pull the president's carriage, Mr. Clark was never introduced to Theodore nor was Postmaster Hartson, who was a personal acquaintance of the president. They also noted that Harvard men "were ignored," and although the newspaper heavily covered the planned events and listed the members of the reception committee, the newspaper was informed they could have a carriage at the rear of the procession "providing they paid for it themselves."[6] The committee quickly blamed secretary Loeb for its events being ignored by the president. (It is hard to imagine that Theodore, no matter how tired, would have ignored speaking to schoolchildren, albeit briefly, had he been made aware.)

The *Spokane Press* was so infuriated with the committee's actions that it sent a telegram to a Scripps-McRae reporter, R. H. Hazzard, traveling on Theodore's train, to ask secretary Loeb who was responsible for the disappointment to the schoolchildren and the Salvation Army. "As Secretary Loeb says the fault lies with the local committee and the school children, their parents and the Athletic Club members now know who is responsible."[7]

The evening before Theodore's arrival in Helena, he was "saved the annoyance of receiving a letter which may be characterized as threatening," reported the *Anaconda Standard*. Niculae Tarcea had gone to the city's post office and asked a clerk to give a letter to Theodore when he arrived in town. The clerk, May Franklin, refused to accept the letter as she suspected the man was "a maniac or an anarchist." She notified police, who then arrested Tarcea a few hours later. In his letter to the president, he claimed to be a poor inventor who had a "flying machine," and its success "depended upon assistance in a financial way." He demanded that the president furnish him money in order to "bring his airship to a state of completion." Tarcea never made any physical threats toward the president, and "officers concluded that the man was insane and harmless." In the early morning hours, newspaper reporters were allowed to speak to Tarcea in his jail cell, where he told them he was originally from Hungary, where he had a wife and two children. He had been in America for sixteen months and worked as a barber. "Tarcea manifestly is crazy" noted the *Anaconda Standard* reporter, adding that the man's plans for his airship were made up of "pieces of paper cut from various colored journals." Tarcea claimed he got the idea after reading about Santos-Dumont's experiments with airships in Paris. "There is no thought now that the man is an anarchist or that he is more than a simpleton," the newspaper stated.[8]

John ("Jack") Willis had no use for Theodore Roosevelt.

In 1888, Theodore had seen the head of a mountain goat at a local taxidermist in Medora that was shot by John Willis. The mountain goat had always eluded Theodore's hunting rifle, but now there was an opportunity to have a man guide him to his target. He dashed off a letter to Willis, who lived in Thompson Falls, Montana, asking, "If I come to Montana, will you act as my guide, and do you think I can kill a white goat?" Willis was not amused, especially by Theodore's crabbed handwriting. "If you can't shoot any better than you can write, NO!" replied Willis. Believing the matter settled, Willis was going about his business when he received a telegram from Theodore, who said he'd arrive in Thompson Falls in two days. Out of curiosity, Willis went to the train station and spotted Theodore immediately ("He looked like a dude to make any hit with me.") Theodore said he was eager to begin his hunt, but Willis stopped him cold. He informed the dude that he did not work for anyone and goes and does "as I damn well please."[9] Theodore's charm and earnestness eventually won Willis over, who said the longer they talked, "the better I liked him." They quickly became good friends.

As Theodore made his way into Montana at the end of May 1903, he dashed off a telegram to John Willis asking that he meet him at his stop in the state's capitol, Helena. Willis agreed, but he said the reception committee was concerned about his presence at the train station. The committee, who "took themselves very seriously," informed Willis both "collectively and individually" of the manners he must exhibit when the president arrived. As the train came to a stop, Theodore walked out onto the station platform and asked for Willis. Hurriedly shaking the extended hands of committee members, Theodore brushed past them to see Willis, whereupon they both exchanged happy greetings as the wary committeemen watched.

Not having seen one another since Theodore's vice presidential inauguration, they looked each other over. Willis asked, "Where in hell did you get that pot belly?" The remark nearly caused the committee members to collapse. Theodore roared with laughter, "I didn't get it riding a cayuse."

"You know I made a man of you, and don't you spoil my work," Willis replied.

"Yes, and I made a Christian of you, and don't you spoil my work!"[10]

The smiles and laughter between the two old friends relieved the committeemen.[11] Theodore insisted his friend travel with him to Butte, refusing to take no for an answer. In a letter to John Hay, Theodore referred to Willis as "A Donatello of the Rocky Mountains—wholly lacking, however, the morbid self-consciousness which made Hawthorne's faun go out of his head because he had killed a man."[12]

Seth Bullock greeted Theodore as he got to his carriage. Turning to Mayor Frank Edwards and Senator J. M. Dixon, Theodore mentioned that he was going to take a sixty-mile horseback ride when he got to Laramie, Wyoming. "I didn't intend to go alone, and he would have to go with me," he stated, nodding to Bullock.

The procession parade made its way to the state capitol, where Theodore gave his speech from a granite coping next to the stairway. As Theodore stepped onto the coping, "a tawny St. Bernard dog, that had seemed greatly interested in the proceedings, jumped up beside the president." The dog looked at Theodore and then out at the crowd. Theodore petted the dog's head before someone grabbed the dog's collar to pull him down. "Don't hurt him, don't hurt him! Let him go, that's all right!" Theodore demanded. The dog was gently removed before he began his speech.[13] Theodore told the citizens that the state was "assured promise of a future greatness." Although the mines and ranches counted for much, he stated that water would be equally important to the state, observing that the "rapid fall of the rivers from the mountains" provides an "inexhaustible source of power" that would help in building up businesses. Irrigation would also play an important part in the state's success through irrigation ditches and reservoirs, making "this whole state blossom like the rose."[14]

As he left the state capitol for the train station, Reverend S. P. Watson of the African Methodist Episcopal Church presented him with a silver-bladed trowel with a gold-mounted ebony handle on behalf of the black people of Helena. The blade held the inscription "Spread the cement of human kindness to all mankind."[15]

The citizens of Helena were ecstatic with Theodore's visit, but the plans to cut one speech out left members of the trade and labor assembly "greatly disappointed." While many union members were assembling in the city auditorium expecting Theodore to deliver a speech relating to labor, they learned that the president would make a speech only at the state capitol. The union members were "up in arms," according to Howard O. Smith, president of the trades and labor assembly. Smith went on to ask "who is responsible for the president not speaking to the labor organizations, and this question 'someone' will have to answer."[16]

— ✦ —

In Butte, mine whistles signaled the president's arrival. As in other towns, people came from surrounding areas to see and hear Theodore speak. This wasn't his first time coming to Butte to make a speech. In 1900 Theodore was on a cross-country trip as the Republican vice presidential candidate, making numerous stops on behalf of the McKinley-Roosevelt ticket. "I had gone through Butte in the campaign of 1900, the major part of the inhabitants receiving me with frank hostility and enthusiastic cheers for Bryan. However, Butte is mercurial and its feelings had changed. The wicked, wealthy, hospitable, full-blooded little city welcomed me with wild enthusiasm of the most disorderly kind," he wrote John Hay.[17]

The town was broken into two different factions, based on rival mine owners. "National party lines count very little in Butte, where the fight was [Fritz Augustus] Heinze and anti-Heinze, ex-Senator [Thomas] Carter and Senator [William A.] Clark being the opposition," he recalled. Neither side was willing to relinquish control over Theodore's events in the city.[18] For Theodore, these actions "drove [him] wild" until he settled matters. The afternoon parade and speech would be "managed by the Heinze people," and the evening speech would fall to the anti-Heinze group. He also demanded that the banquet "contain fifty of each faction," presided over by the city's mayor, Patrick Mullins.[19]

The procession through the town "was rather more exhilarating than usual," and, Theodore noted, it "reduced the faithful secret service men very nearly to the condition of Bedlamites."[20]

> The crowd was filled with whooping enthusiasm and every kind of whiskey, and in their desire to be sociable broke the lines and jammed right up to the carriage. There were a lot of "rednecks" or dynamiters, the men who had taken part in the murderous Coeur d'Alene strike, who had been indulging in threats as to what they would do to me, and of course the city is a hotbed of violent anarchy.[21]
>
> Seth Bullock accordingly had gone down three days in advance and had organized for my personal protection a body-guard composed of old friends of his on whom he could rely, for the most part rough citizens and all of them very quick with a gun. By occupation they were, as he casually mentioned, for the major part gamblers and "sure thing" men. But they had no sympathy whatever with anarchy in any form.... They kept close watch over all who approached me, and I was far less nervous about being shot myself than about their shooting some exuberant enthusiast with peaceful intentions. Seth Bullock rode close beside the rear wheel of the carriage, a splendid-looking fellow with his size and supple strength, his strongly marked aquiline face with its big mustache, and the broad brim of his soft hat drawn down over his hawk eyes. However, nobody made a motion to attack me.[22]

Theodore's carriage arrived at the Finlen Hotel, and he made his way to the second-floor balcony of the hotel to speak to the crowd. As a band played before his introduction, Theodore asked Seth Bullock if he liked the music. "It's all right, but it's a little too far up the gulch," he replied.[23]

Glancing at the crowd, Theodore yelled out, "I want to see Fred Henrick when he comes along. He was on my ranch and he was in my regiment. Fred and I have punched cows and hunted and been in the campaign together." People in the crowd said they'd find him and bring him to the front. Eager people quickly shoved Fred to the front and Theodore told him to come up to the balcony. Shaking hands, Theodore said, "This beats embalmed beef, don't it?" He then related a story of how Fred had asked Theodore if he could go shoot *gorillas* in Cuba. Surprised at the request, Theodore asked why. "Them Spanish *gorillas*," Fred replied. Not only did Fred shoot some of the Spanish guerillas, Theodore noted, but he came back to camp with a guinea hen for dinner.[24]

Introducing Theodore to the crowd, Butte mayor Patrick Mullins mistakenly stated that the president was a "brave and gallant soldier who rode up the heights of San Diego Hill." Theodore smiled at the comment and replied, "You are heaping new honors on me, my good mayor."

Theodore said fifteen years ago he and John Willis were "traveling rough" in their hunt for a mountain goat. Stopping in Butte one morning, Theodore noted that he had "the best breakfast I ever ate at a two-bit restaurant."[25] He then talked about the need for a strong navy, the importance of laws, and how the average citizen must have decency, honesty, courage, and common sense. "In addition to honesty we need sanity, common sense, the cool head that knows what can be done and what cannot be done and shapes the course of man accordingly," he concluded.[26]

Theodore was presented with a gift from the black citizens of the city and later said, "I was genuinely touched by a representative of the colored citizens of Butte giving me a present from them, a miniature set of scales with a design of Justice holding them even." Walking across the street to the Thornton Hotel, he spent some time in a private room with John Willis. He asked his old friend about Romeo, the horse he had ridden on their hunting trips. Willis assured him that for his age, Romeo was in excellent health and running loose on his property, adding that he never let anyone else ride Romeo after their hunting trip. "We sat there quietly for two hours talking over old days and about hunting," Willis later recalled.[27]

The banquet in the hotel was called to order when Mayor Mullins used the handle of his knife and banged on the table, yelling, "Waiter, bring on the feed!" As Theodore later noted, the dinner "was interesting in many regards." Looking out at the people in the dining room, he noted the prominent citizens of Butte were made up of millionaires, professional gamblers, or labor leaders, and each man likely had been all three. Observing the hundred men from the two factions who were now his hosts, Theodore guessed half of them "had killed their man in a private war, or had striven to compass the assassination of an enemy." The two groups "fought one another with reckless ferocity," and could be allies or enemies in "every kind of business scheme, and companions in brutal revelry." Gazing at their "hard, strong, crafty faces," Theodore understood the millionaires had once been laborers, while the labor leaders hoped to become millionaires or, failing that, "pull down all who were." These millionaires spent their wealth in "every form of vicious luxury," but they were the men who "had built up their part of the West." Although these men detested each other, Theodore recognized they "were accustomed to taking their pleasure when they could get it, and they took it fast and hard with the meats and wines" at this banquet.[28]

As the meal proceeded, Conrad Kohrs, an old friend from their cattle days in the mid-1880s, told stories of hunting, prospecting, and Indian fighting in the early days of the state when it was still a territory. "This started Willis upon our feats when we had hunted bear and elk and caribou together in the great mountain forests," Theodore reminisced.[29] These stories continued, he related, as "many a man spoke up" to recall a story or incident in which he had met the president in those days. As the talking went on, Theodore discovered ("to my horror") that Seth Bullock had drunk too much *Who-Hit-John*. "I wanted him to go back to the train and go to bed," Theodore stated. "This he felt was ignominious. But he took off his gun, a long forty-four, and solemnly handed it to Loeb as a compromise."[30]

After the banquet, Theodore was driven in his carriage to Columbia Gardens in what was called "record time"—twenty-seven minutes. The *Anaconda Standard* noted that Theodore's carriage ride "was a novel experience and he [Theodore] was enough of a westerner thoroughly to enjoy it. His driver, John ("Fat Jack") Jones, was an experienced man with horses, something Theodore was quick to recognize and he complimented his skills. Malcolm Gillis of the trade and labor assembly told Jack what the president had said about his proficiency with the lines. "I knew that long before the president told me," Jack replied, which caused Theodore to break into one of his "hearty laughs."[31]

A "Roosevelt" banner was illuminated in red, white, and blue incandescent lights above the covered speaker's stand at Columbia Gardens. Noting that it was a pleasure to be invited to speak to the wageworkers of Butte, Theodore stated that the speech he was about to make was one that he would "make in just exactly the same language to any group of employers or any set of our citizens in any corner of this Republic."

I do not think so far as I know that I have ever promised beforehand anything I did not make a strong effort to make good afterward. It is sometimes very attractive and very pleasant to make any kind of a promise without thinking whether or not you can fulfil it; but in the after event it is always unpleasant when the time for fulfilling comes; for in the long run the most disagreeable truth is a safer companion than the most pleasant falsehood. . . . The man who by the use of his capital develops a great mine, the man who by the use of his capital builds a great railroad, the man who by the use of his capital either individually or joined with others like him does any great legitimate business enterprise, confers a benefit, not a harm, upon the community, and is entitled to be so regarded. He is entitled to the protection of the law, and in return he is to be required himself to obey the law. The law is no respecter of persons. The law is to be administered neither for the rich man as such, nor for the poor man as such. It is to be administered for every man, rich or poor, if he is an honest and law-abiding citizen; and it is to be invoked against any man, rich or poor, who violates it, without regard to which end of the social scale he may stand at, without regard to whether his offence takes the form of greed and cunning, or the form of physical violence; in either case if he violates the law, the law is to be invoked against him; and in so invoking it I have the right to challenge the support of all good citizens and to demand the acquiescence of every good man. I hope I will have it; but once for all I wish it understood that, even if I do not have it, I shall enforce the law. . . . My friends, it is sometimes easier to preach a doctrine under which the millennium will be promised off-hand if you have a particular kind of law, or follow a particular kind of conduct it is easier, but it is not better. The millennium is not here; it is some thousand years off yet. Meanwhile there must be a good deal of work and struggle, a good deal of injustice; we shall often see the tower of Siloam fall on the just as well as the unjust. We are bound in honor to try to remedy injustice, but if we are wise, we will seek to remedy it in practical ways.[32]

A man in military uniform attempted to secure a brief audience with Theodore as he made his way to his carriage, but a Secret Service agent pushed him back. "Let him alone," Theodore said. "Any man in the uniform of a United States soldier is my friend. I want to shake his hand." Theodore and the man in uniform spoke briefly, and he gave the president his address on a slip of paper.[33]

They waited three miles north of Pocatello, Idaho, for the train as the sun began warming them. Horses stamped their feet, occasionally snorting as they stood waiting for their riders to turn them loose. In the distance the train whistle shouted its lonely wail. The ears of the horses went up, alerted by the change of attitude in their riders, who quietly mumbled among themselves. As the train came closer, the riders suddenly kicked their mounts in the flanks with their feet and they were off at a mad gallop.

Fifty mounted Indians from the nearby Fort Hall Reservation let out a variety of war whoops and yells as they charged Theodore's train. As they drew closer, the train slowed and Theodore stepped out to the rear platform smiling broadly at the Indians "garbed in their old-time regalia." The riders escorted the train all the way to the city limits, where eight thousand people were waiting at the train station to greet the president.[34]

After the requisite procession through the city, Theodore spoke to the people from the pavilion at the local high school. Commenting that Pocatello was "a railroad town," he said his trip and his safety depended, night and day, "upon the vigilance, skill, nerve and fidelity of the railroad men." Relating his last talk with General William T. Sherman, Theodore said the war veteran told him that if he had to choose men from one occupation to make up his army, he would choose railroad men. Those men, related Theodore, had five qualities that make a good soldier: he accepts risk and danger, endures physical hardships, lives with irregular hours for sleep, acts on his own in time of emergency, and, finally, takes orders. "The qualities thus developed are of as good service in the field of citizenship in ordinary civil life as in military life," Theodore said.

He paid a "special acknowledgment" to the Indians who greeted his train, noting that many of them "are traveling along the white man's road and beginning not only to send their children to school, but to own cattle and to own property." Theodore stressed that the only outcome relating to the "Indian question" was to help them become property owners and be law-abiding and hard-working citizens. "When he is traveling that path and when he is doing his duty he is entitled to and he shall receive exactly as square a deal as anyone else," he asserted.

> After all, that is the fundamental principle of our government. In the last analysis what America stands for more than for aught else is for treating each man on his worth as a man; if he acts well in whatever walk of life, whatever his ancestry, his creed, his color, give him a fair chance; if he acts badly let nothing protect him from the hand of the law.[35]

Leaving Pocatello at nine o'clock, Theodore made stops in Shoshone, Glenn's Ferry, Mountain Home, Nampa, and finally Boise, the state capitol. The police were on alert as Police Chief Francis had received three letters threatening to blow up the grandstand during the president's speech. The letters all bore the same style of handwriting and were unsigned. The reason for the threat was that the grandstand was built by non-union carpenters. After checking the entire area, it was patrolled by a heavy police presence until Theodore's departure. Reporters and citizens were unaware of the potential threat that day, which was "thought to be the work of some irresponsible crank."[36]

Once Theodore's carriage arrived at the state capitol, he planted a rock sugar maple tree, not far from the red oak tree that President Benjamin Harrison planted on his visit in 1891. (The tree, dubbed "the Roosevelt Tree," was blown down in a 2006 windstorm.) Making his way up to the grandstand, Theodore passed "through a lane of children," often stopping to say hello and shake a child's hand. He reminded the assembled group of citizens that unlike mining, where the material is to be used up, forests and grasses cannot be treated that way. "On the contrary, we must recognize the fact that we have passed the stage when we can afford to tolerate the man whose object is simply to skin the land and get out," he stressed. "That man is not a valuable citizen. We do not want the absentee proprietor. It is not for him that we wish to develop irrigation. It is not for him that we must shape the grazing lands, or handle our forests. We must handle the water, the woods and the grasses, so that we will hand them on to our children, and our children's children in better, and not worse, shape than we got them." Commenting on how he was impressed with the "beautiful and fertile valley" as he arrived in Boise, it was accomplished by "the application of industry, intelligence, and water, to the soil." Having spent a large portion of his life in the mountains and the plains, Theodore said he felt "a peculiar pride" when he signed the National Irrigation Act.[37]

Throughout his presidency, Theodore continued to exhort the importance of conserving the forest and the land as a whole, as he noted in an Arbor Day speech in 1907:

> We of the older generation can get along with what we have, though with growing hardship, but in your full manhood and womanhood you will want what nature once so beautifully supplied and man so thoughtlessly destroyed; and because of that want you will reproach us, not for what we have used, but for what we have wasted.[38]

Once More in the Saddle: Utah and Wyoming

Don't draw unless you mean to shoot.

THEODORE ARRIVED IN OGDEN, UTAH, "UNDER A SKY AS AZUREOUS AS that famed to spread above the Grecian seas." The *Ogden Standard* observed his ride "through the gaily decked streets was one continuous ovation, a testimonial of the loyalty of the Utah citizens and an endorsement of the record of the nation's Chief Executive."[1]

In his speech, Theodore lauded the citizens of the state who had shown "the wisdom of trying to develop in every way the irrigated agriculture of the country." He added that there was "nothing of greater importance" to the well-being and prosperity of the country than the use of irrigation, noting the aftereffect to one portion of our country was an upshot to all. Acknowledging that neither prosperity nor adversity stops at a state line, Theodore observed that although prosperity "may come unequally," it does come somewhat to all, as does adversity. "And now you know the proverb 'The Lord helps those who help themselves'? If you throw all the duty of helping you on the Lord, he will throw it back on you," he said. "Now, it is the same way with your fellow men. Providence is not going to do everything for you, and the National Government cannot. All that the National Government can do is to try to give you a fair show to help you to the chance of doing your work under favorable conditions, and then the work has got to be done by you yourselves." Once again, he paid tribute not just to the men who fought in the Civil War, but also to the

195

women who endured the hardships of staying at home while the family's breadwinner went off to war. Theodore praised these women who did their best, accepting the possibility that their husbands might never come back; they deserved "just as much recognition" as the men who fought. "In fact, when I speak of good citizenship, I am just as apt to think of a woman as a man," he said, adding "no other citizen in the country has the equal claim upon us as the woman" who raised her children to be honorable citizens.[2]

With the "tremendous growth of our complex industrial civilization" raising new and unchartered problems, Theodore suggested there was a need to meet them with "advanced new methods." One approach he heartily endorsed was unflappable sanity. "If there is one quality which we must try to eradicate from our dealings with any of the social and industrial problems which arise from time to time, it is the quality of hysterics—hysteria," Theodore said. "Banish brutality, envy, greed, hatred—banish them all; and banish with them all forms of emotional hysteria. We need cool-headed, sane common sense in dealing with the problems that confront the nation, just as we need it in dealing each with the problems that confront him or her in his or her own household."[3]

As Theodore was calling for untroubled sanity to solve problems, the Secret Service agents and Ogden local police were dealing with just the opposite. Advised by Theodore's Secret Service men, Ogden police took a man into custody and held him "until the departure of the presidential party." The man, identified as A. Corn, was a suspected anarchist and had arrived in the city a few days ahead of Theodore. Police officers had observed him handing out "inflammatory literature with a decided anarchistic flavor." When he was arrested, Corn was found to be carrying a "long, sharp murderous dagger," and he was charged with "distributing forbidden literature." Officers also arrested a Spaniard who had been boasting he could outshoot the president and intended to challenge him to a target contest. Newspapers stated the man, who claimed he would "make more bullseyes than President Roosevelt," was likely harmless, but he would never get the opportunity to see who was the better shot.[4]

Salt Lake City presented a parade in Theodore's honor. Before taking his place on the grandstand in front of the city and county building, he spoke briefly to several hundred schoolchildren, reminding them of his often-quoted adage "when you play, play hard; when you work, don't play at all."

A marching band passing the grandstand played "*Garryowen*," a personal favorite of the president. "By George, that's bully!" Theodore said with his typical broad smile. A group of schoolchildren stood in front of the grandstand as many Rough Riders and cowboys rode by at a gallop, some getting their horses to buck in front of the president. Theodore stood up and yelled at the riders, "Boys, don't gallop your horses! The little folk might get hurt!" Riders quickly pulled up their horses to a walk as they went by, and Theodore nodded in approval, yelling to a group of Rough Riders, "Boys, you are all right!" When the last rider passed the grandstand, he jokingly stated, "Now come the prominent citizens in carriages."[5]

At the conclusion of the parade, Theodore and his party "made a flying start for the Tabernacle." Crowds had formed at the south gate of the tabernacle by eight o'clock in the morning. "The minute they opened, the mass surged toward the aperture, crowding, pushing and struggling as crowds will even when there is not the slightest need for it," commented the *Salt Lake Tribune*. Squeezing past the gateway, the crowd broke into a "cow trot" toward the tabernacle.[6]

Inside the tabernacle, the word "Welcome" stood above the huge organ "ablaze with electric lights." Under it was a life-sized portrait of Theodore in his Rough Rider uniform, and a national flag hung full length between the welcome sign and portrait. The front of the choir loft was "festooned with bunting and broad strips of red, white and blue cloth" that were intertwined around the entire face of the gallery. Emma Ramsey, knighted the "Nightingale of Utah," sang "The Flag without a Stain." Theodore was so taken by Miss Ramsey's voice that he requested she sing the song again. "The singer then repeated the last verse of this beautiful composition. At the close of this stanza President Roosevelt took her hand and thanked her again," noted the *Salt Lake Tribune*.[7] Senator Thomas Kearns introduced the president, and Theodore was greeted by a "tempest of cheers" and a sea of hats, handkerchiefs, canes, and newspapers "dancing madly" inside the tabernacle.

Theodore began his speech by noting how the pioneers and those who came after them chose a land that had been called a desert and "you literally, not figuratively, you literally made the wilderness blossom as the rose." Those pioneers, he observed, chose to keep the land and pass it on to their children and their children's children. He wished that "all our people from one ocean to the other," but specifically those living in the arid and semiarid regions, the great plains, and the mountains would "approach the problem of taking care of the physical resources of the country in the spirit which has made Utah what it is."

> Here you have shown your wonderful capacity to develop the earth so as to make both irrigated agriculture and stock-raising in all its forms two great industries. When you deal with a mine you take the ore out of the earth and take it away, and in the end exhaust the mine. The time may be very long in coming before it is exhausted, or it may be a short time; but in any event, mining means the exhaustion of the mine. But that is exactly what agriculture does not and must not mean. So far from agriculture properly exhausting the land, it is always the sign of a vicious system of agriculture if the land is rendered poorer by it. The direct contrary should be the fact. After the farmer has had the farm for his life, he should be able to hand it to his children as a better farm than it was when he had it.
>
> In these regions, in the Rocky Mountain regions, it is especially incumbent upon us to treat the question of the natural pasturage, the question of the forests, and the question of the use of the waters, all from the one standpoint the standpoint of the far-seeing statesman, of the far-seeing citizen, who wishes to preserve and not to exhaust the resources of the country, who wishes to see those resources come into the hands not of a few men of great wealth, least of all into the hands of a few men who will speculate in them; but be distributed among many men, each of whom intends to make his home in the land.[8]

After his speech, Theodore was taken to the home of Senator and Mrs. Kearns for lunch, which he said "had points of merits." The guests included a Catholic bishop, an Episcopal bishop, and a Mormon apostle, as well as various men and women of distinction. "Among the latter was one of the plural wives of the Mormon elder," Theodore wrote. "Most of the women were just such as one would meet at Washington, and some of them just such as one would meet in Boston. We discussed *The Virginian*, and the Passion Play, and Wagner, and the flora of the Rocky Mountains, and John Burroughs' writings, and Senator Ankeny's fondness for Bacon's *Essays*; and there at the table were two bishops and the apostle, the plural wife, one Gentile who had done battle with the Danites in the long past; and in short, every combination of beliefs and systems of thought and civilizations that were ages apart." Theodore also noted the "queer combination" he found in many of the leading men in Utah with a "fanaticism" in their ages of faith, yet in nonreligious matters the men displayed "the shrewdest and most materialistic common sense."[9]

———

Secretary of the Navy William Moody was "delighting in the conversations" with Seth Bullock as the Roosevelt Special headed into Wyoming, especially when "Seth happened to be touching upon incidents in the past in which he and I had both taken part," Theodore recalled. He related Seth's story of when he first wore a sheriff's badge and was forced to kill two men. The lawman commented that he felt like getting out of politics. During their trip through Wyoming, Seth crossed paths with men he had arrested but who were now reformed, as well as others he had either fought for or against.[10]

When Seth was relating a tale of an Indian fight he was involved in, the name Bill Hamilton came up. Theodore brought up an incident of the man's son, known as Three-Seven Bill Jones.

I knew the son well. He had on one occasion stopped a mail train by shooting at the conductor's feet to make him dance. Two or three days after, I had been over at Mingersville *[Mingusville]*, and in a wretched little hotel had been put in a room with two beds and three other men, one of them was Bill Jones. He and I had slept in the same bed. In the middle of the night there was a crash, the door was burst in, a lantern was flashed in my face, and as I waked up I found a gun had been thrust in my face too. But I was dropped at once, a man saying "He ain't the man. Here—here he is. Now Bill, come along quietly." Bill responded, "All right, don't sweat yourselves. I'm coming quietly," and they walked out of the room. We lit a light. I tried to find out from my companions if they knew the reasons for what had happened, but they possessed an alkali etiquette in such matters, the chief features of which are silence, wooden impassiveness, and uncommunicativeness. So, we blew out the light and went to sleep again.[11]

———

"The sun was shining warm and pleasant; the streets were free from dust; the air crisp and invigorating, and the town, in honor of the day, was handsomely decorated with flags and bunting, and pictures of the distinguished guest," exalted the *Cheyenne Daily Leader* covering Theodore's arrival in Laramie.[12] When his train came to a stop at the depot, Theodore, who was wearing a cutaway coat, riding trousers, leather leggings, cavalry hat, and spurs, stepped off the rear platform and walked up to thank the engineer, Tom McHugh. He then greeted the reception committee, Senator Francis Warren and members of the Grand Army of the Republic.

The Rawlins band and a troop of cowboy cavalry consisting of many former Rough Riders led Theodore's carriage to the entrance of the University of Wyoming. Standing before a crowd of citizens, Grand Army of the Republic and Spanish-American War veterans, students, and military cadets, Theodore stated that the man in civilian life, as in the military, must be "a decent man first of all, or else no amount of strength or courage will have the power to make his life anything but an evil one." Loyalty to himself and his associates were equally important, for without them, he commented, it will not make him a power for good. "In fact, the greater his strength, the greater his skill, the more influence for evil he will exert. The foundation of every character, whether that of a man or of a nation, must be a spirit of decency. The sum of every nation's character is made up of individual characters, and as the stream can rise no higher than its source, it follows that the character of every single individual tends to raise or lower to that of the nation. A man who does a wrongful act sins against the State as well as against himself," Theodore discerned. He reminded the students that the greatness of the state depended on how they play their part. The education they were receiving granted them "no special privileges, but on the contrary adds responsibility."[13]

He was then ushered by Senator Warren to the east side of the university's main building where a "beautiful grey horse" with "a silver mounted saddle" stood patiently waiting. Senator Warren stated that his friends in Cheyenne, learning of his desire to ride into the city, had the saddle made especially for this "powerful and fleet charger which will carry you over the first section of your journey." Presenting a pair of silver inlaid spurs, Warren teased Theodore he should not establish a "new rough riding record" on his sixty-mile jaunt. The senator also commented that the people of Laramie and Cheyenne appreciated that he was "willing to exchange the luxury of a Pullman for man's four-footed friend."[14]

Theodore and thirteen invited guests would now head off on a sixty-mile horseback ride from Laramie to Cheyenne. When this ride was first suggested to him, Theodore leapt at the chance, waving aside any objections by the Secret Service agents or secretary Loeb. For Theodore, this was another adventure, something boys dream about. "The mounts provided for the President between Laramie and Cheyenne are a magnificent lot of horses, the finest types of Wyoming's celebrated riding animals, famed for endurance, speed and easy gaits," noted the *Cheyenne Daily Leader*. Theodore wasted no time and quickly mounted the horse named Teddy. He was known to have "a slow rack and an easy canter," which made for a very comfortable ride. "He was selected with particular care for the first relay, which crosses the high rides of the hills east of Laramie, the hardest portion of the trip," a newspaper stated.[15]

The cowboy cavalry escorted Theodore and his party toward the eastern end of the city. Reaching the south end of Second Street, the group of cowboys and Rough Riders rode to one side of the road, letting Theodore and his party pass by. Trotting past the riders, he raised his hat to them, "I thank you gentlemen. Goodbye." Nudging his horse in the flanks Theodore led his party off in a gallop. A mile out of town, the group dismounted "to tighten their saddle-girths." While they did this, Senator Warren read rules for the riders. No one was to ride beside the president except upon his invitation, and then must be careful not to let his horse's head get beyond the president's stirrup. The rest of the group, unless "called upon by the president" must ride at least ten yards behind him, and anyone with "an unruly horse must keep well in the rear."[16]

The group rode to Tie City, fifteen miles southeast of Laramie, where they changed mounts. Theodore would now ride a buckskin named Yellowbird, who was known for its speed and endurance. The horse would "carry the President over this relay without turning a hair." Ora Haley, the owner, stated nobody would ever ride the horse again "after the President gets off his back."[17] Theodore led the group without slowing his pace. It was observed that the pace "while not unusually fast, was speedy enough to make several of the escort look, if they did not feel, uncomfortable."[18]

From there they made their way to McGee's ranch, crossing over a ridge with an altitude of eight thousand feet. "As mile after mile was left behind, the President seemed to enjoy the outing more and more, and frequently addressed jovial remarks to the escort. There was little ceremony observed," reported the *Cheyenne Tribune*.[19] At McGee's ranch, horses were once again changed, this time Theodore riding a roan, Rosy Roan. R. S. Van Tassell, who owned a twenty-one-thousand-acre ranch in the area, considered the horse to be one of the "best in the bunch."[20] Theodore and his group arrived at the Van Tassell ranch at 12:45, while a half-mile from the ranch, his train stopped in Islay, and the rest of those traveling with the president were taken by carriage to the ranch. After a bountiful lunch, the guests returned to the train while Theodore and his group continued their ride. The horse Theodore rode this time was a familiar one. Jim was a bay horse that stood sixteen hands high and was known as "one of the finest saddle horses in the west." During his 1900 vice presidential campaign, Theodore had ridden Jim when he visited the area and requested to have the animal in his string of horses.[21]

This portion of the ride continued at a "more somber pace" as they drew closer to Cheyenne. Six miles from the city, Governor Fenimore Chatteron and a "delegation of Cheyenne citizens" rode out to greet

Theodore and his party. It was one of the more unusual greetings the president was given by elected officials on his grand tour. All seated on horseback, Governor Chatteron stated that they greeted him not only as the nation's chief executive, "but because you are Theodore Roosevelt, the man who has dared to do, and daring has done, things ever looking to the highest thought, to the material uplifting of all conditions of men, and to the honor and integrity of our nation." Theodore thanked the governor for his "kind welcome and generous words." Referring to his ride, he noted that he had "enjoyed it beyond expression."[22]

The party swung into Fort Russell, which was headquartered in Cheyenne, where the Thirteenth Artillery fired a salute. The blast of the cannon alerted the city's citizens that their honored guest would soon arrive. At Fort Russell, he spent twenty minutes in Major Foster's building before he and the major rode past the Thirteenth Cavalry, explaining that time constraints did not allow him to review the troops.[23] As they rode past, "the Thirteenth wheeled into line and followed into the city."

The Roosevelt Special pulled into the Union Pacific depot and people rushed to see the president exit the train. They were disappointed when they saw only members of his group exiting onto the depot walkway.

> Almost before people were aware of it, Theodore Roosevelt had entered Cheyenne. . . . Down a mountain valley he came in a whirl of dust, and at his heels there clattered a gallant company. Superbly mounted, he rode with a plainsman's ease, forward in the saddle and with shoulders loose. The west was written in every line of his frame, and clothes and bearing; he might have been a ranchman leading a round-up gang for all the chance observer knew—yet there was something about him, an indescribable air of subdued authority; that marked him a greater leader of man. . . . Many presidents have made trips through states over which they rule, and in the very early days presidents rode through the country on horseback for lack of a better means of transportation, but it remained for President Roosevelt to ride fifty miles over hill and dale for the joy that a gallant steed and crisp cool air gives to a man who has learned them both.[24]

Theodore refused to trade in his horse, Ragalong, for a carriage to ride through the city. (He switched horses for the final ride when the party reached Tassell's windmill.) Along the parade route, he would greet the children "with a special wave of his hat and a smile which meant volumes. The responsive little hands that returned the greeting completed a picture prettier than the brush of any artist could portray." As his ride came to an end when he reached the grandstand at Fifteenth and Ferguson Streets, a newspaper reporter commented that Theodore's power of endurance was "remarkable for a man so little used of late years to strenuous western life." Of all who accompanied him on the long ride, Theodore looked, according to the reporter, "the freshest."[25]

Noting to the crowd that this was Decoration Day,[26] Theodore paid tribute to the veterans of the Civil War and Spanish-American War. Praising the men who "proved their truth by their endeavor, whose metal rang true on war's red blood-stained fields," he also was very proud of the men of the Grand Army who gave him "the most cordial response when I pay tribute to the valor of the men who wore gray." Returning to his recurring theme that the lessons learned in the military could also be used in civil life, he stressed that to "make this republic true to its promise," they could not, as citizens, "afford to sunder in the deep matters along lines other than the lines of conduct which separates good citizens from bad citizens." Theodore reminded the audience that there was good and bad "in every class, in every creed, in every occupation." He again stated his long-held belief that a man who was a "decent citizen" and good to his family, his neighbors, and the country was more worthwhile than the man who acted the opposite.[27]

"I would preach to my countrymen not the life of ease; not the effortless life of comfort, of avoidance of risk, and avoidance of trouble," he went on. "I would ask them not to strive to find out the things that are easiest to do, but the things that are best worth doing." Theodore observed that the nation must confront the great problems it faces from within and without. "We are not to be excused if we blink at them, or if with selfish timidity we say we don't have to settle it in our day, let those that come after us attend to it," he cautioned.

Each one of us is his brother's keeper, each one of us is the keeper of his sons, the son of each one of us is the keeper of the generations that are to come after us, and we must strive so to handle ourselves that when those generations arise they will find that we have taken the right steps in beginning the solution of the problems that will confront them, as they confront us. And we must attack them in a spirit of courage; in a spirit of love and also in a spirit of common sense.

This nation in dealing with foreign affairs with other nations should follow just that which we regard as right for a private citizen. In my day there was one kind of man who was not respected in the West. It was a man who talked and boasted and threatened, and when the pinch came, didn't make good. Just so with our nation. In other words, act in accordance with a proverb I heard in the old days when I myself lived in the cow country. The proverb ran: "Don't draw unless you mean to shoot."[28]

———

Sunday morning, May 31, Theodore refrained from any public speeches or processions. After breakfast in his room at the Inter-Ocean Hotel, he held meetings with Secretary of Agriculture James Wilson and Secretary of the Navy William Moody and then dictated necessary letters. Carriages arrived at 10:30 to take him and his party to the First Methodist Church for Sunday services. As with other previous church services during his trip, the pastor, Reverend Forsyth, was told not to deviate from his normal sermon and to make no mention of Theodore. When the services concluded, parishioners waited in their pews until Theodore and his group had exited the church. He then went to the residence of Mr. and Mrs. Joseph Carey, a former senator for the state. The luncheon "was informal, but elegantly appointed."[29]

As on other Sundays, Theodore went on a horseback ride to the Terry Ranch, which was part of the Warren Livestock Company, owned by Senator Warren. Although Theodore and his party left Cheyenne at 3:30 in the afternoon, they did not reach Terry Ranch until after six o'clock in the evening, primarily due to visiting the "numerous ranches of the company." Waiting to greet Theodore were about "one hundred prominent Wyomingites," who were introduced to Theodore by Senator Warren. The five-course meal was held in the dining room of the ranch house for Theodore, Senator Warren, Joseph Carey, Dr. Rixley, and a few others; the other guests ate in a large tent erected on the ranch. When dinner was completed, Theodore and his party rode back to Cheyenne, covering the nearly thirty miles in one hour.[30]

Since he would not be in Cheyenne for its traditional "Frontier Days" in July, a special exhibition was held for him at Frontier Park on Monday morning. Once Theodore and his party were seated in the stands, Senator Warren brought Ragalong to the front of the grandstand. He stated that on behalf of the citizens of Douglas, Wyoming, he had the honor of presenting the horse as a gift to Theodore. Proving his loyalty and affection to his new owner, Ragalong knelt down on his two front legs and bowed his head. Theodore was delighted by the horse's actions and announced he would call him Wyoming. Speaking to the nearly twelve thousand people in Frontier Park, Theodore said he would be proud to ride so fine a horse in Washington, adding that the cow country of Wyoming "produces the finest horses in the world." He told reporters that the horse was "a rocking chair to ride," even across rough country. "I couldn't have had a gift that would have pleased me more."[31]

The exhibition began with a display of "the dexterity of Wyoming cowboys in that daring and nerve-trying ordeal" a cowboy goes through every day during a roundup. Other events included bucking horses, a stakes race, steer roping, riding wild steers, and a ladies' cow-pony race. Thad Sowder, the champion rodeo rider in the world, rode Steamboat, "one of the most notorious buckers in the country." Theodore later said, "As for the gentlemen who have been riding these horses, while I wish it distinctly understood that personally I prefer the gait of the one that was given to me—I like my horse to do things horizontally rather than vertically—still I am very proud of them as Americans."[32]

When Theodore saw the Cowboy chuck wagon in Hugo, Colorado, he could not resist sharing a meal. He shakes hands with the lead cook, Jack Kepple, as John Hayman (in cowboy hat) looks on. Kepple, who hired Hayman as his assistant, called him "as good a camp man that ever drew a breath." THEODORE ROOSEVELT COLLECTION, HOUGHTON LIBRARY, HARVARD UNIVERSITY

Theodore helps himself to a steak from the Dutch oven. As he ate his steak from the back of the chuck wagon, he exclaimed, "This is bully!" AUTHOR'S COLLECTION

As his train took on water at Deer Trail, Colorado, Theodore stepped down from the train and spent several minutes speaking with nearly two dozen people who had hoped to get a glimpse of him. They were not disappointed.
THEODORE ROOSEVELT COLLECTION, HOUGHTON LIBRARY, HARVARD UNIVERSITY

Throughout his tour, Theodore made it a point to thank the various train engineers and firemen, as illustrated here during a stop at Emery Gap in New Mexico Territory.
AUTHOR'S COLLECTION

Above: Theodore speaking to a large crowd in Albuquerque. THEODORE ROOSEVELT COLLECTION, HOUGHTON LIBRARY, HARVARD UNIVERSITY AUTHOR'S COLLECTION

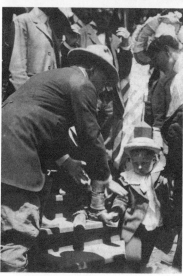

Theodore loved children and never missed an opportunity to greet a child, like this young boy at the Grand Canyon. THEODORE ROOSEVELT COLLECTION, HOUGHTON LIBRARY, HARVARD UNIVERSITY AUTHOR'S COLLECTION

As Theodore began his ride around the Grand Canyon, a photographer caught a Secret Service agent holding back a man as the president rode by.

When his train arrived in Redlands, California, Theodore was sitting in the fireman's seat, to the delight of onlookers.

Theodore watches the Fiesta of the Flowers as it makes its way up Broadway in Los Angeles.
THEODORE ROOSEVELT COLLECTION, HOUGHTON LIBRARY, HARVARD UNIVERSITY

Visiting the Redwoods in Santa Cruz, Theodore was incensed by the signs placed on the trees, like the one behind him. He made his feelings known, and after he returned from a walk among the trees, all signs had been removed.
AUTHOR'S COLLECTION

Theodore struck this iconic pose while camping on Glacier Point in Yosemite. This image came to represent his determination to preserve and to protect America's wilderness for generations to come. AUTHOR'S COLLECTION

ON THIS SITE PRESIDENT THEODORE ROOSEVELT SAT BESIDE A CAMPFIRE WITH JOHN MUIR ON MAY 17. 1903 AND TALKED FOREST GOOD. MUIR URGED THE PRESIDENT TO WORK FOR PRESERVATION OF PRICELESS REMNANTS OF AMERICA'S WILDERNESS. AT THIS SPOT ONE OF OUR COUNTRY'S FOREMOST CONSERVATIONISTS RECEIVED GREAT INSPIRATION.

The Bridalveil Meadows, where Theodore and John Muir camped on their last night in Yosemite, is now designated with this sign. AUTHOR'S COLLECTION

Theodore and his group of riders during the sixty-mile horseback ride from Laramie to Cheyenne, Wyoming. (Left to right: W. W. Daley, Otto Gramm, Senator Francis Warren, Deputy Marshal Joe Lefors, Theodore, Dr. Rixley, F. A. Hadsell, J. Atherley, Fred Porter, and John Ernest. Seth Bullock and W. L. Park are obscured by others.) THEODORE ROOSEVELT COLLECTION, HOUGHTON LIBRARY, HARVARD UNIVERSITY

Theodore was the first U.S. president who was part of the emerging new media of the twentieth century. Whether it was in newspapers, magazine articles, infant newsreels, or stereoscopic cards, Theodore was constantly before the public's eyes. Underwood and Underwood of New York City produced numerous stereo cards detailing Theodore's 1903 Great Loop Tour, allowing the public to "see" their president in an early version of 3-D. AUTHOR'S COLLECTION

Theodore once said, "It is hard to fail, but it is worse never to have tried to succeed." AUTHOR'S COLLECTION

Last Stops: Iowa, Illinois, and Indiana

I'd rather hear them sing than that they'd hear me screech.

THE WEATHER FRONT MOVING THROUGH THE GREAT PLAINS IN LATE May was expected to provide some rain in various states. No one was concerned at first, since rainstorms on the plains at that time of year were expected occurrences.

However, the storm proved to be anything but normal. Heavy rains unleashed their wrath on areas of Oklahoma, Kansas, Nebraska, Iowa, and Missouri starting May 28. During the next four days, rivers overran their banks, flooding cities and farmlands alike. Farmers watched helplessly as their crops washed away, and the rising waters in towns and cities forced residents onto their roofs. (One woman rescued from the roof of her second-story home in Iowa was still holding her dead child.) In Nebraska, the loss of the corn crop was estimated to be $1,500,000.[1] Railroad lines were "seriously crippled" in certain locations, and many telegraph lines were damaged or destroyed. Tornados only increased the misery, touching down in parts of Iowa and Ohio. As the rain subsided and rivers began to recede, a new problem loomed: contagious diseases raised their ugly heads.[2] The May 29 headline of the *Topeka Daily Capital* summed up the situation: "Heavy Rains Put Kansas in a Bad Fix."

Theodore received news of the flooding while in Cheyenne and quickly dashed off a telegram to Kansas governor Willis Bailey to ask if federal authorities could be of assistance. Bailey responded that "our people deeply appreciate the solicitude shown by your dispatch." He added that the town of Topeka is "heroically meeting the situation," but future developments would show "extent of need."[3] As Theodore's train passed through much of the flooded districts in Iowa, he had a firsthand view of the damage. "For many miles no land was in sight," commented Davenport's *Daily Times*. "Trees, farm houses and telegraph poles seemed growing from a great sea, as tracks of the Illinois Central were just on a level with the crest of the flood."[4]

Due to the heavy rains, the Rock Island Railroad brought in "a train load of gravel" to fill in the Denison depot grounds in order to provide the big crowd "standing room out of the mud and water." (Denison was not experiencing any floodwaters.) Upon his arrival, Theodore participated in a carriage ride through the city before returning to the train depot. As he stepped up to speak, hundreds of white doves were released from the crowd in front of him.[5]

> At this time, as I enter your beautiful State, there have come calamities upon our people here in Iowa, and to an even greater degree, in Kansas and Missouri. . . . We have Biblical authority, as well as the authority of common sense, for the statement that the rain falls on the just and the unjust alike. When the hand of the Lord is heavy upon any body of men, the wisdom of man can do but little. Now and then in our country, from drought, from floods, from pestilence, trouble and misfortune will come, but, oh friends, as I drove through your city this morning, and now as I look at you, the men and women of this State, I know that all of your troubles are temporary, that misfortunes will be met and overcome, because in heart and hand the American citizen is able to win his way in the long run.[6]

After leaving Denison, Theodore made six additional stops before spending the night in Dubuque.[7] In Cedar Falls, Theodore was serenaded by schoolchildren singing their school song. Theodore was waiting to speak, and Treasury Secretary Leslie Shaw attempted to quiet the children. "Never mind," Theodore told Shaw. "I'd rather hear them sing than that they'd hear me screech."[8] After a banquet at the Dubuque Club, Theodore retired to his train for the evening. His train was parked in the station yard, under guard of a group of volunteers made up of members of the Grand Army of the Republic and National Guard. Before he went to his room, Theodore thanked the men for offering to protect him and wished them "a quiet night."[9]

———

The following morning, June 3, would be "the busiest day of his trip," with Theodore giving nine speeches, eight of them outdoors and several in the rain. The Roosevelt Special pulled into the Freeport, Illinois, depot and, after the customary greetings, Theodore was taken to the site of the 1858 debate between Abraham Lincoln and Stephen Douglas. Although his time in the city was brief, he "could not resist" the opportunity to dedicate a monument and honor the memory of his favorite president.

> In all history I do not believe that there is to be found an orator whose speeches will last as enduringly as certain speeches of Lincoln. And in all history, with the sole exception of the man who founded the republic, I do not think there will be found another statesman at once so great and so single hearted in his devotion to the weal of his people. We cannot too highly honor him.[10]

In Aurora, former Civil War colonel and steel magnate John Lambert intended to travel to Joliet with Theodore and had his private car attached to the Roosevelt Special. When Theodore learned of the man's actions—Lambert never asked the president for permission—he immediately vetoed the arrangement "in emphatic terms." Theodore informed Lambert that such action would not be allowed, as many other men wanted to attach their private cars to his train during the trip. He refused every request and no exception would be made.[11] Returning to his train in Joliet after giving a speech, Theodore found several Civil War veterans standing alongside the train "as guard of honor." Delaying his departure, he spoke to the men, stating they were always entitled to a place of honor in American affairs.

Comments by the mayor of the small town of Dwight likely caused many in the Democratic Party a severe case of apoplexy. The mayor, a Democrat, stated to the crowd at the train station that he considered Theodore "the ideal American citizen." He went on to say that he supported the president's actions and would "support [him] for re-election." Touched by the man's words, Theodore told the audience that if they were all good Americans, there was "enough platform for all of us to stand on." In closing, Theodore once again thanked the mayor for his words: "I prize more than I can say such words as have been uttered by the mayor and I assure you I shall do my best to try and deserve them."[12]

After staying overnight at the Illinois Hotel in Bloomington, Theodore was scheduled to arrive in the town of Lincoln at nine o'clock. It would be a simple stop, greeting reception members and speaking to the public before leaving for Springfield.

All that changed when policemen found a satchel of dynamite.

The satchel was found near the Chicago Alton tracks, only a few feet from where Theodore would step off his train. Police wired Secret Service agents and informed them of their ongoing investigation, which suggested that it was most likely another plot to kill the president. The *Chicago Tribune* offered a different version in its story, titled "Dynamite, but No Plot." The newspaper reported that police officers found a single stick of dynamite in a corncrib, near the tracks of the railroad. The single explosive stick belonged to a workingman who claimed he used dynamite as part of his job. He placed the stick in the corncrib rather than risk carrying it home and having it there overnight.[13] Although the report about lawmen finding a satchel of dynamite was carried by several newspapers across the country, the *Chicago Tribune* is the only one to state that it was a single dynamite stick belonging to an unnamed worker. It appears that the latter version was never picked up by any of the news wires. Was it an assassination attempt? Or did a worker simply forget to leave the stick of dynamite at work? It appears no one will ever know for certain.

Arriving in Springfield at 10:15 the following morning, Theodore's carriage took him through the streets of the state capitol and on to Oak Ridge Cemetery. Standing at the monument that was President Lincoln's gravesite, Theodore looked out at the crowd, which included numerous members of the Grand Army of the Republic, as well as the guard around the monument. (The guards were black soldiers from the Twenty-Fourth and Twenty-Fifth Infantry Regiment of the U.S. Army.) "It is a very great pleasure for me to see you today, the veterans in a double sense, you who represent the navy, the Union, and the army, and all else to which Americans should, without regard to any minor differences, be one in their allegiance," he said. "Let me say one word: It seems fitting that the guard around the tomb of Lincoln should be composed of colored soldiers. It was my own good fortune at Santiago to serve beside colored troops. A man who is good enough to shed his blood for his country is good enough to be given a square deal afterwards."[14]

From the cemetery, he went to the dedication ceremonies of the new Springfield arsenal.[15] The immense hall was "packed to the doors" with an audience waiting to hear the president. Theodore told the audience that over the years he had met many men who knew Abraham Lincoln personally. Commenting that Lincoln and his memory of greatness will "loom ever larger through the centuries to come,"

It is a good thing for us, by speech, to pay homage to the memory of Abraham Lincoln, but it is an infinitely better thing for us in our lives to pay homage to his memory in the only way in which that homage can be effectively paid, by seeing to it that this republic's life, social and political, civic and industrial, is shaped now in accordance with the ideals which Lincoln preached and which all his life long he practiced. The greatness of our forefathers must serve not as an excuse to us for failing to do our duties in return, but as a spur to make us feel that we are doubly recreant to them as well as to ourselves if we fail to rise level with the standards they set. . . . I envy no man a life of ease, and I feel little but contempt for him if his only ideal is to lead a life of ease. We should reserve our feeling of admiration for the men who have difficult work to do but work eminently worth doing and do it well. The problems that face us as a nation today are different from the problems which Lincoln and the men of his generation had to face. Different methods must be devised for solving them, but the spirit in which we approach them must be the same as the spirit with which Lincoln and his fellows in council, his followers in war, approached their problems, or else this nation will fail. But it will not fail—it will succeed because we still have in us the spirit of the men of '61. . . . This is not and never shall be a government of a plutocracy. This is not and never shall be a government of a mob. It is a government of liberty, by, under and through the law. A government in which no man is to be permitted either to domineer over the less well off or to plunder the better off. It is a government in which man is to be guaranteed his rights and in return in which it is to be seen that he does not wrong his fellows. The supreme safety of our country is to be found in the fearless and honest administration of the law of the land. And it makes not the slightest difference whether the offense against the law takes the form of cunning and greed on the one hand, or of physical violence on the other. In either case the law breaker must be held accountable and the law breaking stopped. And when any executive undertakes to enforce the law, he is entitled to the support of every decent man, rich or poor, no matter what form the law breaking has taken, he is entitled to the support of all men in his efforts. And if he is worth his salt, he will enforce the law whether he gets the support or not. All men are not merely wicked, but foolish, if they ask privileges to violate the law. All men are not only wicked but foolish if they complain because they are forced to obey the law. But the most foolish man in making such complaints is the rich man; for the rich man owes his very existence, his prosperity to the fact that the law throws its mantle around him, and he therefore is twice over foolish, if in any way he permits reverence for the law to be broken down in a community like ours. . . . I ask that as a nation we approach the new problems in the spirit with which Lincoln and the men of Lincoln's time approached the problems they solved—a spirit of courage and resolution, a spirit of the broadest kindliness, a spirit of genuine brotherhood and love for all men.[16]

As his train headed to Indianapolis, the newspaper reporters who had been traveling for two months with Theodore brought him the keys to the dining car, *Gilsey*. "Fellow Americans, I accept the keys of the diner in the same proud spirit in which they are offered," he said. As he was led by the reporters to the dining car, the two porters, Letcher and Smith, lined up with brooms held in the military stance of present arms and stated to Theodore that they were his national guard. Entering the dining car, Theodore was greeted "with a wild yell by the entire party." He usually ate dinner in his car during the trip, but tonight he was one of the boys.[17]

———

Theodore's last official stop and speech was in Danville, Illinois. Arriving just after six o'clock in the evening, Theodore greeted the waiting crowd, which had gathered and waited at the city's train station since noon. (Newspapers estimated that the crowd numbered more than ten thousand people.) The city was the hometown of Congressman Joseph Cannon, who would take over as Speaker of the House in November 1903.[18] Theodore praised Cannon's actions in protecting "the interests of the nation, the interest of the people as a whole, from the improper demands of localities and individuals." He went on to thank the members of the Grand Army of the Republic, noting "to whom we owe it that we have a nation to be proud of today." Theodore also paid thanks to the officers and men of the National Guard. "As a nation we must ever keep in mind the debt we owe to the regular army of the United States and the national guard of the several states; and nothing can be done better than to show in every way by our actions that we support them," he stated.[19]

Theodore made one last stop in Indianapolis while his train took on water. A crowd of five thousand people waited to catch a glimpse of their president, who stepped out on the train's rear platform. "I have been to the Atlantic to the Pacific and now well nigh back again to the Atlantic, and the thing that has struck me more than aught else wherever I have been is the fundamental unity of our people. And another thing, I went on my trip a pretty good expansionist; I come back a better one, because, having seen our people on the Atlantic coast, in the Mississippi valley, in the great plains, and among the Rockies and on the Pacific coast, I fail to see how any man can look at them and not see that inevitability they belong to the expanding and not to the stationary races of mankind," he commented.[20]

With the conclusion of his speech, the Roosevelt Special headed east toward Washington, DC, and home.

Home and the Horizon

And now I am going in to my own folks.

THE WHITE HOUSE HAD BEEN GIVEN AN "UNUSUALLY THOROUGH cleaning and dusting" in advance of the president's arrival. "Crash coverings," which protected the mahogany desks in the president's office, the cabinet room, and Secretary Loeb's office were removed and given a detailed polishing by "Uncle Jerry" Smith, who had been working at the White House since President Grant's first term. Summer furnishings replaced "the heavy winter upholstery and hangings."[1]

The Roosevelt Special steamed into the Baltimore and Potomac Railroad Station at seven o'clock on the evening of June 5, marking the end of Theodore's sixty-five-day tour. After greeting various officials, Theodore made his way to his carriage. Along the route to the White House, a group of high school cadets served as his escort, and Theodore stood up to greet the crowd lining the sidewalks who gave "a hearty greeting to their long-absent neighbor." As his carriage approached the entrance of the White House, it moved slowly by the group of cadets for Theodore to review with his ever-present smile.

The U.S. Marine Band, which had provided a concert for the citizens waiting in front of the White House, broke into "Hail to the Chief" when Theodore stepped out on the south portico to address the crowd.[2]

> I thank you very, very much for coming here to greet me this afternoon, and I have appreciated more than I can say the welcome back home that I have received today. I have been absent over two months and I have traveled many miles. During that

215

time one thing has struck me, and that is the substantialness of the American people. One can travel from ocean to ocean and from Canada to the Gulf and always be at home among one's fellow Americans. I thank you again, my friends, and now I am going in to my own folks.[3]

With that, Theodore went back inside to have "dinner with his family in the good old White House."

Whatever concerns Theodore may have held about being chosen as the 1904 Republican Party nominee for president quickly vanished on July 27, when he swept all 994 delegate votes.[4] That November, Theodore won in a landslide election against the Democratic candidate Alton Parker. Theodore won 336 electoral college votes to Parker's 140; in the popular vote, Theodore received 7,630,457 versus Parker's 5,083,880. He won every northern and western state, losing only twelve southern states. Given his support of Minnie Cox and John Crum, this was hardly unexpected.[5]

After learning he had won, Theodore told reporters he would not seek a third term. It was a comment he regretted for the rest of his life, once saying he would cut one of his arms off to take it back. Though he remained popular with the public and likely would have been reelected in 1908, Theodore stood by his word, no matter how much it hurt.

During his second term, Theodore became the first U.S. president to win the Nobel Peace Prize for negotiating a peace treaty between Russia and Japan, ending their eighteen-month war. He donated the $40,000 in prize money to create a foundation for industrial peace.

His administration filed forty-four antitrust lawsuits, including the regulation of Standard Oil, the country's largest oil and refinery company, and pushed Congress to approve the Meat Inspection Act and the Pure Food and Drug Act in 1906.[6] Theodore became the first U.S. president to travel abroad while in office, visiting the construction site of the Panama Canal. In typical fashion, he even operated one of the large steam shovels.

Perhaps his most important and far-reaching action was signing the 1906 Antiquities Act into law. The legislation gave the president the power to create national monuments on federal land based on their significant natural, cultural, and scientific features, without requiring congressional approval. Theodore wasted no time in using the law to preserve many of the country's landmarks such as Devil's Tower (the first national monument), Gila Cliff Dwellings, Jewel Cave, Montezuma Castle, Muir Woods, and Natural Bridges.

March 4, 1909, marked Theodore's last day in office. Even the weather was unhappy with his departure, as a blizzard forced the swearing-in ceremony of William Howard Taft (Theodore's choice to succeed him) to take place inside the Senate chamber instead of outside the Capitol. It had to be a bittersweet moment for Theodore. Once the new president was sworn in, Theodore shook Taft's hand and exchanged greetings with a few others before making his way out of the Supreme Court side of the Capitol to his carriage. As the carriage slowly made its way through the snow to the train station, a band played "Auld Lang Syne."

"Our hand in parting, strenuous friend! Shake!" began the *Washington Herald* editorial at the end of Theodore's term.

> May good luck attend you and big game continue to be your portion!
>
> We shall miss you. Words would be vain, even if italicized, to tell you how much we shall miss you.
>
> If you have not always won our approbation; if you have, indeed, sometimes provoked our criticism and called forth our censure, we have known, nevertheless, great and good friend, that you really did not care a rap whether we approved or disapproved—whether we agreed or disagreed. And this knowledge has but led us to esteem you and respect your independence all the more.
>
> Your impetuosity, under high tension, now and then displeased us. If your going off at a tangent occasionally roused our righteous wrath, or moved us to regretful tears, your courageous spirit invariably challenged our admiration, your honesty of purpose steadily gave us increasing confidence in you and in your undertakings; and your square deal principles, day in and day out, appealed to us through and through. Of this we are very sure.
>
> Taking you all in all, we have approved you heartily. Having never kowtowed in the past, we do not intend to kowtow now,

but we do not mind letting you know—whether you care to know it or not—that deliberately reviewing the several administrations we have seen come and go, and calmly summing up in retrospect the things other Presidents did, and left undone, we have reached the firm conviction that you, strenuous friend, have done more for the common good of this glorious republic than any of your predecessors—in our day.

Honesty is more prevalent than it was seven years ago.

Fair-dealing is now the rule rather than the exception.

The business world thinks twice before consuming its money-making transactions.

Wealth, unless honestly acquired, has lost much of its potency.

Man and his fellow-man are getting on better together.

Partisanship is crowded to the rear by citizenship.

The Rooseveltian road has come to be a generally, if not exclusively, traversed thoroughfare.

And to you, strenuous friend, is the credit largely due for this wholesome readjustment and transformation in our everyday affairs. You have made for better things throughout this land of ours.

Perhaps you do not appreciate it, but your teachings have been an inspiration in the press. The number of honest and cou-rageous and independent newspapers is greater as the result of your precepts and example. It has been easier to print an hon-est newspaper in the last seven years than it was before. It has become more popular. Editorial sneers may follow this expres-sion, strenuous friend, but it is so. That is the reason the fact is chronicled here.

Good wishes, again, and au revoir! We are not full of faith that we shall see your like again. But you are young yet. Your good work is not finished by any manner of means, and we do expect to see, if not your like, you yourself many times and oft in the not too distant future.

Meanwhile, in the tranquil days which come upon us, we shall miss you—miss you every hour.

Then, God bless you, strenuous friend! Peace and more big game be yours![7]

An American Original

It is better to be an original than an imitation.

THEODORE'S GREAT LOOP TOUR WAS A ROUSING SUCCESS.

He crossed party lines, sharing grandstands with Republicans and Democrats alike. In his speeches he avoided partisanship, choosing to speak to all Americans no matter their party affiliation. Several Democratic officials endorsed his reelection (either openly or confidentially) even before he had secured the Republican nomination. This was just one small demonstration of Theodore's popularity and leadership.

Of course, he had opposition. Democrats longed to have one of their own running things in the White House. The Republican Party pro-business faction and Wall Street quietly hoped for a candidate more to their liking and did what they could to thwart his attempts at being nominated. In the end they came to realize that Theodore's leadership made a potent adversary. No doubt they also figured it was easier to deal with the devil they knew than one they didn't.

The tour solidified Theodore's approval with the people of the states he visited. They heartily responded to his genuine, honest approach when it came to dealing with problems, domestic and foreign. The public understood the meaning of speaking softly and carrying a big stick. In Theodore, they perceived a man who truly cared about the country and its citizens, one who urged them to succeed and to do what was right. Unlike other politicians, Theodore Roosevelt meant what he said. There was no double-talk, no obfuscation in his meaning. The words he spoke were clear, honest, to the point, and sometimes blunt. He stressed using common sense in solving problems, something the average American citizen easily understood even if those in Washington did not.

Although Theodore was well-educated, well-read, and could entertain and discuss affairs with world leaders, he was equally at home (and likely more comfortable) with a bunch of cowboys eating off the back of a chuck wagon or talking with farmers. This ability to connect with the average person was one of Theodore's innate qualities that endeared him to the American people. He was one of *them*. "You need not consider me a tenderfoot even if I do come from the east," Theodore said to a group in Montana. "I have been a rancher myself and long enough to grow a Westerner like the rest of you."[1]

There was something else about Theodore that the American people responded to.

He led by example.

Theodore would not ask the American public to do anything he wasn't willing to do—and, in many cases, had already done himself. He was at the forefront, whether it was taking on a trust or speaking out for conservation. His leadership was evident as far back as his days in the Dakota Territory, when he refused any preferential treatment during a roundup simply because he was the cattle owner. Theodore was not afraid to get his hands dirty, doing the job of a regular cowboy, from rounding up strays or branding cows to riding night herd.[2] (The only thing he could not do was lasso cattle, due to his poor eyesight.)

When he captured the three men who stole his boat from his Dakota ranch, he eschewed the traditional action of the day of hanging or shooting the thieves. Instead, he put them in a wagon, walking behind it in ankle-deep mud (in the middle of February!) for forty-five miles to turn them into local law officers. Ranchers and cowboys did not understand why he did not execute them on the spot.

They simply did not understand Theodore. He wanted justice, not revenge.

When he received word to take Kettle Hill in Cuba during the Spanish-American War, Theodore, astride a horse while bullets whizzed around him, yelled to his Rough Riders, "Follow me!" He led them up the hill while other officers directed troop action from below the line of fire.

Theodore's actions on Kettle Hill and San Juan Hill made him a national hero. When he learned there was no effective plan to evacuate his sick and wounded men to America for necessary medical care, he was not afraid to castigate Secretary of War Russell Alger. His comments regarding the secretary's incompetence led to Alger's resignation, and speaking out against the secretary cost Theodore his chance to receive a much-deserved Medal of Honor.[3]

Like his favorite president, Abraham Lincoln, Theodore Roosevelt was the right man at the right time to lead the country. It is easy to understand why he was so popular as president. His words and actions resounded with the people. Even though he disliked being called Teddy, he could not stop the public from referring to him as "our Teddy." They embraced him as one of the family.

Since his passing in 1919, streets, schools, and even a national park have been named in his honor. People still quote his words and books continue to be written about him. He is even given a significant mention in the Hall of Presidents attraction at Walt Disney World's Magic Kingdom, often eliciting applause at the mention of his name. Voters from both parties pine for his leadership.

Why, after a hundred years since his passing, is Theodore Roosevelt still ranked as one of the top U.S. presidents in so many polls?

In an age of double-speaking politicians who say whatever it takes to get a vote, Theodore Roosevelt stands out as a true man of his word. Though some may not agree with everything he did or said, they respect the man and his actions. The words Theodore spoke during his 1903 tour are just as meaningful, just as important, and just as honest today as when he originally spoke them. The actions he took as president were always for the betterment of the country and its people. The land he set aside, not just for the current population, but for their children's children, is something everyone still appreciates. He was looking to the future, knowing that if we continued skinning the land of its resources without careful renewal plans or outright protection, nothing would be left for future generations. As we all should be, Theodore was a steward of the country's resources.

Theodore's spirit demonstrates we should all lead by his example.

No one, even a president, is without faults. Like others, Theodore had his own. But in the end, the positive actions he took far outweigh any of his missteps. We all owe Theodore Roosevelt a debt of gratitude for leading by example. His actions are an inspiration to all of us. His words still resonate, inspire, and encourage us to do better. Our lands, our parks, our wildlife, our country, and even we ourselves are all better because of his efforts.

Theodore once said, "It is hard to fail, but it is worse to never have tried to succeed."

Bully, indeed.

Cities and Towns Visited

April 1—Washington, DC, and Pennsylvania:
    Leaves Washington, DC
    Altoona (Pennsylvania)
    Harrisburg (Pennsylvania) (Overnight on his train)
April 2—Illinois:
    Chicago
    Evanston (Overnight on his train)
April 3—Wisconsin:
    Madison
    Lake Mills
    Jefferson Junction
    Waukesha
    Milwaukee (Overnight on his train)
April 4—Wisconsin and Minnesota:
    LaCrosse (Wisconsin)
    St. Paul (Minnesota)
    Minneapolis (Minnesota) (Overnight on his train)
April 5—South Dakota:
    Sioux Falls (Overnight on his train)
April 6—South Dakota and North Dakota:
    Yankton (South Dakota)
    Scotland (South Dakota)
    Tripp (South Dakota)
    Parkston (South Dakota)
    Mitchell (South Dakota)
    Woonsocket (South Dakota)
    Alpena (South Dakota)
    Tulare (South Dakota)

Redfield (South Dakota)
Aberdeen (South Dakota)
Edgeley (North Dakota) (Overnight on his train)

April 7—North Dakota:
Fargo
Casselton
Tower City
Valley City
Dawson
Mandan
Dickinson
Medora (Overnight on his train)

April 8–24—Yellowstone (Montana/Wyoming):
Theodore spent seventeen days in Yellowstone and did not give any speeches.

April 24—Montana:
Gardiner (Overnight on his train)

April 25—Montana, Wyoming, South Dakota, and Nebraska:
Billings (Montana)
Gillette (Wyoming)
Moorecroft (Wyoming)
New Castle (Wyoming)
Edgemont (South Dakota)
Ardmore (South Dakota)
Crawford (Nebraska)
Alliance (Nebraska) (Overnight on his train)

April 26—Nebraska:
Grand Island (Overnight on his train)

April 27—Nebraska:
Hastings
Lincoln
Wahoo
Fremont
Crete
Omaha (Overnight on his train)

April 28—Iowa:
Shenandoah
Clarinda
Sharpsburg
Van Wert
Osceloa
Des Moines
Oskaloosa
Ottumwa (Overnight on his train)
April 29—Iowa, Illinois, and Missouri:
Keokuk (Iowa)
Quincy (Illinois)
Hannibal (Missouri)
St. Louis (Missouri) (Overnight as a guest of David R. Francis)
April 30—Missouri:
St. Louis (Overnight on his train)
May 1—Missouri and Kansas:
Kansas City (Missouri)
Lawrence (Kansas)
Topeka (Kansas) (Overnight on his train)
May 2—Kansas:
Manhattan
Junction City
Chapman
Detroit
Abilene
Solomon
Salina
Bavaria
Brooksville
Carneira
Kanopolis
Ellsworth
Black Wolf
Wilson

Dorrance
Bunker Hill
Russell
Gorham
Walker
Victoria
Hays
Ellis
Collyer
WaKeeney (Overnight on his train)

May 3—Kansas:
Sharon Springs (Overnight on his train)

May 4—Wyoming and Colorado:
Cheyenne (Wyoming)
Hugo (Colorado)
Denver (Colorado)
Colorado Springs (Colorado)
Pueblo (Colorado)
Trinidad (Colorado) (Overnight on his train)

May 5—New Mexico Territory:
Santa Fe
Albuquerque (Overnight on his train)

May 6—Arizona Territory:
Grand Canyon
Seligman (Overnight on his train)

May 7—California:
Barstow
Victorville
San Bernardino
Redlands
Riverside (Overnight at Mission Inn)

May 8—California:
Claremont
Pasadena
Los Angeles (Overnight on his train)

May 9—California:
Oxnard
Ventura
Surf
San Luis Obispo
Paso Robles (Overnight on his train)
May 10—California:
Monterey (Overnight at Hotel Del Monte)
May 11—California:
Parjaro
Watsonville
Santa Cruz (Visits Redwoods)
Campbell
San Jose (Overnight on his train)
May 12—California:
Palo Alto
Burlingame
San Francisco (Overnight at the Palace Hotel)
May 13—California:
San Francisco (Overnight at the Palace Hotel)
May 14—California:
San Francisco
Oakland
Berkeley
Vallejo (Overnight at the Palace Hotel)
May 15—California:
Raymond (Travels to Yosemite)
May 15–17—California:
In Yosemite with John Muir
May 18—California:
Berenda
Merced
Modesto (Overnight on his train)
May 19—California and Nevada:
Sacramento (California)

Auburn (California)
Colfax (California)
Truckee (California)
Carson City (Nevada) (Overnight on his train)

May 20—California and Oregon:
Redding (California)
Dunsmuir (California)
Sisson (now Mt. Shasta) (California)
Montague (California)
Hornbrook (California)
Ashland (Oregon)
Medford (Oregon
Grants Pass (Oregon)

May 21—Oregon:
Roseburg
Eugene
Albany
Jefferson
Salem
Portland (Overnight at the Portland Hotel)

May 22—Oregon and Washington:
Portland (Oregon)
Chehalis (Washington)
Centralia (Washington)
Olympia (Washington)
Tacoma (Washington) (Overnight at the Tacoma Hotel)

May 23—Washington:
Bremerton
Seattle
Everett
Seattle (Overnight at the Washington Hotel)

May 24—Washington:
Seattle (Overnight on his train)

May 25—Washington:
Ellensburg

North Yakima
Pasco
Wallula
Walla Walla (Overnight on his train)
May 26—Washington and Idaho:
Tekoa (Washington)
Spokane (Washington)
Wallace (Idaho)
Harrison (Idaho) (Overnight on his train)
May 27—Montana:
Helena
Butte (Overnight at the Thornton Hotel)
May 28—Idaho:
Pocatello
Shoshone
Glenn's Ferry
Mountain Home
Nampa
Boise (Overnight on his train)
May 29—Utah:
Ogden
Salt Lake City
Echo (Overnight on his train)
May 30—Wyoming:
Evanston
Rawlins
Laramie
Cheyenne (Overnight at the Inter-Ocean Hotel)
May 31—Wyoming:
Cheyenne
June 1—Wyoming and Nebraska:
Cheyenne (Wyoming)
Sidney (Nebraska)
North Platte (Nebraska) (Overnight on his train)

June 2—Iowa:
Denison
Fort Dodge
Webster City
Iowa Falls
Cedar Falls
Waterloo
Independence
Dubuque (Overnight on his train)

June 3—Illinois:
Freeport
Rockford
Rochelle
Aurora
Joliet
Dwight
Pontiac
Lexington
Bloomington

June 4—Illinois and Indiana:
Lincoln (Illinois)
Springfield (Illinois)
Decatur (Illinois)
Danville (Illinois)
Indianapolis (Indiana) (Overnight on his train)

June 5—Returns to Washington, DC

Acknowledgments

A writer relies on several people along the way from the initial idea to research, writing, and, eventually, the final book.

The Theodore Roosevelt Center at Dickinson State University was of great help in allowing access to Theodore's various speeches and letters. Thank you to Sharon Kilzer, project manager, and to all of the staff for their assistance.

The Houghton Library at Harvard, which houses the Theodore Roosevelt Collection, was equally helpful in providing me numerous materials used in this book. My thanks to Christine Jacobson for all her assistance.

Jayne Pearce, of the Fort Wallace Museum in Wallace, Kansas, was extremely generous and helpful in sharing information about Theodore's visit to Sharon Springs, Kansas.

Jack Burgess provided information about the history of the Yosemite Valley Railroad.

Betty Uyeda at the Seaver Center for Western History Research at the Los Angeles Natural History Museum generously answered my questions about Los Angeles during Theodore's visit.

The Billings Public Library in Montana, the Cheyenne Public Library in Wyoming, the Western History section of the Denver Public Library, the Los Angeles Public Library, the Pasadena Public Library, and the special collections department of the Penrose Library of the Pike's Peak Library District in Colorado Springs were tremendous resources. My thanks to the staff members of these institutions for their generous suggestions and assistance.

I always am beholden to Beth Werling, collections manager of the American History Collection at the Natural History Museum in Los Angeles. Her knowledge and advice always have provided me with a wealth of information. Thank you is not enough.

Jenny Lerew, a fellow admirer of Theodore Roosevelt, graciously shared valuable information relating to Theodore's trip through California. I am very grateful for her help and friendship.

Once again, Erin Turner of Two Dot had faith in this book when it was simply an idea. Her support is gratefully appreciated.

I am beholden to Kristen Mellitt and Erin McGarvey at Two Dot for their help in putting this book together.

Thank you to those who helped me along the way: Cliff and Dawn Allen, John Allen, Rich Allen, Terese Mary Allen, Marie Behar, James Benesh, Larry Blanks, James and Barbara Columbo, Johnny D. Boggs, Jamie Capps, Tony and Tina Chong, Chris Enss, Capt. Remy Garner, USA, George Gold, Richard Day Gore, Mike Hawks, Lolita Jerigan, Lisa Kelly, Kevin Kenney, Robert Knott, Jim Krause, Kathy Krause, Michael Kriegsman, Bill and Mary Ann Lagnerse, Terry and Nancy Lamfers, Craig Lindberg, George and Nancy Loomis, Mary Mahler, William Malin, Geri Mars, Lydia Milars, Sherry Monahan, Major Tom Oblak, USA (Ret.), Keith Palmer, Dan and Patti Richmond, Carrie Renfro, Celeste Rush, Todd Roberts, Stuart Rosebrook, Rosemary Schiano, Terry Shulman, David C. Smith, Winter Stezaker, Steve Tanner, Mitch Trimboli, and Teresa Vest.

Finally, thank you to my wife, Linda. The past thirty-one years I have shared with her have been absolutely "Bully!"

Endnotes

Preface

1. *Webster's Unabridged Dictionary* (New York: Barnes and Noble, 1996), 276.
2. Although some believe that Theodore took to using this word during his presidency, one story traces it back to his days at Harvard University. On one bitingly cold day accompanied by an equally harsh wind, he and a friend, Richard Welling, went ice skating. After a few minutes, Welling wanted to seek warmer quarters and expected his friend to quickly give up. To his dismay, Theodore exclaimed, "Isn't this bully!"
3. *Washington Herald*, March 4, 1909.
4. *Kalispell (MT) Bee*, June 23, 1903.
5. *Salt Lake (UT) Tribune*, May 30, 1903.
6. *Caldwell (ID) Tribune*, June 6, 1903.

A Presidential Tour Unlike Any Other

1. The tour stopped in Baltimore, Maryland; Philadelphia, Pittsburgh, and Harrisburg, Pennsylvania; New York City; West Point Military Academy; Albany, Auburn, Niagara Falls, and Buffalo, New York; Cleveland, Cincinnati, Columbus, and Toledo, Ohio; Detroit, Michigan; Chicago, Springfield, and Alton, Illinois; St. Louis, Missouri; Indianapolis, Indiana; and Louisville, Kentucky. *Minneapolis Journal*, April 2, 1903.
2. Hayes's tour stopped at Chicago, Illinois; Des Moines, Iowa; Omaha, Nebraska; Cheyenne in Wyoming Territory; Ogden, Utah; Sacramento, San Francisco, Yosemite, and Los Angeles, California; Portland, Oregon; Walla Walla, Tacoma, Victoria, and Seattle, Washington; Tucson in Arizona Territory; Santa Fe in New Mexico Territory; St. Louis, Missouri; and Toledo, Ohio. "Exhibit Looks at Travel before There Were Highways or Cars," *Past Times*, vol. 11, Rutherford B. Hayes Presidential Center, Fremont, OH, 2012.
3. The U.S. Secret Service was formed on July 5, 1865. Its duty at that time was to stop counterfeit currency within the nation. It wasn't until the assassination of President McKinley that Congress appointed the Secret Service to protect the president.
4. President Hayes was the first U.S. president to visit the Pacific Coast. *Morning Oregonian*, September 30, 1880.
5. Cleveland's trip stopped in Baltimore, Maryland; York, Harrisburg, and Pittsburgh, Pennsylvania; Indianapolis and Terre Haute, Indiana; St. Louis, Missouri; Chicago, Illinois; Milwaukee, Madison, and La Crosse, Wisconsin; St. Paul and Minneapolis, Minnesota; Omaha, Nebraska; Sioux City, Iowa; Kansas City, Missouri; Memphis, Nashville, and Chattanooga, Tennessee; Atlanta, Georgia; and Montgomery, Alabama. Cleveland

declined to run again in 1896, and the Democratic Party chose William Jennings Bryan as its nominee. Bryan would lose to William McKinley.

President James Garfield (1881), the victim of an assassination, died after serving only two hundred days in office. President Chester A. Arthur (1881–1885) made a visit to Yellowstone during his time in office.

6. The total mileage of this trip was 9,232 miles. Harrison's route visited Charlotte, Roanoke, and Lynchburg, Virginia; Bristol, Knoxville, Memphis, and Chattanooga, Tennessee; Atlanta, Georgia; Birmingham, Alabama; Little Rock, Arkansas; Texarkana, Longview Junction, Palestine, Houston, Galveston, San Antonio, Logier, Valentine, and El Paso, Texas; Tucson and Yuma, Arizona Territory; Los Angeles, San Diego, Riverside, Pasadena, Santa Barbara, Saugus, Tehachapi, Bakersfield, Fresno, Merced, San Francisco, Sacramento, Tehama, and Sisson, California; Ashland, Portland, The Dalles, Umatilla Junction, Pendelton, La Grande, and Huntington, Oregon; Tacoma and Seattle, Washington; Boise and McCammon, Idaho; Ogden and Salt Lake City, Utah; Grand Junction, Glenwood Springs, Leadville, Salida, Pueblo, Colorado Springs, and Denver, Colorado; McCook, Lincoln, and Omaha, Nebraska; Moberly and Hannibal, Missouri; Springfield and Decatur, Illinois; Indianapolis, Indiana; Dayton, Xenia, and Columbus, Ohio; Pittsburgh, Altoona, and Harrisburg, Pennsylvania.

7. McKinley's trip consisted of visits to Memphis, Tennessee; New Orleans, Louisiana; Houston, Austin, and Del Rio, Texas; New Mexico and Arizona Territories; Redlands, Ontario, Alhambra, Los Angeles, Ventura, Santa Barbara, Surf, Monterrey, Oakland, and San Francisco, California.

8. The Pullman Company supplied the passenger cars.

9. The *Elysian* train car was sold in 1920 to the Western Pacific Railroad, where it served as a passenger car until 1942, when it was retired. From December 1945 until April 1951, it was used as a locker room at the Stockton, California, roundhouse before being scrapped. Chris Epting, *Teddy Roosevelt in California: The Whistle Stop Tour That Changed America* (Charleston, SC: History Press, 2015), 128.

10. *Chicago Daily Tribune*, April 1, 1903.

11. *Minneapolis Journal*, April 3, 1903.

12. The merger of the Great Northern Railway, Union Pacific, and Northern Pacific into the Northern Securities Company would make it the largest trust in the country. The term "trust" was applied when two or more corporations merged, creating a monopoly. Trusts, such as Northern Securities Company, controlled essential services to businesses and the general public and held a monopoly on a specific product (in this case, shipping and passenger travel). With no competition, they were free to charge whatever price the market would support. The case went all the way to the Supreme Court, where, in a 1904 five-to-four ruling, the court stated that the trust did indeed violate the Sherman Antitrust Law and was ordered broken up.

13. *The New York Sun* was owned by J. P. Morgan, one of the defendants in the Northern Securities Antitrust lawsuit. Letter dated August 25, 1903, Theodore Roosevelt Papers, Library of Congress.

14. (Washington, DC) *Evening Star*, March 30, 1903.

15. *Saint Paul Globe*, April 5, 1903.

16. In 1792, Napoleon, who was a brigadier general at the time, witnessed the mob storm the Tuileries (a royal palace in Paris) during the French Revolution. He believed the military should have fired at the mob, sweeping "four or five hundred of them" from the street, forcing others to scatter. It was a tactic he used three years later against a Parisian mob.

17. (Washington, DC) *Evening Star*, April 24, 1903.

18 Elting E. Morris, ed., *The Letters of Theodore Roosevelt: The Square Deal 1901–1903, Volume 3* (Cambridge, MA: Harvard University Press, 1951), 482.

19. Morris, *The Letters of Theodore Roosevelt*, 481.

20. Douglas Brinkley, *The Wilderness Warrior: Theodore Roosevelt and the Crusade for America* (New York: HarperCollins, 2009), 222.

21. Letter dated March 7, 1903, in *The Letters of Theodore Roosevelt: The Square Deal 1901–1903*, 441–42.

22. John Burroughs, *Camping and Tramping with Roosevelt* (Boston: Houghton Mifflin, 1907), viii.

23. Burroughs left Washington, DC, with Theodore on April 1, 1903. Letter dated March 7, 1903, in *The Letters of Theodore Roosevelt: The Square Deal 1901–1903*, 447.

24. Brinkley, *The Wilderness Warrior*, 493.

The Journey Begins: Pennsylvania to Minnesota

1. The station was located at the corner of B Street NW (now Constitution Avenue) and Sixth Street NW. It was demolished with the opening of Union Station in 1907.

2. *Chicago Tribune*, April 2, 1903.

3. *Washington Times*, April 1, 1903.

4. (Washington, DC) *Evening Star*, March 30, 1903.

5. Alfred Henry Lewis, ed., *A Compilation of Messages and Speeches of Theodore Roosevelt, 1901–1905* (Washington, DC: Bureau of National Literature and Art, 1906), 212–13.

6. *Altoona (PA) Tribune*, April 2, 1903.

7. The Horseshoe Curve was built in 1850 without the use of any machinery, using only men with picks, shovels, and horses to drag and level the ground. It opened in 1854 and is still in use today.

8. *Minneapolis Journal*, April 3, 1903.

9. (Chicago) *Inter-Ocean*, April 3, 1903.

10. Lewis, *A Compilation of Messages and Speeches of Theodore Roosevelt*, 215–17.

11. On September 3, 1902, Theodore's carriage was struck by a trolley car in Pittsfield, Massachusetts. The trolley line was supposed to be closed off until Theodore's carriage had reached its destination, but witnesses claim people on the trolley urged the driver to go faster so that they could greet Theodore at the Lennox Country Club. The trolley came on fast, clanging its bell. People waved at the trolley to stop with no success. The trolley smashed into the left side of the carriage, just clipping the left rear wheel. The front left wheel took the full impact, which sent Secret Service agent Bill Craig (who was seated next to the carriage driver) under the wheels of the moving trolley, crushing his body and killing him instantly. Theodore, Governor Winthrop Crane, and George Cortelyou were thrown from the carriage.

Theodore lay on his face and didn't move for a few seconds. Everyone feared the worst. Regaining his senses, he stood up and nodded when asked if he was all right. Blood ran from his chin and the right side of his face would soon begin swelling. Learning that Craig was killed, all Theodore could say was "Poor Craig. How my children will feel." Quentin quickly came to mind, as he and Craig had formed a close friendship, often reading comics together. Craig became the first Secret Service agent to die in the line of duty.

Theodore's sadness turned to fury when he saw Luke Madden, the driver of the trolley. Balling his hand into a fist, he stared straight at the driver yelling, "This is the most damnable outrage I ever knew. If you lost control of your car, there is some excuse, but if you tried to pass us, disregarding all our warnings, you ought to be punished." Madden and the conductor, James Kelly, were arrested on charges of manslaughter. Madden was given a six-month jail sentence and fined $500, while Kelly's case was placed "on file."

12. (Chicago) *Inter-Ocean*, April 3, 1903.

13. The doctrine was written by the secretary of state (and future president) John Quincy Adams.

14. In 1904, Theodore added what is now called the "Roosevelt Corollary." It stated that the United States would intervene in conflicts between European and Latin American countries to enforce legitimate claims by European powers, rather than have those European countries press their own claims directly, which could possibly lead to an armed conflict.

15. Letter dated August 9, 1903, in *The Letters of Theodore Roosevelt: The Square Deal 1901–1903, Volume 3*, ed. Elting Morison (Cambridge, MA: Harvard University Press, 1951), 548.

16. *Minneapolis Journal*, April 4, 1903.

17. This letter was in reply to Sprague's congratulating Theodore for forcing the Republicans to withdraw support from a corrupt financial adviser. Letter dated January 26, 1900, in *The Letters of Theodore Roosevelt: The Years of Preparation 1898–1900, Volume 2*, ed. Elting E. Morris (Cambridge, MA: Harvard University Press, 1951), 1141.

18. This was on September 2, 1901, four days before President McKinley was shot.

19. (Minneapolis, MN) *Star Tribune*, September 3, 1901.

20. *Wisconsin State Journal*, April 3, 1903.

21. (Washington, DC) *Evening Star*, April 3, 1903.

22. *Wisconsin State Journal*, April 3, 1903.

23. *Wisconsin State Journal*, April 3, 1903.

24. *Wisconsin State Journal*, April 3, 1903.

25. *New York Times*, April 4, 1903.

26. Speech given on April 3, 1903, Theodore Roosevelt Digital Library, Dickinson State University, Dickinson, ND.

27. Letter dated August 9, 1903, in *The Letters of Theodore Roosevelt: The Years of Preparation 1868–1898*, 549–50.

28. *Minneapolis Journal*, April 4, 1903.

29. Speech given on April 3, 1903.

30. Lewis, *A Compilation of Messages and Speeches of Theodore Roosevelt*, 225–32.

31. John Burroughs, *Camping and Tramping with Roosevelt* (Boston: Houghton Mifflin, 1907), 10.

32. *Altoona (PA) Tribune,* April 6, 1903.

33. *Washington Times,* April 4, 1903.

34. "Hurricane deck" was a western term for the saddle on a bucking horse.

35. Lewis, *A Compilation of Messages and Speeches of Theodore Roosevelt,* 245–49.

36. Lewis, *A Compilation of Messages and Speeches of Theodore Roosevelt,* 245–49.

37. An ad in the *Saint Paul Globe* noted a reduced fare would be offered on "all railroads within one hundred miles" of St. Paul to enable the public to "join in the welcoming of the Nation's chief." *Saint Paul Globe,* April 2, 1903.

38. *Saint Paul Globe,* April 5, 1903.

39. *Saint Paul Globe,* April 5, 1903.

40. Burroughs, *Camping and Tramping with Roosevelt,* 10–11.

41. Lewis, *A Compilation of Messages and Speeches of Theodore Roosevelt,* 249–52.

42. *Saint Paul Globe,* April 6, 1903.

43. (Minneapolis, Minnesota) *Star Tribune,* April 5, 1903.

44. (Minneapolis, Minnesota) *Star Tribune,* April 5, 1903.

45. Lewis, *A Compilation of Messages and Speeches of Theodore Roosevelt,* 257.

Old Stomping Grounds: North and South Dakota

1. John Burroughs, *Camping and Tramping with Roosevelt* (Boston: Houghton Mifflin, 1907), 8–9.

2. Letter dated August 9, 1903, in *The Letters of Theodore Roosevelt: The Square Deal 1901–1903, Volume 3,* ed. Elting Morison (Cambridge, MA: Harvard University Press, 1951), 548.

3. Three of the nine Sundays while on tour would be spent in Yellowstone and Yosemite. Seattle was the largest town in which he would spend a Sunday; the other cities had populations less than fourteen thousand.

4. Theodore met Sylvane and Joe Ferris and Bill Merrifield during his 1883 trip to the Dakota Territory to hunt buffalo. Joe served as Theodore's guide and Sylvane and Merrifield wound up managing his newly purchased Maltese Cross ranch. The three men remained close friends with Theodore until his death. Bill Sewall and Wilmot Dow met Theodore in September 1878 and later came with Theodore to the Dakotas in 1884. Both men remained close friends with Theodore.

5. Letter to John Hay dated August 9, 1903, in *The Letters of Theodore Roosevelt: The Square Deal 1901–1903,* 550.

6. (Sioux Falls, SD) *Argus-Leader,* April 6, 1903.

7. (Sioux Falls, SD) *Argus-Leader,* April 6, 1903.

8. (Sioux Falls, SD) *Argus-Leader,* April 6, 1903.

9. *Minneapolis Journal,* April 6, 1903.

10. Alfred Henry Lewis, ed., *A Compilation of Messages and Speeches of Theodore Roosevelt, 1901–1905* (Washington, DC: Bureau of National Literature and Art, 1906), 257–62.

11. (Sioux Falls, SD) *Argus-Leader,* April 6, 1903.

12. Speech given in Mitchell, South Dakota, April 6, 1903, Theodore Roosevelt Digital Library, Dickinson State University, Dickinson, ND.

13. Speech given in Aberdeen, South Dakota, April 6, 1903.

14. *Minneapolis Journal*, April 7, 1903; *Jamestown (ND) Weekly Alert*, April 16, 1903.

15. *New York Times*, April 7, 1903.

16. *Minneapolis Journal*, April 7, 1903.

17. *Minneapolis Journal*, April 7, 1903.

18. The Philippine Islands came under Spanish rule with Magellan's discovery in 1521. In that same year the first Hispanic settlements were created and the islands remained under Spanish rule until the Spanish-American War in 1898. With Spain's defeat, the islands (and Cuba) were ceded to U.S. control. In 1899, a war broke out between Philippine insurgents and the U.S. Army, ending in 1902. That same year Congress passed the Philippine Organic Act, which created a Philippine Assembly that was voted in by all males living on the islands. (Women had no voting rights at that time.) The Philippines were to be granted independence by 1941, but the Japanese occupation of the islands during World War II stalled the implementation of Philippine independence until 1946. Addison Thomas, *Roosevelt among the People* (Chicago: L. W. Walter, 1910), 129–31.

19. *Jamestown (ND) Weekly Alert*, April 12, 1903; Burroughs, *Camping and Tramping with Roosevelt*, 12.

20. *Jamestown (ND) Weekly Alert*, April 9, 1903.

21. *Jamestown (ND) Weekly Alert*, April 9, 1903.

22. Letter to John Hay dated August 9, 1903, in *The Letters of Theodore Roosevelt: The Square Deal 1901–1903*, 549.

23. Speech given on April 7, 1903, Theodore Roosevelt Digital Library, Dickinson State University, Dickinson, ND.

24. (Washington, DC) *Evening Star*, April 9, 1903.

25. (Washington, DC) *Evening Star*, April 4, 1903, (Washington, DC) *Evening Star*, April 8, 1903.

26. *Bismarck Tribune*, April 8, 1903.

27. *Bismarck Tribune*, April 8, 1903.

28. *Bismarck Tribune*, April 8, 1903.

29. Letter to John Hay dated August 9, 1903, in *The Letters of Theodore Roosevelt: The Square Deal 1901–1903*, 551.

30. Joe Ferris and his wife moved to Sidney, Montana, to run another general store akin to their store in Medora. From Montana they moved to California in 1922, where Joe died in 1937. Sylvane Ferris became a bank president in Dickinson, North Dakota, before moving to California where he died in 1933.

31. Burroughs, *Camping and Tramping with Roosevelt*, 12–14.

32. Michael F. Blake, *The Cowboy President: The American West and the Making of Theodore Roosevelt* (Helena, MT: Two Dot, 2018), 92.

33. The marquis returned to France where he became involved in politics, which included a plan to overthrow the French government. He attempted to build a railroad in Indochina, but that also failed. A rabid anti-Semite, he hatched a ludicrous plan to unite all of Islam against the English and the Jews. The marquis traveled to Libya to attack British colonialism but was killed by a Tuareg Tribe in June 1896.

34. Theodore, along with William Hornaday, instituted a buffalo breeding program at the Bronx Zoo. They were able to reintroduce buffalo to the Wichita Mountains area of Oklahoma, as well as persuade Congress to establish the National Bison Range in western Montana. Both places now have large, healthy herds of buffalo, in addition to the more than six hundred buffalo at Theodore Roosevelt National Park in Medora, North Dakota.

35. Letter to John Hay dated August 9, 1903, in *The Letters of Theodore Roosevelt: The Square Deal 1901–1903*, 551.

36. Lewis, *A Compilation of Messages and Speeches of Theodore Roosevelt, 1901–1905*, 271.

37. Letter to John Hay dated August 9, 1903, in *The Letters of Theodore Roosevelt: The Square Deal 1901–1903*, 552.

Interlude with Nature: Yellowstone

1. In 1902, Theodore went on a black bear hunt in Mississippi. He came up empty handed until his guide caught an old beat-up black bear and tied it to a tree. Theodore found shooting a tied-up animal to be unsporting and refused. He ordered the sickly bear to be put down. Reporters had a field day making fun on the president's lack of killing a bear until Clifford Berryman, a cartoonist for *Washington Post* drew a cartoon of Theodore refusing to shoot a small black bear cub. The cartoon became hugely popular with the public, boosted Theodore's approval and gave birth to the "Teddy Bear" doll.

2. Letter to Ethan Hitchcock dated February 14, 1903, in *The Letters of Theodore Roosevelt: The Years of Preparation 1868–1898, Volume 3*, ed. Elting Morison (Cambridge, MA: Harvard University Press, 1951), 425.

3. Letter to Major John Pitcher dated March 2, 1903, in *The Letters of Theodore Roosevelt: The Square Deal 1901–1903*, 437–38.

4. Letter to Major John Pitcher dated March 2, 1903, in *The Letters of Theodore Roosevelt: The Square Deal 1901–1903*, 437–38.

5. John Burroughs, *Camping and Tramping with Roosevelt* (Boston: Houghton Mifflin, 1907), 7.

6. Burroughs, *Camping and Tramping with Roosevelt*, 6–7.

7. *Butte (MT) Inter-Mountain*, April 9, 1903.

8. *Anaconda (MT) Standard*, April 9, 1903.

9. The Newlands Reclamation Act gave the government the authority to divert, retain (such as in reservoirs), and transmit water to arid or semiarid lands for the purpose of irrigating farmlands. This act was considered (next to the 1862 Homestead Act) one of the most significant steps in the westward expansion movement. Whereas the Homestead Act granted farmers the right to claim land, the new irrigation bill helped them to make their land fertile by giving them access to water. California, Colorado, Idaho, Kansas, Montana, Nebraska, Nevada, North Dakota, Oklahoma, Oregon, South Dakota, Utah, Washington, and Wyoming, as well as two territories, Arizona and New Mexico, benefitted from this new law. Texas was added to the list in 1906. By 1907, twenty-four projects had been authorized, including the Lower Yellowstone District, which runs water from the Yellowstone River to the thirsty border of Montana and North Dakota, an area Theodore knew well.

10. *Butte (MT) Inter-Mountain*, April 9, 1903.

11. *Butte (MT) Inter-Mountain*, April 10, 1903.

12. *Butte (MT) Inter-Mountain*, April 9, 1903.

13. Burroughs, *Camping and Tramping with Roosevelt*, 23–25.

14. Of the sixty structures that were built between 1891 and 1913, roughly thirty-two remain standing. These buildings serve as the park's headquarters, visitor's center, museum, and housing for park employees. The military ended its role of protecting Yellowstone on October 31, 1918, when it was turned over to the National Park Service, which was founded in 1916.

15. Burroughs, *Camping and Tramping with Roosevelt*, 27–28.

16. *Butte (MT) Inter-Mountain*, April 9, 1903.

17. Today, the buffalo in Yellowstone number close to four thousand.

18. *Anaconda (MT) Standard*, April 9, 1903.

19. Cinnabar was built in 1883 by the Northern Pacific Railroad as the last stop on its branch line to Yellowstone Park. The town was abandoned in 1903, after Theodore's visit, when the railroad extended the line to Gardiner. Nothing remains of the town today.

20. *Butte (MT) Inter-Mountain*, April 10, 1903.

21. *Anaconda (MT) Standard*, April 14, 1903.

22. *Butte (MT) Inter-Mountain*, April 16, 1903; *Butte (MT) Inter-Mountain*, April 20, 1903.

23. Burroughs, *Camping and Tramping with Roosevelt*, 31–33.

24. Burroughs, *Camping and Tramping with Roosevelt*, 34–37.

25. Thomas Elwood "Billy" Hoffer (sometimes spelled Hofer) arrived in Colorado in 1872 with high hopes of finding his fortune by mining. With little luck in that regard, he moved on to Montana and eventually arrived in Yellowstone, working for a freighting outfit. Later he built a sailboat that he used to take tourists around Yellowstone Lake. From that enterprise he began taking tourists into the wilds, and this is where he met Theodore in 1890 and 1892. In 1907, he operated a boat rental company at Yellowstone Lake, but three years later lost his business because of poor management. He sold his property in Gardiner and moved to the state of Washington. He was often referred to as "Billy" or "Uncle Billy," a nickname he was given for reasons unknown.

26. Burroughs, *Camping and Tramping with Roosevelt*, 38–40.

27. Theodore Roosevelt, *Theodore Roosevelt: An Autobiography* (Norwalk, CT: Easton Press, 1996), 347.

28. Burroughs, *Camping and Tramping with Roosevelt*, 43–45.

29. Tower Falls is south of today's Roosevelt Lodge area. Contrary to popular belief, Theodore never camped in that area. Originally, in 1906, the area consisted of tents and was called Camp Roosevelt. In 1919 and 1920, the lodge and cabins were built. It was claimed that this was where Theodore camped in 1903, but that is inaccurate. Their camp was closer to present-day Calcite Springs Overlook. Burroughs, *Camping and Tramping with Roosevelt*, 46–47.

30. *Butte (MT) Inter-Mountain*, April 11, 1903.

31. Letter to Clinton Merriman dated April 16, 1903, in *The Letters of Theodore Roosevelt: The Square Deal 1901–1903, Volume 3*, ed. Elting Morison, 461–62.

32. The Sibley tent, designed in 1856 by U.S. Army major Henry Sibley, was a conical-shaped tent that could house a dozen men comfortably. Measuring twelve feet high and eighteen feet wide, it was supported by a central pole that attached to a tripod and tent pegs on the outside. The tripod could be placed over a firepit for cooking or heating, and a cowl over the center pole provided ventilation and allowed smoke to escape. This tent was very similar to the Plains Indian lodges. Sibley was paid five dollars for each tent built by the War Department but forfeited future payments when he joined the Confederacy during the Civil War. After his death in 1886, his family fought the War Department for unpaid royalties, but they were unsuccessful.

33. Burroughs, *Camping and Tramping with Roosevelt*, 51–54.

34. *Butte (MT) Inter-Mountain*, April 17, 1903.

35. *Anaconda (MT) Standard*, April 15, 1903.

36. Burroughs, *Camping and Tramping with Roosevelt*, 63–67.

37. Burroughs, *Camping and Tramping with Roosevelt*, 64–65.

38. Letter to Clinton Merriman dated April 22, 1903, in *The Letters of Theodore Roosevelt: The Square Deal 1901–1903*, 463.

39. Letter to Clinton Merriman dated April 22, 1903, in T*he Letters of Theodore Roosevelt: The Square Deal 1901–1903*, 463.

40. Earle Looker, *The White House Gang* (New York: Fleming H. Revell, 1929), 146.

41. *Butte (MT) Inter-Mountain*, April 24, 1903.

42. Burroughs, *Camping and Tramping with Roosevelt*, 70–71, 73–74.

43. Burroughs, *Camping and Tramping with Roosevelt*, 74.

44. Today, the entrance arch is known as the Roosevelt Arch, the northern entrance to the park. *Billings (MT) Gazette*, April 25, 1903.

45. *Billings (MT) Gazette*, April 25, 1903.

46. Alfred Henry Lewis, ed., *A Compilation of Messages and Speeches of Theodore Roosevelt, 1901–1905* (Washington, DC: Bureau of National Literature and Art, 1906), 273–75.

Heading East in the West: Montana to Iowa

1. Letter to John Hay dated August 9, 1903, in *The Letters of Theodore Roosevelt: The Square Deal 1901–1903, Volume 3*, ed. Elting Morison (Cambridge, MA: Harvard University Press, 1951), 554.

2. *New York Times*, April 29, 1903.

3. Speech given on April 25, 1903, Theodore Roosevelt Digital Library, Dickinson State University, Dickinson, ND.

4. Speech given on April 25, 1903.

5. *New York Times*, April 26, 1903.

6. *Alliance (NE) Herald*, May 1, 1903.

7. *Lincoln (NE) Journal Star*, April 27, 1903.

8. Theodore's comment about the regiment and Montana referred to his visit to Fort Russell, outside Cheyenne. Seth's reputation as a lawman was widely known and respected not just in the Dakotas, but in Montana as well. Letter dated April 27, 1903, Theodore Roosevelt Collection, Library of Congress, Washington, DC.

9. *Omaha (NE) Daily Bee*, April 28, 1903.

10. *Lincoln (NE) Daily Star*, April 27, 1903.
11. Speech given on April 27, 1903, Theodore Roosevelt Digital Library, Dickinson State University, Dickinson, ND.
12. *Omaha (NE) Daily Bee*, April 28, 1903.
13. *Lincoln (NE) Daily Star*, April 27, 1903.
14. *Omaha (NE) Daily Bee*, April 28, 1903.
15. *Omaha (NE) Daily Bee*, April 28, 1903.
16. *Omaha (NE) Daily Bee*, April 28, 1903.
17. *Omaha (NE) Daily Bee*, April 28, 1903.
18. *Omaha (NE) Daily Bee*, April 28, 1903.
19. The hooligans were part of those threatening an industrial strike at several Omaha businesses on May 1. *St. Louis Post-Dispatch*, April 28, 1903.
20. Alfred Henry Lewis, ed., *A Compilation of Messages and Speeches of Theodore Roosevelt, 1901–1905* (Washington, DC: Bureau of National Literature and Art, 1906), 283–84.
21. *Omaha (NE) Daily Bee*, April 29, 1903.
22. *Des Moines (IA) Register*, April 29, 1903.
23. *Des Moines (IA) Register*, April 29, 1903.
24. *Des Moines (IA) Register*, April 29, 1903.
25. Lewis, *A Compilation of Messages and Speeches of Theodore Roosevelt*, 298.
26. *Des Moines (IA) Register*, April 29, 1903.

Louisiana Purchase Centennial: St. Louis

1. The territory included land from what is now Arkansas, Missouri, Iowa, Oklahoma, Kansas, Nebraska, and portions (of varying sizes) of Minnesota, North and South Dakota, New Mexico, Texas, Montana, Wyoming, Colorado, Louisiana (including New Orleans), as well as small portions of the present-day Canadian provinces of Alberta and Saskatchewan. In 1818, the sections of land in Canada were ceded to Great Britain.
2. The World's Fair in St. Louis would open the following year in the same location, still celebrating the accomplishments of Lewis and Clark. Theodore would open the World's Fair via a telegraph message. The plot for the movie *Meet Me in St. Louis* (1944) follows the Smith family as the World's Fair is about to debut.
3. Alfred Henry Lewis, ed., *A Compilation of Messages and Speeches of Theodore Roosevelt, 1901–1905* (Washington, DC: Bureau of National Literature and Art, 1906), 304–6.
4. This was only the third time the Grand Act ever took place in America. Previously, it was held twice in Woodstock, Maryland, in 1874 and 1890. *St. Louis Post-Dispatch*, April 29, 1903.
5. Edmund Morris, *Theodore Rex* (New York: Random House, 2001), 83.
6. William Jennings Bryan, who ran three times for the Democratic presidential nomination (1896, 1900, and 1908), also chose not to run. Other people considered as potential nominees were William Randolph Hearst and Lieutenant General Nelson Miles. In the end, Alton B. Parker, chief judge of the New York Court of Appeals, won the nomination.

7. Letter dated May 11, 1903, in *Selections from the Correspondence of Theodore Roosevelt and Henry Cabot Lodge 1884–1918, Volume 2*, ed. Henry Cabot Lodge (New York: Charles Scribner's Sons, 1925), 13.

8. *St. Louis Republic*, May 1, 1903.

9. Letter to John Hay dated August 9, 1903, in *The Letters of Theodore Roosevelt: The Square Deal 1901–1903, Volume 3*, ed. Elting Morison (Cambridge, MA: Harvard University Press, 1951), 554.

10. (New York) *Sun*, May 1, 1903.

11. *Minneapolis Journal*, May 1, 1903.

12. (New York) *Sun*, May 1, 1903.

13. Lewis, *A Compilation of Messages and Speeches of Theodore Roosevelt*, 307–18.

Ruffians and Jayhawkers: Missouri and Kansas

1. *Salina (KS) Evening Journal*, May 1, 1903.

2. Speech given on May 1, 1903, Theodore Roosevelt Digital Library, Dickinson State University, Dickinson, ND.

3. Speech given on May 1, 1903, Theodore Roosevelt Digital Library.

4. *St. Louis Post-Dispatch*, May 1, 1903.

5. *Topeka (KS) Daily Capital*, May 2, 1903.

6. *Topeka (KS) Daily Capital*, May 2, 1903.

7. *Topeka (KS) Daily Capital*, May 2, 1903.

8. *Topeka (KS) Daily Capital*, May 2, 1903.

9. Speech given on May 2, 1903, Theodore Roosevelt Digital Library, Dickinson State University, Dickinson, ND.

10. (Washingon, DC) *Evening Star*, May 2, 1903.

11. *Junction City (KS) Republic*, May 1, 1903.

12. *Abilene (KS) Daily Reflector*, May 2, 1903.

13. *Salina (KS) Daily Union*, May 2, 1903.

14. *Wilson (KS) World*, May 7, 1903.

15. *Russell (KS) Reformer*, May 8, 1903.

16. *Hays (KS) Free Press*, May 2, 1903.

17. (WaKeeney, KS) *Independent*, May 8, 1903.

18. In 1869 Sharon Springs was originally named Eagle Tail after the creek that ran through the town. It was rechristened with its current name in 1886. The town's founding was exclusively due to the transcontinental railroad situated nearby.

19. (Sharon Springs, KS) *Western Times*, May 8, 1903.

20. Jayne Pearce, *The Great Sabbath Day*, Sharon Springs Methodist Church, December 19, 2013.

21. Reverend H. H. Carter of the First Presbyterian Church in Kansas City was brought in to deliver the sermon, Reverend E. J. Stevens gave a prayer, and Reverend John Wickstrand gave the benediction. *Denver Republican*, May 4, 1903.

22. Letter to John Hay dated August 9, 1903, in *The Letters of Theodore Roosevelt: The Square Deal 1901–1903, Volume 3*, ed. Elting Morison (Cambridge, MA: Harvard University Press, 1951), 554.

23. *Russell (KS) Reformer*, May 8, 1903.

24. (Sharon Springs, KS) *Western Times*, May 8, 1903.

25. Jayne Pearce to the author, October 1, 2018.

26. Jane Paterson Kerr, *A Bully Father: Theodore Roosevelt's Letters to His Children* (New York: Random House, 1995), 116.

27. Josiah became a favorite of Theodore's son Archie, who could be seen carrying the badger around with him in the White House. Theodore once warned his son, who was once again picking up Josiah, that the animal could bite his face. Archie replied that Josiah only nibbled on his toes. Within a year, Josiah would display his natural instincts and temperament and was given to the Bronx Zoo, which Theodore helped found.

Letter to John Hay dated August 9, 1903, in *The Letters of Theodore Roosevelt: The Square Deal 1901–1903*, 555.

28. The six girls were Pearl Gorsuch, Leta and Marie Halsey, Annabelle Perry, and Bernice and Bessie Ward.

29. (Sharon Springs, KS) *Western Times*, May 8, 1903.

A Cowboy Breakfast: Colorado

1. The term "rawhides" was given to Texas cowboys by their counterparts of the northern plains. In this case, Keppel meant that some Texas cowboys in Denver came to the dinner.

2. *Valentine (NE) Democrat*, December 24, 1903.

3. *Colorado Springs Gazette*, May 4, 1903.

4. Letter to John Hay dated August 9, 1903, in *The Letters of Theodore Roosevelt: The Square Deal 1901–1903, Volume 3*, ed. Elting Morison (Cambridge, MA: Harvard University Press, 1951), 555.

5. *Denver Republican*, May 4, 1903.

6. *Denver Republican*, May 4, 1903.

7. *Denver Republican*, May 4, 1903.

8. *Valentine (NE) Democrat*, December 24, 1903.

9. *Denver Republican*, May 3, 1903.

10. *Denver Post*, May 3, 1903.

11. *Denver Republican*, May 3, 1903.

12. (Denver, CO) *Rocky Mountain News*, May 4, 1903.

13. *Denver Post*, May 3, 1903.

14. *Denver Republican*, May 5, 1903.

15. Alfred Henry Lewis, ed., *A Compilation of Messages and Speeches of Theodore Roosevelt, 1901–1905* (Washington, DC: Bureau of National Literature and Art, 1906), 323–25.

16. Lewis, *A Compilation of Messages and Speeches of Theodore Roosevelt*, 323–25.

17. *Denver Republican*, May 4, 1903.

18. Nebuchadnezzar, the king of Babylon, had a dream about a tall tree with beautiful foliage and fruit. A holy man ordered the tree to be cut down, leaving just the stump and the roots. When he asked Daniel the meaning of the dream, Nebuchadnezzar was told that he was the tree, and God would make him live with the beasts in the field and eat grass as an animal. *Colorado Gazette*, May 5, 1903.

19. During the Antlers Hotel rebuild in 1900, an eighteen-year-old Colorado Springs resident named Lon Chaney helped to install carpets and hang wallpaper. He later became one of the major movie stars of the American silent film era, known as "the man of a thousand faces." The second version of the Antlers Hotel was torn down in 1964 to make way for a more modern, and less appealing, version.

20. *Colorado Springs Gazette*, May 5, 1903.

21. *Colorado Springs Gazette*, May 5, 1903.

22. *Colorado Springs Gazette*, May 5, 1903.

23. *Colorado Springs Gazette*, May 5, 1903.

24. The Mineral Palace was the brainchild of William H. Harvey, who wanted to display Colorado's mineral wealth in a museum-style setting. It opened on July 4, 1891, but within five years was facing financial hardship. By 1897, state bonds helped to fund the enterprise, turning the area around the museum into a park, complete with a lake, boathouse pavilion, bandstand, and small zoo. By 1935, the building had fallen into disrepair and was torn down. Today, Mineral Palace Park remains with its lake and a new bandshell.

25. *Arizona Republican*, May 5, 1903.

26. Letter to John Hay dated August 9, 1903, in *The Letters of Theodore Roosevelt: The Square Deal 1901–1903*, 555.

The Southwest: New Mexico

1. *Las Vegas (NM) Daily Optic*, May 5, 1903.

2. *Las Vegas (NM) Daily Optic*, May 5, 1903.

3. Pat Garrett, former lawman who killed Billy the Kid in 1881 at Fort Sumner, New Mexico, was also in attendance. Garrett never missed a chance to bolster himself and being seen with the president was a perfect opportunity. Theodore had appointed Garrett collector of customs in El Paso in 1902. Despite complaints of his lack of people skills, he remained on the job, even inviting himself to the 1905 Rough Riders reunion in San Antonio. Garrett brought along his friend Tom Powers, who was the owner of El Paso's "most notorious saloon," and introduced Powers to Theodore as a "cattle man." When photos of the president posing with Garrett and Powers were published, Garrett's detractors were quick to inform Theodore of Powers's real profession. Theodore would not forget the embarrassment. When it appeared to Garrett that he likely would not be reappointed to his post, he went to the White House with Powers in tow to talk to Theodore, but it became obvious to Garrett that his career as collector of customs was finished.

4. Alfred Henry Lewis, ed. *A Compilation of Messages and Speeches of Theodore Roosevelt, 1901–1905* (Washington, DC: Bureau of National Literature and Art, 1906), 324–26.

5. Since the early 1880s, when cattle ranching exploded in the area, there had not been any severe summer droughts and winters had been fairly mild. All that changed in the summer of 1886, when the sun dried up the grass and rain was a distant memory. The arrival of artic owls in October was another warning, as it indicated a harsh winter. Few paid heed to these signs. The blizzard of 1886–1887 proved to be a grim and painful

lesson, as most cattle owners lost upward of 80 percent of their herds, and some suffered nearly 100 percent losses. Theodore, it has been estimated, lost about 65 percent of his herd. One explanation for his losses not being as severe as others was the fact that his two ranches, the Maltese Cross and the Elkhorn, had wooded bottoms, which provided some shelter for his herd during the bitter winter months. Even so, his net loss by 1899 was estimated to be $20,292.63, not including any lost interest.

6. *Las Vegas (NM) Daily Optic*, May 5, 1903.

7. Armijo had been shot in the wrist during the battle of Las Guásimas. He mustered out with the other Rough Riders after a thirty-day quarantine on September 15, 1898. Theodore's letter reads: "My Dear Sergeant, I congratulate you heartily. Give my warm regards to the bride. Faithfully yours, Theodore Roosevelt." Theodore Roosevelt's Letter to George W. Armijo, dated January 15, 1902, Theodore Roosevelt Digital Library, Dickinson State University, Dickinson, ND.

8. The fight in the Netherlands to which Theodore refers was the Dutch Revolt (also called the Eighty Years' War, 1568–1648), in which the largely Protestant Seven Provinces of the Low Country rebelled against the Catholic Church and King Phillip II of Spain. The war ended with a peace treaty signed in January 1648. Letter to John Hay dated August 9, 1903, in *The Letters of Theodore Roosevelt: The Square Deal 1901–1903, Volume 3*, ed. Elting Morison (Cambridge, MA: Harvard University Press, 1951), 557.

9. *Albuquerque Citizen*, May 5, 1903.

10. *Albuquerque Citizen*, May 5, 1903.

11. Speech given on May 5, 1903, Theodore Roosevelt Digital Library, Dickinson State University, Dickinson, ND.

12. Speech given on May 5, 1903, Theodore Roosevelt Digital Library.

13. Lewis, *A Compilation of Messages and Speeches of Theodore Roosevelt*, 326.

14. The Albuquerque Commercial Club had been formed by various businessmen in the city. It was a forerunner of what would now be a city's chamber of commerce.

15. The Harvey Curio Shop was owned and run by Fred Harvey, who developed the Harvey House lunch rooms, restaurants, souvenir shops, and hotels to serve the rail passengers on the Atchison, Topeka, and Santa Fe Railway, the Gulf Colorado and Santa Fe Railway, the Kansas Pacific Railway, and the St. Louis–San Francisco Railway. As an innovative restaurateur and marketer, Fred Harvey is credited with creating the first restaurant chain in the United States and was a leader in promoting tourism in the American Southwest during the late nineteenth century. *Albuquerque Citizen*, May 5, 1903.

16. Theodore was also given a "leather cowboy suit" from the Rio Grande Woolen Company. *Albuquerque Citizen*, May 5, 1903.

17. The Wright and Shinick Carriage Builders worked on several carriages belonging to Theodore's father.

18. *Santa Fe New Mexican*, May 6, 1903.

19. *Los Angeles Record*, May 7, 1903.

20. *Arizona Daily Star*, May 7, 1903.

The Big Ditch: Arizona

1. The "youngest" layer, at 250 million years old, is called the Kaibab Limestone. When viewed from the canyon rim, it has a cream to gray-white color, resembling what many refer to as the canyon's "bathtub ring." Many fossils have been found in this layer of rock such as brachiopods, mollusks, and sea lilies.
2. Diamond Creek is now part of the Hualapai Indian Reservation.
3. Powell later published an account of his river trip in 1875, calling the Grand Canyon "our granite prison," as well as describing a harrowing ride down the rapids.
4. Cameron bought Berry's rights to Bright Angel Trail and extended his franchise of the trail until 1906. Grand Canyon Railway, completed in 1901, had an arrangement with a competing hotel that prevented Cameron from soliciting visitors at the canyon's new railroad station. Cameron caused problems when he began charging people to use Bright Angel Trail and eventually closed his hotel after the 1905 opening of El Tovar Hotel.
5. The brothers separated in 1913, with Emery continuing to operate the studio until his death in 1976. Today the studio is a museum, sharing the history of the two brothers and their efforts.
6. The Atchison, Topeka, and Santa Fe railroad opened its rail line to the Grand Canyon on September 17, 1901. It made the canyon readily available to tourists with a ticket price of $3.95, compared to the $18 ticket for the eight-hour stagecoach ride from Flagstaff. The railroad ceased operations in 1968 due to declining business, but the Grand Canyon Railway reopened on September 17, 1989, eighty-eight years to the day after the first train traveled to the canyon. It continues to transport tourists, helping to reduce the number of cars—nearly 50,000—that would otherwise drive into the national park.
7. *Bisbee (AZ) Daily Review,* May 7, 1903.
8. Although Daniels had been forced to resign and the situation proved a public embarrassment to Theodore, he did not abandon his friend. Theodore managed to get Daniels appointed warden at the Arizona Territorial Prison in Yuma and in June 1905 awarded Daniels a presidential pardon. When Daniels attended Theodore's 1905 swearing-in ceremony, Theodore informed him that he would again nominate him for U.S. marshal in Arizona. This time, Theodore had numerous letters of support from notable citizens, judges, and law officers, and Daniels's appointment was easily approved by the Senate in 1906. Daniels served as U.S. marshal in Arizona until 1909, when he was asked to resign his position by President Taft. At the age of sixty-eight, he won election as Pima County sheriff and two years later headed a posse that captured some killers. Defeated in 1922 when he ran for reelection, Daniels died on April 20, 1923, after suffering a stroke. The *Arizona Republican,* May 7, 1903.
9. *Bisbee (AZ) Daily Review,* May 7, 1903.
10. The group included secretary Loeb, Dr. Rixley, Nicholas Murray Butler (president of Columbia University), Arizona Territory governor Alexander Brodie, and several Secret Service agents. Brodie, a graduate of West Point (1866) and veteran of the Indian Wars, served with Theodore in Cuba. He was appointed senior regimental officer of the Arizona group with a rank of major. Brodie was wounded during the battle at Las Guásimas.

11. *Bisbee (AZ) Daily Review*, May 7, 1903.

12. Bucky O'Neill was a true pioneer of Arizona. Graduating from Georgetown Law School, he moved to the Arizona Territory where he worked as a printer for a Phoenix newspaper. When he tired of the job, he went to Tombstone, working briefly on the town's newspaper, the *Tombstone Epitaph*. After serving as a lawman in Phoenix, O'Neill moved to Prescott, Arizona, where he worked as a news reporter, starting his own paper called *Hoof and Horn*, which catered to the local cattle business. He was elected judge of Yavapai County, then served three terms as the county sheriff, where he gained a reputation as a fearless and honorable lawman. O'Neill was elected unanimously as mayor of Prescott before joining the Rough Riders in 1898. Waiting to charge Kettle Hill, O'Neill's Troop A came under heavy fire from the Spaniards. He stood up and walked the line in front of his men to calm them. When one soldier warned him he might get shot, O'Neill said there wasn't a Spanish bullet made that could kill him. Moments later he was shot in the mouth and died instantly. He is buried at Arlington National Cemetery.

13. Alfred Henry Lewis, ed., *A Compilation of Messages and Speeches of Theodore Roosevelt, 1901–1905* (Washington, DC: Bureau of National Literature and Art, 1906), 327.

14. Lewis, *A Compilation of Messages and Speeches of Theodore Roosevelt*, 326–27.

15. (Flagstaff, AZ) *Coconino Sun*, May 9, 1903.

16. Teddy was born in the mountains of northern Mexico in June 1902. He was only a few weeks old when he was captured by a party of loggers near Cananea. The mother bear went into camp in search of her cub and was shot by one of the loggers. *Bisbee (AZ) Daily Review*, May 7, 1903; the *Spokane (WA) Press*, May 26, 1903.

17. *Bisbee (AZ) Daily Review*, May 7, 1903.

18. Lewis, *A Compilation of Messages and Speeches of Theodore Roosevelt*, 327.

19. Letter dated May 10, 1903, in *A Bully Father: Theodore Roosevelt's Letters to His Children*, ed. Jane Paterson Kerr (New York: Random House, 1995), 116.

20. In 1910 and 1911, attempts were made in Congress to grant the Grand Canyon national park status but both failed. In December 1932, nearly 310 square miles adjacent to the park were designated as a second Grand Canyon national monument. Marble Canyon National Monument, covering forty-one square miles, was established on January 20, 1969. President Gerald Ford signed a bill on January 3, 1975, which doubled the size of the Grand Canyon by incorporating these two national monuments and additional federal land. At the same time, Havasu Canyon was returned to the Havasupai Tribe.

The Golden State: Southern California

1. At his first two stops, Barstow and Victorville, he spoke for fewer than ten minutes. Both of Theodore's speeches, given from the train's rear platform, consisted of a total of seventy-seven words.

2. California Promotion Committee, *California Addresses by Theodore Roosevelt* (San Francisco: Tomoyé Press, 1903), 1.

3. *Los Angeles Record*, May 6, 1903.

4. *Los Angeles Times*, May 8, 1903.

5. Citrus fruits were first introduced by Spanish padres in 1769, with the first recorded orchard being planted in 1804 at the San Gabriel Mission. In 1841, the first commercial orchard was planted in the area that is now the center of downtown Los Angeles. By 1901, there were 4.5 billion citrus trees planted within three counties of Southern California (Los Angeles, San Bernardino, and San Diego).

6. The memorial bust and granite pedestal were covered by a stone canopy with columns. The canopy and columns have long disappeared, but the bust remains on the lawn of the Lincoln Shrine, behind the public library.

7. California Promotion Committee, *California Addresses by Theodore Roosevelt*, 4–10.

8. Letter to John Hay dated August 9, 1903, in *The Letters of Theodore Roosevelt: The Square Deal 1901–1903, Volume 3*, ed. Elting Morison (Cambridge, MA: Harvard University Press, 1951), 557–58.

9. *San Bernardino (CA) Daily Sun*, May 7, 1903.

10. *San Bernardino (CA) Daily Sun*, May 7, 1903.

11. California Promotion Committee, *California Addresses by Theodore Roosevelt*, 11.

12. *San Bernardino (CA) Daily Sun*, May 7, 1903.

13. *San Bernardino (CA) Daily Sun*, May 7, 1903.

14. *San Bernardino (CA) Daily Sun*, May 7, 1903.

15. *San Bernardino (CA) Daily Sun*, May 7, 1903.

16. California Promotion Committee, *California Addresses by Theodore Roosevelt*, 12–16.

17. *Los Angeles Record*, May 6, 1903.

18. The palm tree still stands at that location.

19. California Promotion Committee, *California Addresses by Theodore Roosevelt*, 17.

20. *Los Angeles Record*, May 6, 1903.

21. That tree died from a fungal infection in 1922. The other original navel tree is still thriving on Magnolia Avenue.

22. California Promotion Committee, *California Addresses by Theodore Roosevelt*, 19–23.

23. California Promotion Committee, *California Addresses by Theodore Roosevelt*, 19–23.

24. *Pasadena (CA) Daily News*, May 5, 1903.

25. *Pasadena (CA) Daily News*, May 5, 1903.

26. *Pasadena (CA) Daily News*, May 5, 1903.

27. California Promotion Committee, *California Addresses by Theodore Roosevelt*, 24–28.

28. California Promotion Committee, *California Addresses by Theodore Roosevelt*, 24–28.

29. California Promotion Committee, *California Addresses by Theodore Roosevelt*, 24–28.

30. *Los Angeles Times*, May 9, 1903.

31. *Pasadena (CA) Daily News*, May 8, 1903.

32. The term "snowbird" originated during the Indian Wars period (late 1860s to 1880s), when a soldier enlisted in the army during the winter for food and shelter, only to desert in the spring. Today it is a term generally used to describe people who leave the cold climates during the winter for warmer locations, like Arizona.

33. Before the real estate boom, land prices were ten to thirty dollars an acre, without water for irrigation. When the land boom exploded, the prices jumped to between one thousand and ten thousand dollars per acre.

34. Beth Werling to the author, Hollywood, September 18, 2018.

35. The Fiesta of Flowers would continue for many years until 1919, when it was discontinued due to lack of interest and population growth. In addition, another flower parade had become much more popular and still is today. The Rose Parade, known today as the Tournament of Roses Parade, promoted the area and its mild winters to boost tourism and business. Originally, the parade was made up of horse-drawn carriages decorated with roses. By 1895, motorized floats began to appear, and the first football game was played in 1902. The next game, held in 1916, was called the Tournament of Roses football game, and has been held annually ever since. The Rose Bowl, where the game is still played, was built in 1923. *Los Angeles Record*, May 6, 1903.

36. *Los Angeles Record*, May 7, 1908.

37. *Los Angeles Record*, May 9, 1903.

38. *St. Louis Republic*, May 2, 1903.

39. The "embalmed beef" is a reference to the horrible rations the Rough Riders endured while in Cuba. *Los Angeles Times*, May 9, 1903.

40. *Los Angeles Times*, May 9, 1903.

41. *Los Angeles Times*, May 9, 1903.

42. California Promotion Committee, *California Addresses by Theodore Roosevelt*, 29–30.

43. California Promotion Committee, *California Addresses by Theodore Roosevelt*, 29–30.

44. No doubt the escalating issues between Russia and Japan over China may have required him to be updated. Nine months later, on February 8, 1904, Japan issued a declaration of war against Russia.

45. *Los Angeles Times*, May 7, 1903.

46. California Promotion Committee, *California Addresses by Theodore Roosevelt*, 31.

47. *Los Angeles Times*, May 10, 1903.

48. *Los Angeles Times*, May 10, 1903.

49. California Promotion Committee, *California Addresses by Theodore Roosevelt*, 36–42.

50. California Promotion Committee, *California Addresses by Theodore Roosevelt*, 43.

The Golden State: Northern California

1. *San Francisco Examiner*, May 9, 1903.

2. *Los Angeles Times*, May 10, 1903.

3. Del Monte is now part of the city of Monterey. Hotel Del Monte was created by Charles Crocker, one of the four California railroad barons. The original hotel, opened in 1880, was destroyed by a fire in 1897. The second hotel, the one where Theodore stayed, was also destroyed by fire in 1924. The third hotel, built in 1926, was purchased by the U.S. Navy in 1947. Today, the grounds serve as the Naval Academy's postgraduate school, and the third version of the hotel now is renamed Herrmann Hall.

4. *San Francisco Examiner*, May 11, 1903.

5. Letters dated May 10, 1903, in *A Bully Father: Theodore Roosevelt's Letters to His Children*, ed. Jane Paterson Kerr (New York: Random House, 1995), 115–18.

6. California Promotion Committee, *California Addresses by Theodore Roosevelt* (San Francisco: Tomoyé Press), 1903, 53–54.

7. California Promotion Committee, *California Addresses by Theodore Roosevelt*, 53–54.

8. California Promotion Committee, *California Addresses by Theodore Roosevelt*, 55–56.

9. Since Theodore's visit, none of the trees have a sign attached to them.

10. *San Francisco Examiner*, May 12, 1903.

11. California Promotion Committee, *California Addresses by Theodore Roosevelt*, 63–73.

12. California Promotion Committee, *California Addresses by Theodore Roosevelt*, 63–73.

13. Letter dated May 11, 1903, *Selections from the Correspondence of Theodore Roosevelt and Henry Cabot Lodge 1884–1918, Volume 2*, ed. Henry Cabot Lodge (New York: Charles Scribner's Sons, 1925), 13.

14. *San Francisco Examiner*, May 12, 1903.

15. *San Francisco Examiner*, May 12, 1903.

16. *San Francisco Examiner*, May 12, 1903.

17. The dinner, which was scheduled to start at 7:40 p.m., was a long one. When the speeches began, M. H. DeYoung, head of the city's reception committee, spoke first. He was then followed by Mayor Eugene Schmitz, then Governor George Pardee, who introduced Theodore. When Theodore finished his speech, Major General MacArthur and Secretary of the Navy William Moody were the final speakers. *San Francisco Examiner*, May 13, 1903.

18. California Promotion Committee, *California Addresses by Theodore Roosevelt*, 84.

19. *San Francisco Call*, May 14, 1903.

20. *San Francisco Call*, May 14, 1903.

21. Cliff House has gone through four incarnations. The one Theodore visited was built in 1896. It survived the 1906 earthquake only to burn to the ground a year later. *San Francisco Chronicle*, May 14, 1903.

22. *San Francisco Examiner*, May 14, 1903.

23. California Promotion Committee, *California Addresses by Theodore Roosevelt*, 92–93.

24. *San Francisco Call*, May 14, 1903.

25. *San Francisco Call*, May 14, 1903.

26. California Promotion Committee, *California Addresses by Theodore Roosevelt*, 94–101.

27. California Promotion Committee, *California Addresses by Theodore Roosevelt*, 102–4.

28. California Promotion Committee, *California Addresses by Theodore Roosevelt*, 102–4.

29. *San Francisco Chronicle*, May 15, 1903.

30. California Promotion Committee, *California Addresses by Theodore Roosevelt*, 105–11.

31. California Promotion Committee, *California Addresses by Theodore Roosevelt*, 112–13.

32. California Promotion Committee, *California Addresses by Theodore Roosevelt*, 114–15.

33. *San Francisco Chronicle*, May 15, 1903.

34. California Promotion Committee, *California Addresses by Theodore Roosevelt*, 119–23.

35. *San Francisco Call*, May 15, 1903.

Tramping with Muir: Yosemite

1. The Yosemite Valley Railroad ran from Merced to El Portal on the park's western boundary, with the first passenger train arriving on May 15, 1907. In addition to carrying passengers, the railroad also hauled freight. By the mid-1920s, passenger traffic began to slip due to a new highway that allowed automobiles and buses access to the park. Yosemite Valley Railroad dropped ticket prices to compete with the bus service,

but it proved to be a money-losing effort. In 1935, the railroad incorporated under a new name, Yosemite Valley Railway, and managed to stay afloat with its freight business. With the outbreak of World War II, passenger travel halted and the freight business quickly declined. The railroad's last run was on August 24, 1945. The equipment was sold off and the rails were quickly scrapped.

2. *Raymond (CA) Tattler*, March 1933.

3. California Promotion Committee, *California Addresses by Theodore Roosevelt* (San Francisco: Tomoyé Press, 1903), 124–25.

4. The Wawona Tunnel Tree fell in 1969. Throughout the 1903 tour, photographers from the New York City studio of Underwood and Underwood took the images of Theodore on his trip, including those in Yosemite.

5. *San Francisco Call*, May 17, 1903.

6. Charlie Leidig's Report of President Roosevelt's Visit in May 1903, Yosemite Research Library, Yosemite National Park.

7. Theodore Roosevelt, *Theodore Roosevelt: An Autobiography* (Norwalk, CT: Easton Press, 1996), 347–48.

8. *San Francisco Chronicle*, May 18, 1903.

9. Charlie Leidig's Report of President Roosevelt's Visit in May 1903.

10. The theory accepted by scientists at the time was that Yosemite was created by a violent convulsion of the Earth. Muir's theory was that Yosemite was created by a mighty glacier from the Ice Age. There is no evidence of any dislocation of the Earth's crust, though there is abundant proof of glacier movement. However, it is not believed that a massive glacier created the valley and canyons; they were most likely created by streams of water. François Matthes, "John Muir and the Glacial Theory of Yosemite," *Sierra Club Bulletin*, vol. 23, no. 2 (April 1938): 9–10.

11. Douglas Brinkley, *The Wilderness Warrior: Theodore Roosevelt and the Crusade for America* (New York: HarperCollins, 2009), 540.

12. Brinkley, *The Wilderness Warrior*, 540.

13. Charlie Leidig's Report of President Roosevelt's Visit in May 1903.

14. Addison Thomas, *Roosevelt among the People* (Chicago: L. W. Walter, 1910), 250.

15. Hank Johnston, "Camping Trip with Roosevelt and Muir," *Yosemite*, vol. 56, no. 3 (summer 1994): 4.

16. *San Francisco Examiner*, May 18, 1903.

17. Charlie Leidig's Report of President Roosevelt's Visit in May 1903.

18. Leidig estimated that the number of people could have been between three to five hundred. Charlie Leidig's Report of President Roosevelt's Visit in May 1903.

19. The Bridalveil Meadow now has a sign indicating the location of the campsite. Charlie Leidig's Report of President Roosevelt's Visit in May 1903.

20. Brinkley, *The Wilderness Warrior*, 538.

21. Roosevelt, *Theodore Roosevelt*, 348–49.

22. Hank Johnston, "Camping Trip with Roosevelt and Muir," 4.

23. California Promotion Committee, *California Addresses by Theodore Roosevelt*, 136.

24. California Promotion Committee, *California Addresses by Theodore Roosevelt*, 139–43.

The Northwest: Oregon and Washington

1. *Daily Oregon Statesman*, May 22, 1903.
2. *Daily Oregon Statesman*, May 20, 1903.
3. *Daily Oregon Statesman*, May 22, 1903.
4. *Daily Oregon Statesman*, May 22, 1903.
5. *Daily Oregon Statesman*, May 22, 1903.
6. Letter dated June 4, 1903, Theodore Roosevelt Collection, Library of Congress, Washington, DC.
7. *Daily Oregon Statesman*, May 22, 1903.
8. *Daily Oregon Statesman*, May 22, 1903.
9. *Daily Oregon Statesman*, May 22, 1903.
10. *Oregon Daily Journal*, May 21, 1903.
11. Alfred Henry Lewis, ed., *A Compilation of Messages and Speeches of Theodore Roosevelt, 1901–1905* (Washington, DC: Bureau of National Literature and Art, 1906), 418–21.
12. *Oregon Daily Journal*, May 21, 1903.
13. *Oregon Daily Journal*, May 22, 1903.
14. *Outlook*, February 23, 1907.
15. *Eugene (OR) Guard*, May 21, 1903.
16. *Oregon Daily Journal*, May 20, 1903.
17. *Oregon Daily Journal*, May 22, 1903.
18. He died in 1926. Hermann was exonerated in 1932 of any wrongdoing by Secretary of the Interior Harold Ickes during the Franklin D. Roosevelt administration.
19. Letter dated May 13, 1903, in *Selections from the Correspondence of Theodore Roosevelt and Henry Cabot Lodge 1884–1918, Volume 2*, ed. Henry Cabot Lodge (New York: Charles Scribner's Sons, 1925), 14.
20. *Oregon Daily Journal*, May 26, 1903.
21. Archie Roosevelt had a Shetland pony, Algonquin, at the White House. Suffering from the measles while Theodore was on his tour, he had asked Edith if he could see his horse at the stables. The request was quickly dismissed, but Quentin had a better idea. With the help of the White House footman, Charles Reeder, they loaded the 350-pound horse into the freight elevator and brought Algonquin up to Archie's room. The sick boy squealed with delight and the horse's whinnies gave away the secret visit. Letter dated May 10, 1903, in *A Bully Father: Theodore Roosevelt's Letters to His Children*, ed. Jane Paterson Kerr (New York: Random House, 1995), 118.
22. *Oregon Daily Journal*, May 22, 1903.
23. *Seattle Star*, May 23, 1903.
24. Lewis, *A Compilation of Messages and Speeches of Theodore Roosevelt*, 421–24.
25. (Friday Harbor, WA) *San Juan Islander*, May 28, 1903.
26. *Seattle Star*, May 23, 1903.
27. "Jack Tar" was an old term for sailors.
28. Lewis, *A Compilation of Messages and Speeches of Theodore Roosevelt*, 435–36.
29. Lewis, *A Compilation of Messages and Speeches of Theodore Roosevelt*, 433–35.
30. *Seattle Star*, May 23, 1903.

31. Lewis, *A Compilation of Messages and Speeches of Theodore Roosevelt*, 429–33.

32. Lewis, *A Compilation of Messages and Speeches of Theodore Roosevelt*, 429–33.

33. *Adams County (WA) News*, May 27, 1903.

34. Lewis, *A Compilation of Messages and Speeches of Theodore Roosevelt*, 436–39.

35. *Seattle Star*, May 23, 1903.

36. *Seattle Star*, May 23, 1903.

37. In some newspaper articles his last name was listed as Becker. Walla Walla's *Evening Statesman* reported his real name was John Bushey. For the sake of clarity, I have chosen to use Joseph Barker.

38. *Butte (MT) Miner*, May 26, 1903.

39. *Kendrick (ID) Gazette*, May 29, 1903.

40. (Walla Walla, WA) *Evening Statesman*, May 26, 1903.

41. *Butte (MT) Miner*, May 26, 1903.

42. When talking about the president, one Sacramento man proclaimed in a loud voice that "One has died, and another might just as well." He was arrested and held until the following day. Nine days after Theodore left Oakland, it was announced that the city's police department had also stopped an attempted assassination.

In the Footsteps of Lewis and Clark: Montana and Idaho

1. *Spokane Press*, May 25, 1903.

2. *Spokane Press*, May 25, 1903. Those arrested in the police sweep included twenty-four-year-old Joseph Schoder, who was arrested for carrying concealed weapons. He was described by the newspaper as having "scars on his face and arms and is regarded as a suspicious character."

3. *Spokane Press*, May 30, 1903.

4. Letter dated May 27, 1903, *Selections from the Correspondence of Theodore Roosevelt and Henry Cabot Lodge 1884–1918, Volume 2*, ed. Henry Cabot Lodge (New York: Charles Scribner's Sons, 1925), 19.

5. No doubt his comments relating to the "man of wealth" were a not-so-veiled jibe at the antitrust lawsuit against J. P. Morgan and the Northern Securities Company. Alfred Henry Lewis, ed., *A Compilation of Messages and Speeches of Theodore Roosevelt, 1901–1905* (Washington, DC: Bureau of National Literature and Art, 1906), 440–41.

6. *Spokane Press*, May 29, 1903.

7. *Spokane Press*, May 29, 1903.

8. *Anaconda (MT) Standard*, May 27, 1903.

9. Jack Willis and Horace Smith, *Roosevelt in the Rough* (New York: Ives Washburn, 1931), 8–11.

10. Theodore's comment about making a Christian out of Willis referred to his giving up killing game only for the skins. Willis later opened one of the largest department stores in Montana. Willis and Smith, *Roosevelt in the Rough*, 155–56.

11. Willis and Smith, *Roosevelt in the Rough*, 155–56.

12. Letter to John Hay dated August 9, 1903, in *The Letters of Theodore Roosevelt: The Square Deal 1901–1903, Volume 3*, ed. Elting Morison (Cambridge, MA: Harvard University Press, 1951), 558.

13. Theodore had a St. Bernard named Rollo that was part of the White House menagerie. *Anaconda (MT) Standard*, May 28, 1903.
14. Lewis, *A Compilation of Messages and Speeches of Theodore Roosevelt*, 443–44.
15. *Anaconda (MT) Standard*, May 28, 1903.
16. *Anaconda (MT) Standard*, May 29, 1903.
17. Letter to John Hay dated August 9, 1903, *The Letters of Theodore Roosevelt: The Square Deal 1901–1903*, 558–59.
18. Fritz Agustus Heinze was known as one of the three "copper kings" of Montana, along with William A. Clark and Marcus Daly.
19. Letter to John Hay dated August 9, 1903, *The Letters of Theodore Roosevelt: The Square Deal 1901–1903*, 558–59.
20. Theodore's description meant the crowd situation drove the secret service agents crazy.
21. In 1892, workers went on strike at several mines in Coeur d'Alene, Idaho, because of low wages and terrible working conditions. Mine owners replaced the miners with non-union workers. The action led to a bloody series of gunfights until martial law was declared.
22. Elting Morison, ed., *The Letters of Theodore Roosevelt: The Square Deal 1901–1903*, 559.
23. Bullock's comment meant that the music was too high class for him to appreciate thoroughly. *Anaconda (MT) Standard*, May 28, 1903.
24. *Anaconda (MT) Standard*, May 28, 1903.
25. Theodore meant that the restaurant charged only twenty-five cents for a meal. *Anaconda (MT) Standard*, May 28, 1903.
26. *Anaconda (MT) Standard*, May 28, 1903.
27. Willis and Smith, *Roosevelt in the Rough*, 157.
28. Morison, *The Letters of Theodore Roosevelt: The Square Deal 1901–1903*, 559–60.
29. Morison, *The Letters of Theodore Roosevelt: The Square Deal 1901–1903*, 560.
30. Who-Hit-John was a western term for liquor. Morison, *The Letters of Theodore Roosevelt: The Square Deal 1901–1903*, 560–61.
31. *Anaconda (MT) Standard*, May 28, 1903.
32. Lewis, *A Compilation of Messages and Speeches of Theodore Roosevelt*, 441–43.
33. *Anaconda (MT) Standard*, May 28, 1903.
34. *Spokane Press*, May 28, 1903.
35. Lewis, *A Compilation of Messages and Speeches of Theodore Roosevelt*, 444–47.
36. *Anaconda (MT) Standard*, May 29, 1903.
37. Lewis, *A Compilation of Messages and Speeches of Theodore Roosevelt*, 450–51.
38. Speech given on April 15, 1907. H. Paul Jeffers, ed., *The Bully Pulpit: A Teddy Roosevelt Book of Quotations* (Lanham, MD: Taylor Trade, 2002), 30.

Once More in the Saddle: Utah and Wyoming

1. *Ogden (UT) Standard*, May 29, 1903.
2. Alfred Henry Lewis, ed., *A Compilation of Messages and Speeches of Theodore Roosevelt, 1901–1905* (Washington, DC: Bureau of National Literature and Art, 1906), 456–60.
3. Lewis, *A Compilation of Messages and Speeches of Theodore Roosevelt*, 456–60.

4. (Salt Lake City, UT) *Deseret Evening News*, May 29, 1903.

5. *Salt Lake Tribune*, May 29, 1903.

6. *Salt Lake Tribune*, May 29, 1903.

7. *Salt Lake Tribune*, May 29, 1903.

8. Theodore also talked about the hazards of overgrazing, something he had proselytized during his time in the Dakota Territory. He said the ranges "must be treated as a great capital investment." The danger of overgrazing came to a horrible culmination in the winter of 1886 and 1887 in the Dakotas, when many cattle ranches saw their stock wiped out or severely diminished, including Theodore's. He also discussed the need for maintaining and increasing forest reserves, as well as avoiding overgrazing in these regions.

9. Lewis, *A Compilation of Messages and Speeches of Theodore Roosevelt*, 452–56.

10. Elting Morison, ed., *The Letters of Theodore Roosevelt: The Square Deal 1901–1903, Volume 3* (Cambridge, MA: Harvard University Press, 1951), 561.

11. In the letter, Theodore misspelled Mingersville; it should be Mingusville. This was the small town just across the Montana border where he was involved in knocking unconscious a drunken cowboy in June 1884. Morison, *The Letters of Theodore Roosevelt: The Years of Preparation 1868–1898*, 561.

12. *Cheyenne (WY) Daily Leader*, May 30, 1903.

13. Lewis, *A Compilation of Messages and Speeches of Theodore Roosevelt*, 460–62.

14. *Laramie (WY) Boomerang*, May 31, 1903.

15. The term "rack" was another word for trot. *Cheyenne (WY) Daily Leader*, May 30, 1903.

16. The riding party consisted of Seth Bullock, Senator Warren, U.S. Marshal Frank Hadsell, Deputy Marshal Joe Lefors, Dr. Marion Rixley, William Daley, Nathaniel Boswell, Otto Gramm, Fred Porter, and W. F. Park. Both Daley and Boswell were well-known figures in Wyoming history. Both men owned large cattle ranches, and Boswell served as Laramie's sheriff. Joe Lefors was known to have obtained a confession from Tom Horn for killing fourteen-year-old Willie Nickell, although some historians believe Lefors set Horn up for the murder. (At the time of this ride, Horn was in a Cheyenne jail awaiting his hanging on November 20, 1903.) Lefors was also part of the posse that chased the Hole-in-the-Wall gang, led by Butch Cassidy, after the Willcox train robbery in 1899. Charlie Siringo, a well-known lawman and Pinkerton agent, said Lefors was, at best, an incompetent lawman. *Cheyenne (WY) Daily Leader*, May 30, 1903.

17. The first horse Theodore purchased in the West was a buckskin named Nell. He bought it from Sylvane Ferris during his buffalo hunt in 1883.

18. Tie City no longer exists. It had been named by the railroad men who cut trees down for railroad ties. Today, the area is known as Tie City Campground, part of the National Forest Service. *Cheyenne (WY) Daily Leader*, May 30, 1903.

19. William Chapin Deming, *Roosevelt in the Bunkhouse and Other Sketches: Visits of the Great Rough Rider to Wyoming in 1900, 1903, and 1910* (Laramie, WY: Laramie Printing, 1927), 23.

20. McGee's Ranch no longer exists. The site of the former ranch is near Laramie County Road #110, close to where the Bunkhouse Bar and Happy Jack Road go over the south fork of Crow Creek.

21. In measuring the height of a horse (from hoof to the withers) a "hand" equals four inches. Therefore, Jim, who was sixteen hands, stood nearly five feet, four inches at his shoulder.

22. Deming, *Roosevelt in the Bunkhouse*, 23.

23. Fort Russell is now known as Warren Air Force Base. Deming, *Roosevelt in the Bunkhouse*, 23–24.

24. (Cheyenne) *Wyoming Tribune*, May 31, 1903.

25. Theodore and his party had spent slightly longer than six hours in the saddle, minus the ninety-minute lunch at Van Tassell's ranch and the time spent switching horses and meeting with Major Foster at Fort Russell. By the time he started his speech, it was seven o'clock. (Cheyenne) *Wyoming Tribune*, May 30, 1903.

26. Decoration Day, which began in 1868, was changed to Memorial Day in the early 1880s. It was officially declared Memorial Day by federal law in 1967.

27. Deming, *Roosevelt in the Bunkhouse*, 28–32.

28. Deming, *Roosevelt in the Bunkhouse*, 28–32.

29. *Cheyenne (WY) Daily Leader*, June 1, 1903.

30. *Cheyenne (WY) Daily Leader*, June 1, 1903.

31. *Cheyenne (WY) Daily Leader*, June 1, 1903.

32. Deming, *Roosevelt in the Bunkhouse*, 37–39.

Last Stops: Iowa, Illinois, and Indiana

1. In today's dollars, the loss would be nearly $43 million.

2. Diphtheria, scarlet fever, and measles were being reported in North Topeka, Kansas, by June 1. *Davenport (IA) Morning Star*, June 2, 1903.

3. Rock Island Railroad sent "a long train of passenger coaches" to house displaced residents who were taken to Atchison, Kansas, or St. Joseph, Missouri, where they would be taken care of. *Des Moines (IA) Register*, June 2, 1903.

4. From Cheyenne, Theodore's train stopped briefly in Sidney, Nebraska, and then at North Platte, Nebraska, before passing through Council Bluffs, Iowa, at 4:30 in the morning. (Davenport, IA) *Daily Times*, June 2, 1903.

5. *Davenport (IA) Weekly Republican*, June 4, 1903.

6. *New York Tribune*, June 3, 1903.

7. Leaving Denison, Theodore's train stopped in Fort Dodge, Webster City, Iowa Falls, Cedar Falls, Waterloo, and Independence before arriving in Dubuque.

8. (Waterloo, IA) *Courier*, June 3, 1903.

9. (Davenport, IA) *Daily Times*, June 3, 1903.

10. *New York Tribune*, June 4, 1903.

11. (Chicago) *Inter-Ocean*, June 4, 1903.

12. *New York Tribune*, June 4, 1903.

13. *New York Tribune*, June 4, 1903; *Chicago Tribune*, June 4, 1903; *Billings (MT) Weekly*, June 5, 1903.

14. (Chicago) *Inter-Ocean*, June 5, 1903.

15. The building, which cost $150,000 in 1903, resembled a medieval fortress. In 1934, the arsenal suffered severe damage from an arson fire and was replaced by a new building in 1937.

16. Alfred Henry Lewis, ed., *A Compilation of Messages and Speeches of Theodore Roosevelt, 1901–1905* (Washington, DC: Bureau of National Literature and Art, 1906), 477–81.

17. *Lincoln (NE) Star Journal*, June 5, 1903.

18. Joseph Cannon was the second-longest continuously serving Republican as House Speaker, serving from 1903 to 1911.

19. Theodore Roosevelt's speech at Danville, Illinois, June 4, 1903, Theodore Roosevelt Digital Library, Dickinson State University, Dickinson, ND.

20. *Chicago Tribune*, June 5, 1903.

Home and the Horizon

1. *Washington Times*, June 5, 1903.

2. *Washington Times*, June 6, 1903.

3. Alfred Henry Lewis, ed., *A Compilation of Messages and Speeches of Theodore Roosevelt, 1901–1905* (Washington, DC: Bureau of National Literature and Art, 1906), 481.

4. Neither Theodore nor his vice presidential candidate, Charles Fairbanks, attended the Republican convention or made any speeches. Instead, others made nominating speeches on their behalf. Former New York governor Frank Black made the speech on Theodore's behalf. Interestingly, Theodore was chosen to replace Black as the Republican candidate for New York governor in 1898.

Theodore and Fairbanks did not get along. Dubbed a "reactionary machine politician" by Theodore, Fairbanks actively worked against the president's Square Deal program. Theodore limited the role Fairbanks played in his administration. During this period in the United States, the president did not choose his vice president. That was left up to the Republican Party at its convention. Fairbanks tried to secure the Republican presidential nomination in 1908 but lost to William Howard Taft. In 1916, he again ran for the presidential nomination only to be defeated by Charles Evans Hughes but agreed to take the vice presidential nomination. The ticket lost to Woodrow Wilson.

5. Arizona, New Mexico, Oklahoma, and Indian Territories did not vote. Parker won the electoral votes in Texas, Arkansas, Louisiana, Mississippi, Alabama, Tennessee, Kentucky, Georgia, Florida, South Carolina, North Carolina, and Virginia. The Socialist Party and the Prohibition Party did little to change the outcome, with neither obtaining any electoral votes. Of the popular votes, these two parties received 2.98 percent and 1.92 percent, respectively.

Minnie Cox was a black woman who was appointed postmaster of Indianola, Mississippi (population three thousand), by Presidents Harrison, McKinley, and Roosevelt. In 1902, James Vardaman, editor of the *Greenwood Commonwealth* and a white supremacist, launched a campaign to oust her. Cox refused to vacate her position until it expired in January 1904. When she and her family were threatened with physical harm, she sent Theodore her resignation and moved away. Theodore refused her resignation, announcing she would continue to be paid her federal salary until the expiration of her term. On

January 2, 1903, he closed the Indianola post office, informing residents that they could get their mail by traveling thirty miles to the town of Greenville. He kept the Indianola post office closed until Minnie Cox's term expired.

Dr. John Crum worked as a physician at the black-run McLennan Hospital in Charleston, South Carolina. (He eventually became the hospital's chief administrator.) An active supporter of Republican politics, his work caught the eye of Theodore, who appointed Crum collector of customs for the port of Charleston. The move infuriated southern whites, since Crum would replace a white man. (Theodore placed another black man in the same position, collector of customs, in Savannah, Georgia, without a single complaint, as well as placing other blacks in various positions.) The Senate deliberately delayed approving Crum's position, but Theodore appointed Crum during a congressional recess and there was nothing they could do to oppose it. He used this option until Crum was finally approved by the Senate in 1905.

6. The Meat Inspection Act made it a crime to adulterate or mislabel meat products for consumption and to ensure that meat was slaughtered and processed under strict sanitary regulations. The law was instigated in part by Upton Sinclair's book *The Jungle*, which revealed the problems in the Chicago meat-packing industry. The Pure Food and Drug Act would ban contaminated and mislabeled food and drugs. It also required companies to provide a label of active ingredients and set a standard of purity levels in the making of drugs.

7. It had been announced before his term expired that Theodore would be taking an extensive African safari sponsored by the Smithsonian Institution and Andrew Carnegie. This explains the newspaper wishing him "more big game be yours." *Washington Herald*, March 4, 1909.

An American Original
1. *Kalispell (MT) Bee*, June 23, 1903.
2. Riding night herd was one of the most dangerous jobs. As the cattle bedded down for the night, two riders circled the herd in opposite directions, often softly singing to calm the animals. This was an important job, as a sound could spook the herd and lead them into a stampede. Theodore was involved in two stampedes during his time in the Dakotas.
3. On January 16, 2001, President Clinton posthumously awarded Theodore a Medal of Honor, which was accepted by his great-grandson, Tweed Roosevelt. The medal, along with his Nobel Peace Prize, is displayed in the Roosevelt Room at the White House. Theodore and his son, Theodore Jr. (who received his Medal of Honor for his actions on D-Day during World War II), are the second set of father and sons to be awarded the Medal of Honor. Arthur MacArthur and his son, Douglas, are the other.

Bibliography

Books

Auchincloss, Louis. *Theodore Roosevelt: Letters and Speeches*. New York: Library of America, 2004.

Blake, Michael F. *The Cowboy President: The American West and the Making of Theodore Roosevelt*. Helena, MT: Two Dot, 2018.

Blevins, Win. *Dictionary of the American West*. Seattle, WA: Sasquatch Books, 2001.

Brands, H. W. *T. R.: The Last Romantic*. New York: Basic Books, 1997.

———. *The Selected Letters of Theodore Roosevelt*. New York: Cooper Square Press, 2001.

Brinkley, Douglas. *The Wilderness Warrior: Theodore Roosevelt and the Crusade for America*. New York: HarperCollins, 2009.

Burroughs, John. *Camping and Tramping with Roosevelt*. Boston: Houghton Mifflin, 1907.

California Promotion Committee. *California Addresses by Theodore Roosevelt*. San Francisco: Tomoyé Press, 1903.

Cutright, Paul Russell. *Theodore Roosevelt: The Making of a Conservationist*. Chicago: University of Illinois Press, 1985.

Deming, William Chapin. *Roosevelt in the Bunkhouse and Other Sketches: Visits of the Great Rough Rider to Wyoming in 1900, 1903, and 1910*. Laramie, WY: Laramie Printing, 1927.

Epting, Chris. *Teddy Roosevelt in California: The Whistle Stop Tour That Changed America*. Charleston, SC: History Press, 2015.

Hagedorn, Hermann. *The Boy's Life of Theodore Roosevelt*. New York: Harpers, 1918.

———. *Roosevelt in the Bad Lands*. Boston: Houghton Mifflin, 1921.

———. *The Theodore Roosevelt Treasury: A Self-Portrait from His Writings*. Norwalk, CT: Easton Press, 1988.

Hart, Albert Bushnell, and Herbert Ronald Feleger, eds. *Theodore Roosevelt Cyclopedia*. Westport, CT: Theodore Roosevelt Association and Meckler Corporation, 1989.

Jeffers, H. Paul. *The Bully Pulpit: A Teddy Roosevelt Book of Quotations*. Lanham, MD: Taylor Trade, 2002.

———. *Roosevelt the Explorer: Teddy Roosevelt's Amazing Adventures as a Naturalist, Conservationist and Explorer*. Lanham, MD: Taylor Trade, 2003.

Kerr, Jane Paterson. *A Bully Father: Theodore Roosevelt's Letters to His Children*. New York: Random House, 1995.

Lewis, Alfred Henry, ed. *A Compilation of Messages and Speeches of Theodore Roosevelt, 1901–1905*. Washington, DC: Bureau of National Literature and Art, 1906.

Lodge, Henry Cabot, ed. *Selections from the Correspondence of Theodore Roosevelt and Henry Cabot Lodge 1884–1918, Volume 1*. New York: Charles Scribner's Sons, 1925.

———. *Selections from the Correspondence of Theodore Roosevelt and Henry Cabot Lodge 1884–1918, Volume 2.* New York: Charles Scribner's Sons, 1925.

Looker, Earle. *The White House Gang.* New York: Fleming H. Revell, 1929.

Mallard, Candice. *The River of Doubt: Theodore Roosevelt's Darkest Journey.* New York: Anchor Books, 2005.

Miller, Nathan. *Theodore Roosevelt: A Life.* New York: William Morrow, 1992.

Morison, Elting E., ed. *The Letters of Theodore Roosevelt: The Years of Preparation 1868–1898, Volume 1.* Cambridge, MA: Harvard University Press, 1951.

———. *The Letters of Theodore Roosevelt: The Years of Preparation 1898–1900, Volume 2.* Cambridge, MA: Harvard University Press, 1951.

———. *The Letters of Theodore Roosevelt: The Square Deal 1901–1903, Volume 3.* Cambridge, MA: Harvard University Press, 1951.

———. *The Letters of Theodore Roosevelt: The Square Deal 1903–1905, Volume 4.* Cambridge, MA: Harvard University Press, 1951.

Morris, Edmund. *The Rise of Theodore Roosevelt.* New York: Random House, 1979.

———. *Theodore Rex.* New York: Random House, 2001.

———. *Colonel Roosevelt.* New York: Random House, 2010.

Morris, Sylvia Jukes. *Edith Kermit Roosevelt.* New York: Modern Library, 2001.

Mullins, Linda. *The Teddy Bear Men: Theodore Roosevelt and Clifford Berryman.* Grantsville, MD: Hobby House Press, 1998.

Robinson, Corrine Roosevelt. *My Brother Theodore Roosevelt.* New York: Charles Scribner's Sons, 1921.

Roosevelt, Theodore. *The Wilderness Hunter.* New York: G. P. Putnam's Sons, 1893.

———. *Addresses and Presidential Messages of Theodore Roosevelt, 1902–1904.* New York: G. P. Putnam's Sons, 1904.

———. *Ranch Life and the Hunting-Trail.* Reprint, Alexandria, VA: Time-Life Books, 1981.

———. *Theodore Roosevelt: An Autobiography.* Reprint, Norwalk, CT: Easton Press, 1996.

———. *Outdoor Pastimes of an American Hunter.* Reprint, Birmingham, AL: Palladium Press, 1999.

Shaw, Albert. *A Cartoon History of Roosevelt's Career.* New York: Review of Reviews, 1910.

Thomas, Addison C. *Roosevelt among the People.* Chicago: L.W. Walter, 1910.

Vietze, Andrew. *Becoming Teddy Roosevelt: How a Maine Guide Inspired America's 26th President.* Lanham, MD: Down East, 2010.

Willis, Jack, and Horace Smith. *Roosevelt in the Rough.* New York: Ives Washburn, 1931.

Wolff, David A. *Seth Bullock: Black Hills Lawman.* Pierre: South Dakota State Historical Society Press, 2009.

Magazine, Newsletters, and Internet

Brands, H. W. "Deliverance." *American History*, April 2013.

Brown, Henry S. "Punishing the Land-Looters." *Outlook*, February 23, 1907.

"Exhibit Looks at Travel before There Were Highway or Cars." *Past Times*, vol. 11, Rutherford B. Hayes Presidential Center. Fremont, OH, 2012.

Johnston, Hank. "Camping Trip with Roosevelt and Muir." *Yosemite* 56, no. 3 (summer 1994).

Koy, Gary. "Theodore Roosevelt and John Muir: 100 Years Ago and Today." *Yosemite* 65, no. 2 (spring 2003).

Matthes, François. "John Muir and the Glacial Theory of Yosemite." *Sierra Club Bulletin* 23, no. 2 (April 1938).

Pearce, Jayne. "The Great Sabbath Day." Sharon Springs Methodist Church, December 19, 2013.

"President Theodore Roosevelt's Horseback Travel Route." Wyoming Historical Society, WyoHistory.org, 2011.

Newspaper Articles

"All Saw the President." *Russell (KS) Reformer*, May 8, 1903.

"Anarchist Suspect Nabbed." (Salt Lake City, UT) *Deseret Evening News*, May 29, 1903.

"Anti-Roosevelt Sentiment." *New York Times*, February 21, 1903.

"Arizona Citizens Angry Because He Wouldn't Appear." *Los Angeles Record*, May 7, 1903.

"Art Notes." (Washington, DC) *Evening Star*, April 4, 1903.

"As Told by the President." *Boston Globe*, September 4, 1902.

"Attack on Roosevelt." (Washington, DC) *Evening Star*, April 23, 1903.

"At the White House." (Washington, DC) *Evening Star*, March 31, 1903.

"Begins Work on Statue Site." *San Francisco Examiner*, May 14, 1903.

"Big Crowd at Gardiner." *Billings (MT) Gazette*, April 25, 1903.

"'Billy' Hoffer, Famous Scout, Will Be President's Guide." (Missoula, MT) *Missoulian*, April 9, 1903.

"Buffalo Jones with the President." *Anaconda (MT) Standard*, April 9, 1903.

"A Calamity Averted." *New York Times*, April 4, 1903.

"California's Welcome Amid Redland's Roses." *Los Angeles Times*, May 8, 1903.

"Change between Candidate and President Roosevelt Slight." (Denver, CO) *Rocky Mountain News*, May 4, 1903.

"Colorado Grasps Hand of President Roosevelt." *Denver Republican*, May 4, 1903.

"Committee Ignored Many." *Spokane Press*, May 29, 1903.

"Cowboy Breakfast." *Saint Paul Globe*, April 2, 1903.

"Crank Tries to Send a Letter to the President at Helena." *Anaconda (MT) Standard*, May 27, 1903.

"The Cross Country Ride to Cheyenne." (Cheyenne) *Wyoming Tribune*, May 31, 1903.

"Crown City's Royal Guest." *Pasadena (CA) Daily News*, May 8, 1903.

"Damnable Outrage." *Boston Globe*, September 4, 1902.

"Defeat Roosevelt." (Washington, DC) *Evening Star*, April 24, 1903.

"At Dinner with the De Youngs." *San Francisco Call*, May 14, 1903.

"Dynamite, but No Plot." *Chicago Tribune*, June 4, 1903.

"Dynamite Plot Alleged." *New York Tribune*, June 4, 1903.

"Eats Luncheon on the Continent's Edge." *San Francisco Chronicle*, May 14, 1903.

"Fifty Thousand Voices Raised." *Daily (Salem) Oregon Statesman*, May 22, 1903.

"Fight on President's Train." *New York Times*, April 29, 1903.

"For Strong Navy." (Friday Harbor, WA) *San Juan Islander*, May 28, 1903.

"Foray into the West." (Washington, DC) *Evening Star*, March 30, 1903.

"Gangs of Pickpockets." *Denver Republican*, May 5, 1903.

"Gay Time." *Lincoln (NE) Star Journal*, June 5, 1903.

"Grand Ovation Awaiting." (*Cheyenne, WY) Daily Leader*, May 30, 1903.

"Great Crowd to Honor the Nation's President." *Spokane Press*, May 25, 1903.

"Growing Weary of His Journey." (Portland) *Oregon Daily Journal*, May 26, 1903.

"He Felt the Kansas Ozone." *Russell (KS) Reformer*, May 8, 1903.

"He Rests." *Lincoln (NE) Journal Star*, April 27, 1903.

"Helena Extends Hearty Greeting to the Nation's Chief." *Anaconda (MT) Standard*, May 28, 1903.

"His Glad Hand Was at Every Function." (Portland) *Oregon Daily Journal*, May 22, 1903.

"His Wild Ride out to the Gardens." *Anaconda (MT) Standard*, May 28, 1903.

"How the President Is to Spend Easter Sunday." *Butte (MT) Inter-Mountain*, April 11, 1903.

"How Roosevelt Will Spend Trip." *Chicago Tribune*, March 15, 1903.

"I Am Tired of My Own Voice." (Davenport, IA) *Daily Times*, June 2, 1903.

"Impromptu Talk." (Minneapolis, MN) *Star Tribune*, April 5, 1903.

"In My Arm Chair." (WaKeeney, Kansas) *Independent*, May 8, 1903.

"Iowa Greets the President." *Davenport (IA) Weekly Republican*, June 4, 1903.

"Insulted the President and the Row Started." *Denver Post*, May 4, 1903.

"Inter-Mountain Gets Only Views of the Departure of Roosevelt." *Butte (MT) Inter-Mountain*, April 9, 1903.

"It's a Rousing Big Reception Butte Gives to the President." *Anaconda (MT) Standard*, May 28, 1903.

"At Kaw's Mouth." *Salina (KS) Evening Journal*, May 1, 1903.

"Kodak Fiend Gets Busy with President." *Saint Paul Globe*, April 5, 1903.

"At Laramie." *Cheyenne (WY) Daily Leader*, May 30, 1903.

"Leaves Dying Son to Welcome President." *Washington Times*, April 4, 1903.

"Lincoln Praised." (Davenport, IA) *Daily Times*, June 3, 1903.

"Loeb Is Not to Blame." *Spokane Press*, June 2, 1903.

"Looked in Face of Death." *Boston Globe*, September 4, 1902.

"Memorable Day at the Grand Canyon." (Phoenix) *Arizona Republican*, May 7, 1903.

"Merry Chase at Sight of a Herd." *Butte (MT) Inter-Mountain*, April 9, 1903.

"Might Makes Right." (New York) *Sun*, April 22, 1903.

"More Details of the President's Visit." (Sioux Falls, SD) *Argus-Leader*, April 6, 1903.

"Mr. Roosevelt Sees a Cowboy Festival." *New York Times*, April 26, 1903.

"Mrs. Roosevelt to Take an Ocean Trip." *Washington Times*, April 1, 1903.

"Nation's Chief Coming Today." *Chicago Tribune*, April 2, 1903.

"Nation's Chief Puts in a Strenuous Day." (Chicago) *Inter-Ocean*, April 3, 1903.

"Nation's Chief Royally Welcomed by St. Paul." *Saint Paul Globe*, April 5, 1903.

"The Nation's Ruler the Honored Guest of San Bernardino." *San Bernardino (CA) Daily Sun*, May 7, 1903.

"Newspaper Man Meets Trouble in Effort to See the President." *Anaconda (MT) Standard*, April 14, 1903.

"Notes on the President's Ride." (Laramie, WY) *Weekly Boomerang*, June 4, 1903.

"Ogden, a Radiant City Greets the Nation's Chief." *Ogden (UT) Standard*, May 29, 1903.

"Omaha—Welcome President—Nebraska." *Omaha (NE) Daily Bee*, April 28, 1903.

"On Board the Special Train." (Portland) *Oregon Daily Journal*, May 22, 1903.

"One Bear Falls Prey to President's Party." *New York Times*, November 15, 1902.

"One Hundred Thousand Saw Him." *Des Moines (IA) Register*, April 29, 1903.

"Our Coming Guests." *Morning Oregonian*, September 30, 1880.

"Pavilion Rafters Ring with Eloquence during an Extraordinary Mass Meeting." *San Francisco Call*, May 14, 1903.

"Plots to Kill Roosevelt." (New York) *Sun*, November 19, 1902.

"Portland Bids the President Godspeed on Northward Trip." (Portland) *Oregon Daily Journal*, May 22, 1903.

"Portland Shouts a Welcome." (Portland) *Oregon Daily Journal*, May 21, 1903.

"Practical Talk by the President at Tabernacle." *Salt Lake Tribune*, May 30, 1903.

"The President at Yankton." (Sioux Falls, SD) *Argus-Leader*, April 6, 1903.

"President Calls Jeerers to Order." *St. Louis Post-Dispatch*, April 28, 1903.

"President Curtails Welcome Program." *Washington Times*, June 5, 1903.

"President Deprecates Class War." (Chicago) *Inter-Ocean*, June 5, 1903.

"President Eats Breakfast at Mess Wagon with Hugo Cowboys." *Denver Republican*, May 4, 1903.

"The President Gets Under a Soft Hat." *Minneapolis Journal*, April 7, 1903.

"President Gives His Guards Hot Chase." (Washington, DC) *Evening Star*, November 13, 1902.

"President Got Meager Lunch." *Minneapolis Journal*, May 1, 1903.

"President Has Come and Gone." *Laramie (WY) Boomerang*, May 31, 1903.

"The President Hunting Bear." *Vicksburg Evening Post*, November 14, 1902.

"The President in Lincoln Today." *Lincoln (NE) Daily Star*, April 27, 1903.

"President in a Wreck." *Indianapolis Journal*, September 4, 1902.

"President in Arizona." *Arizona Daily Star*, May 7, 1903.

"President in Camp, Ready for Bears." *New York Times*, November 14, 1902.

"President in Illinois." *New York Tribune*, June 4, 1903.

"The President in Wilson." *Wilson (KS) World*, May 7, 1903.

"The President off on Tour Today." *Chicago Daily Tribune*, April 1, 1903.

"President on Puget Sound." (Ritzville, Washington) *Adams County News*, May 27, 1903.

"The President Partook of Cowboy Breakfast at Hugo." *Colorado Springs Gazette*, May 4, 1903.

"President Passes through Flagstaff." (Flagstaff, Arizona) *Coconino Sun*, May 9, 1903.

"The President Responds." *Anaconda (MT) Standard*, April 9, 1903.

"President Roosevelt Addresses Gathering at Livingston and Begins Trip into Park." *Butte (MT) Inter-Mountain*, April 8, 1903.

"President Roosevelt Burns the Y.M.C.A. Mortgage." *San Francisco Examiner*, May 12, 1903.

"President Roosevelt in Colorado Springs." *Colorado Springs Gazette*, May 5, 1903.

"President Roosevelt Makes One of His Stirring Speeches." (Minneapolis, Minnesota) *Star Tribune*, April 5, 1903.

"President Roosevelt Royally Received." (Madison) *Wisconsin State Journal*, April 3, 1903.

"President Roosevelt Sees the Grand Canyon." *Bisbee (AZ) Daily Review*, May 7, 1903.

"President Talked on the Philippines." (Sioux Falls, SD) *Argus-Leader*, April 7, 1903.

"President Warmly Greets Denver Newspaper Friend." *Denver Republican*, May 3, 1903.

"President Was Here." *Altoona (PA) Tribune*, April 2, 1903.

"President Welcomed Home by Thousands." *Washington Times*, June 6, 1903.

"President Will Not Shoot at Lions." *Anaconda (MT) Standard*, April 15, 1903.

"President Will Witness Close of the 'Grand Act.'" *St. Louis Post-Dispatch*, April 29, 1903.

"The President's Books." *Minneapolis Journal*, April 3, 1903.

"President's Landau Struck by a Car." *New York Times*, September 4, 1902.

"President's Luncheon Consisted of Coffee and Sandwiches." *St. Louis Republic*, May 1, 1903.

"President's Rest Was Disturbed." *Santa Fe New Mexican*, May 6, 1903.

"President's Southern Trip." (New York) *Sun*, November 11, 1902.

"The President's Sunday." *New York Times*, November 17, 1902.

"President's Train Will Be on Time." *Des Moines (IA) Register*, June 2, 1903.

"President's Trip." (Washington, DC) *Evening Star*, April 1, 1903.

"President's Troubles in Attending Church." *Seattle Star*, May 23, 1903.

"The President's Visit." (Sharon Springs, KS) *Western Times*, May 8, 1903.

"Quiet Sunday." *Cheyenne (WY) Daily Leader*, June 1, 1903.

"A Reporter's Enthusiasm." *Indianapolis Journal*, September 24, 1902.

"Rides in the Rain." *Omaha (NE) Daily Bee*, April 29, 1903.

"Roosevelt Bids Good-By to the West." *Chicago Tribune*, June 5, 1903.

"Roosevelt Called for Fight Results." *Saint Paul Globe*, April 5, 1903.

"Roosevelt Day." (Junction City, KS) *Junction Republic*, May 1, 1903.

"Roosevelt Day a Glorious Occasion for Salt Lake." *Salt Lake Tribune*, May 29, 1903.

"Roosevelt Didn't Get a Bear." (New York) *Sun*, November 19, 1902.

"Roosevelt Enthusiastic over the Wonders of Yosemite." *San Francisco Chronicle*, May 18, 1903.

"Roosevelt Here." *Abilene (KS) Daily Reflector*, May 2, 1903.

"Roosevelt Ignored Hermann." *Eugene (OR) Guard*, May 21, 1903.

"Roosevelt in Danger." *Billings (MT) Weekly*, June 5, 1903.

"Roosevelt Is a Busy Man." *San Francisco Examiner*, May 9, 1903.

"Roosevelt Makes His First Speech during Stop Here." *Harrisburg (PA) Daily Independent*, April 1, 1903.

"Roosevelt on the Trust Problem." *Minneapolis Journal*, April 4, 1903.

"Roosevelt Royally Received." *Bismarck Tribune*, April 8, 1903.

"Roosevelt Scolds Small Boy in Yosemite." *San Francisco Examiner*, May 18, 1903.

"Roosevelt to Iowans." *New York Tribune*, June 3, 1903.

"Roosevelt Wields a Mason's Trowel." *Topeka (KS) Daily Capital*, May 2, 1903.

"Roosevelt's Friends Go into the Park." *Butte (MT) Inter-Mountain*, April 20, 1903.

"Roosevelt's Reception." *Albuquerque Citizen*, May 5, 1903.

"Rushing over South Dakota To-Day." *Minneapolis Journal*, April 6, 1903.

"Sharon Springs Had Glorious Welcome for President Roosevelt." *Denver Republican*, May 4, 1903.

"Shows the Roosevelt Stride." *Chicago Tribune*, April 3, 1903.

"Sister Regina Old Friend." *Indianapolis Journal*, September 24, 1902.

"Situation in Topeka." *Davenport (IA) Morning Star*, June 2, 1903.

"Some Things Not on the Program." *Seattle Star*, May 23, 1903.

"Somebody Is to Blame." *Anaconda (MT) Standard*, May 29, 1903.

"Speak Softly; Carry Big Stick Says Roosevelt." *Chicago Tribune*, April 3, 1903.

"Speaks at Madison." (Washington, DC) *Evening Star*, April 3, 1903.

"Started out in the Rain." (Washington, DC) *Evening Star*, May 2, 1903.

"Strenuous Day in Kansas City." *St. Louis Post-Dispatch*, May 1, 1903.

"Talks in Chapel." (Minneapolis, Minnesota) *Star Tribune*, April 5, 1903.

"Teddy Here Today." *Salina (KS) Daily Union*, May 2, 1903.

"Teddy Remembers All the Pioneers." *Butte (MT) Inter-Mountain*, April 9, 1903.

"Teddy Visits Post after Stay in the Wild." *Butte (MT) Inter-Mountain*, April 16, 1903.

"That Cowboy Breakfast." *Valentine (NE) Democrat*, December 24, 1903.

"Theodore Roosevelt—Au Revoir." *Washington Herald*, March 4, 1909.

"Theodore Roosevelt on New Mexico Soil." *Las Vegas (NM) Daily Optic*, May 5, 1903.

"Thieves Busy at Hastings." *Omaha (NE) Daily Bee*, April 28, 1903.

"Tour Was a Triumph." (Waterloo, IA) *Courier*, June 3, 1903.

"The Tours of the Presidents." *Minneapolis Journal*, April 2, 1903.

"Tramp on Train with Roosevelt." *Butte (MT) Inter-Mountain*, April 9, 1903.

"The Trip from Tacoma." *Seattle Star*, May 23, 1903.

"Tuckered the Bear All Out." (New York) *Sun*, November 15, 1902.

"Tumultuous Welcome to Nation's Executive." *Lincoln (NE) Star Journal*, April 27, 1903.

"Was a Soudan Veteran." *Boston Globe*, September 4, 1902.

"We Must Raise Others while We Are Being Benefited." (Minneapolis, MN) *Star Tribune*, September 3, 1901.

"Welcome of Idaho to Chief Executive." *Anaconda (MT) Standard*, May 29, 1903.

"Welcome to Roosevelt." *Alliance (NE) Herald*, May 1, 1903.

"What the President Had to Say during the Drive." *Pasadena (CA) Daily News*, May 8, 1903.

"What the President Said and Did after the Accident." *Boston Post*, September 4, 1902.

"Where Lincoln and Douglas Met." *New York Tribune*, June 4, 1903.

"The Whole Day of the President." *Los Angeles Times*, May 9, 1903.

"Why He 'Switched.'" *Minneapolis Journal*, April 4, 1903.

"Wild Indians Greet the Great Father." *Spokane Press*, May 28, 1903.

"Will View Geysers." *Butte (MT) Inter-Mountain*, April 17, 1903.

"With the President's Party." *Butte (MT) Inter-Mountain*, April 9, 1903.

"With Roosevelt in Chicago." *Minneapolis Journal*, April 3, 1903.
"Women Blamed." *Boston Globe*, September 4, 1902.
"Works the Fainting Game." *Omaha (NE) Daily Bee*, April 28, 1903.
"Writes Threatening Letters to President." *St. Louis Republic*, May 2, 1903.

Manuscripts

Charlie Leidig's Report of President Roosevelt's Visit in May 1903. Yosemite Research Library, Yosemite National Park.

Theodore Roosevelt's Letter to George W. Armijo, Dated January 15, 1902. Theodore Roosevelt Digital Library. Dickinson State University, Dickinson, ND.

Theodore Roosevelt's Speech at the Soldiers' Home, Milwaukee, Wisconsin, April 3, 1903. Theodore Roosevelt Digital Library. Dickinson State University, Dickinson, ND.

Theodore Roosevelt's Speech at the Exposition Park, Milwaukee, Wisconsin, April 3, 1903. Theodore Roosevelt Digital Library. Dickinson State University, Dickinson, ND.

Theodore Roosevelt's Speech at Mitchell, South Dakota, April 6, 1903. Theodore Roosevelt Digital Library. Dickinson State University, Dickinson, ND.

Theodore Roosevelt's Speech at Aberdeen, South Dakota, April 6, 1903. Theodore Roosevelt Digital Library. Dickinson State University, Dickinson, ND.

Theodore Roosevelt's Speech at Jamestown, North Dakota, April 7, 1903. Theodore Roosevelt Digital Library. Dickinson State University, Dickinson, ND.

Theodore Roosevelt's Speech at New Castle, Wyoming, April 25, 1903. Theodore Roosevelt Digital Library, Dickinson State University, Dickinson, ND.

Theodore Roosevelt's Speech at Edgemont, South Dakota, April 25, 1903. Theodore Roosevelt Digital Library, Dickinson State University, Dickinson, ND.

Theodore Roosevelt's Speech at Lincoln, Nebraska, April 27, 1903. Theodore Roosevelt Digital Library. Dickinson State University, Dickinson, ND.

Theodore Roosevelt's Letter to Seth Bullock, dated April 27, 1903. Theodore Roosevelt Collection, Library of Congress, Washington, DC.

Theodore Roosevelt's Speech at Kansas City, Missouri, May 1, 1903. Theodore Roosevelt Digital Library. Dickinson State University, Dickinson, ND.

Theodore Roosevelt's Speech at Topeka, Kansas, May 2, 1903. Theodore Roosevelt Digital Library. Dickinson State University, Dickinson, ND.

Theodore Roosevelt's Speech at Albuquerque, New Mexico, May 5, 1903. Theodore Roosevelt Digital Library. Dickinson State University, Dickinson, ND.

Theodore Roosevelt's Speech at Danville, Illinois, June 4, 1903. Theodore Roosevelt Digital Library. Dickinson State University, Dickinson, ND.

Theodore Roosevelt Letter to Rev. W. C. Kastner, June 4, 1903. Theodore Roosevelt Collection, Library of Congress, Washington, DC.

Theodore Roosevelt's Letter to Seth Bullock, Dated August 25, 1903. Theodore Roosevelt Collection, Library of Congress, Washington, DC.

Interviews

Jayne Pearce to the author, October 1, 2018.
Beth Werling to the author, September 18, 2018.

Index

About the Author

Michael F. Blake spent sixty years in the film and television industry before his retirement in 2018. A two-time Emmy-winning makeup artist, his credits include *Westworld*, *X-Men: First Class*, *Spider-Man 3*, *Independence Day*, *Tough Guys*, *Soapdish*, *Police Academy II*, *The Munster's Revenge*, and *Happy Days*. As a child actor, Michael appeared in such television shows as *Adam-12*, *The Lucy Show*, *The Munsters*, *Bonanza*, *Kung Fu*, *The Red Skelton Show*, and *Marcus Welby, MD*.

A respected film scholar with a master's degree from UCLA, Michael's three books on silent screen legend Lon Chaney are the definitive works on the actor. His trilogy served as the basis for the Turner Classic Movies documentary *Lon Chaney: A Thousand Faces* (2000), in which he was a special consultant and on-camera interviewee. Michael's two books, *Code of Honor: The Making of High Noon, Shane, and The Searchers* and *Hollywood and the O.K. Corral*, have been recognized as important works about the Western genre.

The Cowboy President: The American West and the Making of Theodore Roosevelt has been praised for showing a side of the man few people knew. *True West* magazine named it their best political biography for 2018, and it was nominated for a Spur Award for best biography by Western Writers of America.

Michael has provided audio commentary for several Lon Chaney films, and has appeared in documentaries about John Ford, Irving Thalberg, and Max Factor. His articles have appeared in *Wild West*, *American Cinematographer*, *True West*, *Round-Up*, and the *Los Angeles Times*. In 2017 he was awarded the Western Writers of America Stirrup Award for his article about the making of *The Searchers*.

Michael lives in Arizona with his wife, Linda, and their dogs.